From Gold to Euro

On Monetary Theory and the History
of Currency Systems

Springer
Berlin
Heidelberg
New York
Barcelona
Hong Kong
London
Milan
Paris
Singapore
Tokyo

Heinz-Peter Spahn

From Gold to Euro

On Monetary Theory
and the History of Currency Systems

With 31 Figures
and 16 Tables

 Springer

Dr. Heinz-Peter Spahn
University of Hohenheim (520 A)
Lehrstuhl für Wirtschaftspolitik
Institut für Volkswirtschaftslehre
70593 Stuttgart
Germany

ISBN 3-540-41605-6 Springer-Verlag Berlin Heidelberg New York

Library of Congress Cataloging-in-Publication Data
Die Deutsche Bibliothek - CIP-Einheitsaufnahme
Spahn, Heinz-Peter: From Gold to Euro: on monetary theory and the history of currency
systems; with 16 tables / Heinz-Peter Spahn. - Berlin; Heidelberg; New York; Barcelona;
Hong Kong; London; Milan; Paris; Singapore; Tokyo: Springer, 2001
    ISBN 3-540-41605-6

Springer-Verlag Berlin Heidelberg New York
a member of BertelsmannSpringer Science+Business Media GmbH

© Springer-Verlag Berlin · Heidelberg 2001
Printed in Germany

Hardcover-Design: Erich Kirchner, Heidelberg

SPIN 10795877   42/2202-5 4 3 2 1 0 - Printed on acid-free paper

Preface

This book deals with the evolution of monetary systems. Firstly, it argues that money forms a constitutional element in any private-ownership economy, establishing a nominal-standard order for the market behaviour of individual agents. The market economy is basically a payment society where money structures and values economic activities, and performs itself as a market asset. The use of resources and the production of commodities are governed by calculations in monetary values which subordinate production and employment to the logic of asset markets. The "veil" of money cannot be withdrawn, as a matter of fact and in theoretical analysis, without changing the economic order of society. Money originates from a credit relation between market agents, thus spot payments replace intertemporal exchange. Problems of low trust and information in mutual economic relations are projected onto the money medium in a monetary economy, thereby enhancing its efficiency and dynamics. The rate of interest is not related to time; it is the price for maintaining the agents' solvency in the current period, and it determines a positive rate of return on capital and production.

Secondly, the book shows that network externalities in the use of money led to monopoly solutions in the national and hegemonic leader-follower relations in the international economy. The management of money supply has always been regulated in order to prevent its misuse, on the part of its creating institutions, and to preserve its reputation as an impartial "arbiter", on the part of society. In the history of banking, it proved to be impossible to found the belief in the future market acceptance of money on its "backing" by some reserve asset. Monetary policy emerged out of the profit-oriented business of private banks. Central banks learned to stabilize the value of money by controlling the scale of monetary transactions via interest rate management. Soon, they were committed to follow rules, imposed as credibility-enhancing devices, but generally practised a discretionary policy aiming to stabilize financial markets. Money provides a order-theoretic framework for micro behaviour, but depends itself on macro demand policy for its own stabilization.

Thirdly, the book studies how on an international level the problem of leadership arose as central banks using some reserve asset for their rule-based note issue were led to defend fixed exchange rates. A simple game-theoretic macro model analyzes the history of the key currency systems in the 20th century and explains the rise and decline of pound sterling, the dollar and the mark. It is shown that the approval of an asymmetric currency system where one country determines the world level of interest rates, and thus growth and employment in other countries, rested on a precarious equilibrium with respect to different economic policy preferences. Key currency systems collapsed because of macroeconomic destabilization or policy failures in the centre countries, accompanied by waning willingness to accept foreign leadership in monetary policy affairs.

Finally, the book argues that the creation of the euro transforms currency policy problems into internal market adjustment challenges. Its establishment corresponds with a world-wide tendency of replacing fixed-exchange-rate systems by flexible non-systems or currency unions. The urge to overcome a state of asymmetric distribution of financial power and to democratize monetary policy decisions was the driving force for the foundation of the European Monetary Union. At the same time, the enthronement of the European Central Bank as a supranational, politically independent body and its sole obligation to maintain price stability may be regarded as a major step toward a depoliticization of central banking. But contrary to the practice of defending a price of a reserve asset, a control of inflation entails a demand management of goods and labour market dynamics so that the central bank may not escape the field of political and economic interests. This is the tragic irony in the legacy of the Keynesian Revolution: Keynes' efforts to come off the gold standard, which he condemned as representing an outdated restraint for maintaining internal equilibrium, i.e. price stability *and* full employment, finally ended up as a concept of stabilization which relied on a stock of unemployment to deter inflation.

The author is deeply indebted to all those who have, consciously or unconsciously, contributed to the completion of this study. I would like to thank the participants of conferences and seminars held in Berlin, Toronto, Vienna, Geneva, London and Chemnitz for valuable comments on presented parts of earlier drafts of the text. Jörg Bibow, Walter Heering and Otto Steiger provided constructive arguments to the line of the theoretical approach. Also I would like to thank Christoph Deutschmann, Rüdiger Dragendorf, Hajo Riese and Hans-Michael Trautwein for inspiring debates over the years. During the final stage of completing the text, I have profited from many discussions with my research assistants Daniel Hartmann, Peter Kühnl, Gerhard Seidel and Udo Vullhorst; in addition, Gerhard Mauch did an excellent job of research assistance in finding and providing literature. And, last but not least, a big thank-you to Maggie Lycett who helped to make the English publication of the book possible.

University of Hohenheim, Stuttgart
December 2000   *Heinz-Peter Spahn*

Contents

Introduction

> It is impossible to pierce the money veil in order to get to the premiums on concrete goods. If one penetrates through it one penetrates into a void.
>
> *Joseph A. Schumpeter*[1]

> The political economy of international monetary systems, good or bad, can only be understood in historical perspective.
>
> *Ronald McKinnon*[2]

The debates on the establishment of the euro have rekindled interest in the monetary foundations of market economies. Quite considerable effort was exerted in designing and codifying the rules of the European Central Bank. An almost constitutional rating was given to the goal of price stability. But the intensity of the discussion on the institutional set-up of the Bank shows a deep-seated uncertainty within society over the priority of that goal and the ability of monetary policy to attain it. The controversy about the compatibility of price stability with other macroeconomic goals as growth and employment and the famous issue of a trade-off between inflation and unemployment capture only a part of the questions related to monetary stability.

The double-nature of this issue stems from the fact that, on the one hand, money – like the judicial system – is a constituent element of a market economy's communicative infrastructure and therefore should be controlled by a constitutional micropolicy aiming at an efficient *order* of society.[3] On the other hand, the monetary system's efficiency and stability is being mainly preserved by means of *demand management*, i.e. by varying the financing conditions of commercial banks, which possibly interferes with the desirable development of other macroeconomic variables. In economic theory, this dual-faceted nature of money is mirrored in the dichotomy of acknowledging the (one-time) efficiency gain due to the existence of money and postulating the neutrality of changes of the quantity of money.

Correspondingly the slogan "money matters", vividly put forward by Post Keynesians[4], can be interpreted to address two different topics: the first refers to the fact (or the puzzle – as seen from the rational-expectations school) that even announced changes in the path of monetary expansion usually have an impact on output and employment, possibly even in the long run. But this type of a "non-neutrality" of money tends to obscure a second question: how does the existence of money affect the market order of a private-ownership economy? The traditional

---

[1] Schumpeter 1934: 184.
[2] McKinnon 1996: 7.
[3] The appropriate German, but hardly translatable, term is "Ordnungspolitik".
[4] Cf. Davidson 1978: 365.

answer, of course, is that money renders the market process more efficient; but apart from that one-time gain, it makes no difference whether money is used in a market system or not. This is the more basic axiom of monetary neutrality which serves as a justification to elaborate economic theories by analyzing an hypothetical non-monetary market system, which then are applied to the "real world".

Economic research has been executed along these lines for more than two centuries, although this practice appears somewhat dubious for epistemological reasons. Social systems can never be properly described by looking only at their personal members and the available resources; the way how people *communicate* with each other and how economic interaction is *organized* is what makes the distinction between different systems. By disregarding these institutions scientific research aims at the discovery of economic "laws" which are valid in all systems and in all periods of time. Such laws may exist; but the analysis of a market economy requires that its social organization is taken serious. Although there has been a growing interest in the analysis of institutions and the economics of the law in the preceding decades, the monetary "language" of the agents' market interaction still is considered to be a phenomenon at the "surface" of economic problems, a "veil" that has to be pulled away if economic essentials are to be explained.

Hence, economic theory does not comprehend money as a category which leads to a differentiation between various economic systems. It is held that all these orders (to a varying degree) use money, and the decision between "plan" and "market" is supposed to settle the question. But there were markets also in socialist planned economies; the term "market" only indicates the location, not the procedure of the necessary coordination of individual economic behaviour. In a private-ownership society, it makes a large difference whether a market is an auction-like event where a mutually exchange of goods is organized, or whether it represents a decentralized institution, in a row with other markets, where agents in a sequential process of search and decision-making buy and sell goods, each on different markets, against money.[5]

For various reasons the first type of barter exchange has played only a minor role, if any, in economic history. Thus the two distinctive features of economic systems are "plan" and "money". In the second case, members of society interact in a competitive, evolutionary process, necessarily marked by imperfect information, where

• money prices provide market agents with information on advantageous economic activities,

• money as a budget constraint shapes the agents' room for manoeuvre, and

---

5   An elaboration of the far-reaching consequences of these two types of markets, the Walrasian and the Marshallian way of organizing a private-ownership economy, is provided by De Vroey (1999).

• stipulating and carrying out money-denominated contracts constitute the formal pattern of the individuals' interaction on markets.

By applying a calculation in terms of the chosen monetary unit, the *coherence*, i.e. the compatibility, of individual economic plans and decisions is checked, established and finally executed by money payments.[6] *A competitive economic order thus implies a monetary economy.* This is almost a truism, but has been suppressed particularly in neoclassical economics because of its long-lasting fixation on the Walrasian idea of a auctioneer-controlled allocation of resources. More astonishingly, the neoliberal school, which emphasized the competitive character of a market system more distinctly than the neoclassicals, also hardly appreciated the monetary framework of the economic order. Hayek always stressed the leading role of law, but hardly the allocative role of money. The fact that the competitive process takes place by using a monetary "language" thus remained rather dim (except from some hints provided by Schumpeter).

Following some mercantilist lines of thought, Keynesian economics led to a renaissance of a monetary understanding of the working of a market economy. The starting point of Keynes' thinking was the quantity theory of money which, at the beginning of the 20th century, represented the dominating school of monetary macroeconomics.[7] Keynes' finding that a monetary expansion acts on prices *and* quantities is considered to be the decisive departure from (neo-) classical orthodoxy.[8] But some other economists, who had grown up in the 1920s debate on value theory and imperfect competition and who were not primarily interested in monetary theory, also saw that employment is determined mainly by goods demand.[9] From both roots various post-Keynesian schools have emerged, which however share a common view: the occurrence of unemployment is interpreted as a way of market failure, where money is taken to be an important (but not exclusive) source of *disturbance* which causes a departure from the full-employment equilibrium. Keynes had the conception of money as a barrier to full employment which ought to be overcome by means of monetary policy. According to Minsky, the existence of money *destroys the coherence* of the economic system, unemployment is the result of a "pathological" market constellation.[10]

But by invoking the hypothetical ideal of a real barter economy as a point of reference (which for no good reason is supposed to be immune to unemployment) this Keynesian approach misses the specific character of a monetary economy: it

---

6   Cf. Laidler 1988, Riese 1990: 1-10, 15-7, Davidson 1994: 97-101.
7   The most prominent representatives of that school were Wicksell, Fisher, Cassel, Hayek, Hawtrey and Robertson (cf. Skidelski 1995).
8   At first, Keynes did not recognize this consequence of his theory of effective demand. His disciple Joan Robinson (1933: 24) spoke of "Mr Keynes' failure to realise the nature of the revolution that he was carrying through".
9   In this context, Kregel (1985) names Kahn, Robinson, Harrod, Kaldor and Kalecki.
10 Cf. Keynes 1936: 235-6, Minsky 1980.

is not an imperfect or flawed variation of a barter system but an economic order of its own, where monetary contracts and money payments form a network, fulfilling the tasks which in a socialist society have to be taken on by a central planning agency. Because money not only serves as a communication medium, but is itself traded and held as a "materialized" wealth asset, the linkage between payment technology and asset holding leaves its mark upon this economic order. The character of the system is shaped by the relations between money, interest, profit and capital, but not by some degree of resource utilization.

Part I of this book therefore aims at the foundation of a theory of a monetary economy which concentrates on questions of allocation and capital theory. It is shown that money constitutes an indispensable element which guides economic calculations, organizes market interaction, manages the transfer of entitlements to resources and settles creditor-debtor relationships. The economics of market societies, which actually have never been characterized by large-scale barter exchange, thus shows in a network of payment processes. The demand for an ability to pay establishes the rate of interest as an option price which covers the yield of money: the option of free-of-charge acquiring resources and of restructuring portfolios; it is *not* the price of time. In contrast to neoclassical *and* Keynesian theory, money does *not* link the present and the future; rather, it serves to eliminate time from economic transactions (money payments being an efficiency-enhancing alternative to intertemporal barter transactions). Money is not neutral; not in the first place because a change of its quantity may influence output and employment, but rather because it determines the economic order of society. The process of production becomes a way of asset holding the yield of which is not based on any physical productivity or efficiency, but on the liquidity premium of money.

The evolution of a monetary economy was an innovation in social history as it allowed economic interaction in low-trust societies where problems relating to imperfect information and a lack of confidence in bilateral economic relations could be shifted on to the money medium; a payment substitutes the holding of a dubiously rated claim to a future delivery of specific goods which may have an uncertain value, in terms of utility, for the recipient. *Part II* of the book describes how high demands on the trustworthiness of the money medium at first forced the banks, being the dominant producers of money, to keep some resources or assets as a form of "backing" of issued money notes. It took some centuries to convince market agents, bankers and politicians that the actual acceptance of a money medium merely depends on a precarious expectation equilibrium with regard to its future acceptance on the part of other agents; this poses a task for the control of the (expected) value of money in terms of goods, but backing money is neither necessary nor sufficient to solve that task.

Money is a public good the use of which yields increasing returns; therefore the process of search for an appropriate money medium might end up in a monopoly solution. At the same time, providing the market with money – unlike supplying other typical public goods – is a profitable business. The market equilibrium tends to be instable because the attainment of the position of a reputable producer of money carries the seeds of its destruction. Hence, *part II* also analyzes the emergence of governmental regulation of the banking system which aimed at a restriction and stabilization of money supply. This task however interfered with the government's own interests with regard to the goals of acquiring easy access to cheap finance and of promoting the macroeconomic development by a rising volume of credit to the private sector. The strategy of reconciling the various motives of banking policy by subordinating the issue of money to a strict rule was a failure in England. Instead, the modern type of a two-tiered banking system evolved in a spontaneous way from the market process as the largest private bank by and by grew into the role of a central bank.

A monetary order has a degree of freedom with regard to the level of all nominal values, i.e. prices of goods and assets. Therefore a nominal anchor is needed which serves as a reference point in market contracts. It can be chosen arbitrarily, but the efforts to preserve the stability of this constitutional price relation has a far-reaching bearing on the macroeconomic process. The typical strategy, prevalent in the late 19th and throughout the 20th century, has been the establishment of key currency systems where the "definition of the monetary unit" is being provided by some hegemonic country; member countries in a way could free-ride on the reputation of the key currency by fixing their exchange rate vis-à-vis to it. This can be envisaged as a further microeconomic gain in efficiency as the problem of low trust, which is so deeply embedded in economic relations, is shifted on to an international level.

Part III of the book is dedicated to this topic; a simple game-theoretic set-up of a two-country model demonstrates the logic and, in each case, the breakdown of the three big currency orders: the gold standard, the Bretton Woods and the European Monetary System (EMS). First, it is explained how an asymmetric constellation of a leader-follower solution is established, i.e. what made the member countries accept the hegemonic position of the key currency country. The analysis yields the somewhat paradoxical result that the "leading" country generally acts a Stackelberg-follower in terms of game theory. Second, with particular reference to the EMS, it is argued that macroeconomic shocks emanating from the key country and a waning political willingness to approve the (monetary) policy power of that country led to the project of the European Monetary Union (EMU).

Thus there is some "logic" in the development of currency systems. But EMU also represents taking a (voluntary?) step backwards to the gold standard: *part IV* of the book describes the attempt to denationalize the money supply and to establish the goal of price stability as an almost constitutional norm, comparable to the sacrosanct gold parity in former times. However, executing the task of stabilizing the monetary economic order will inevitably interfere with conflicting interests particularly on the labour market. It is also argued that the adjustment problems on this market, when the exchange rate cannot be manipulated any longer, might overburden the fragile European political system. The risk is not that Europe is not an "optimal currency area", but rather, that it might turn out to be a "suboptimal governmental area"; the strategy of circumventing national balance-of-payments restrictions then will end up in an inefficient quarrel on European structural, regional and industrial policies.

The end of the era of key currency systems has finally led to a bipolar monetary order in the world economy. The achievement of a common monetary control of the European macro markets will hardly be sacrificed in return for a fixed dollar-euro exchange rate. The exchange rate – being an asset price – cannot be fixed by central banks without abandoning the control of internal monetary stability. Therefore, the options in currency policy matters seem to be narrowed to a choice between monetary union and flexible exchange rates. In the latter case, equilibrium conditions on international financial markets determine only the rates of change, but not the levels of exchange rates. Hence, the new trade-off in international macroeconomics is between misaligned exchange rates, brought about by free capital movements, and the threat of politicized adjustment problems in non-optimal currency unions.

PART I
ON THE THEORY OF A MONETARY ECONOMY

1. Market Organization and Monetary Contracts

1.1 Standard of Value and Means of Payment: A Credit Theory of Money

> Money is the measure by which goods are valued, the value by which goods are exchanged, and in which contracts are made payable.
>
> *John Law*[1]

> He who owes is either a bankrupt, or *must pay*, as long as there is a shilling in the country. But he who buys, or inclines to buy, *must have money*, or he can buy nothing; for if he buys on credit, he then falls immediately into the former category, and *must pay*.
>
> *James Steuart*[2]

> I suppose a person to have lent me a sum of money, on condition that it be restor'd in a few days; and also suppose, that after the expiration of the term agreed on, he demands the sum: I ask, *What reason or motive have I to restore the money?*
>
> *David Hume*[3]

Economies which are characterized by private property of resources and market agents striving for their private interests typically create judicial and monetary systems which then cause the process of economic transactions to look much different compared to the often propagated idea of a direct exchange of goods and services. Social and legal norms establish a framework for individual economic behaviour. Transactions on labour, goods and asset markets are regulated by means of explicit or implicit contracts. They render economic processes – to some extent at least – predictable and less risky and allow some planning in a "spontaneous order". Hence, market relations between firms and households exhibit some degree of stability, which facilitates the employment of optimizing calculations

---

[1] Law 1720: 5.
[2] Steuart 1767b: 212.
[3] Hume 1739/40: 479.

within these decision making units. The terms of these contracts reveal – on the part of the agents involved – the desire for commitment or flexibility.

When designing the contents of contracts, market agents are only restricted by legal regulations. Therefore, they are free to stipulate a delivery of (a bundle of) goods in return for their market supply; dates of delivery could also be settled at will. Obviously, the corresponding system of these "relative prices", i.e. exchange ratios, would imply extremely high information costs. It seems impossible, in practice, to compute the profitability of alternative investment projects and to execute the controlling of ongoing production processes by means of this price system, as the foundations of valuation are subject to permanent changes.[4]

A statistical record of the economic process drawn up by the end of a year generates the impression that goods have been paid for goods, and that real income, i.e. withdrawals of goods, is equivalent to the services of productive factors. This matching of supply and demand may have given support to the Walrasian idea that an economy can be organized by means of a central registration of real supply and demand functions, followed by reciprocal deliveries after the equilibrium vector of relative prices has been computed. Such an allocation procedure may prove to be consistent "ex post", but it does not correspond to a market economy based on permanent competition, because economic activities simply should halt during the time span between the auction dates. A competitive economic order, however, is based on the temporary exploitation of asymmetric information and market imperfections. Economic evolution and social progress result from a permanent "creative" destruction of given equilibria. The notion of rational prediction of future events is at odds with the mechanism of evolutionary selection and freedom of personal choice.[5]

Hence an economy based on a division of labour has to find a *standard of value* which serves as a unit of measurement in economic calculations and market transactions. This task can be carried out by a mere "numéraire" which does not even need physically to exist.[6] If production processes are being calculated by using a *money of account*, supply prices may, obviously, be also denominated in its units. However, this convention does not settle the question what type of equivalent will be demanded in return for a delivery of goods. In any case, the consignee will be-

---

[4]   "Efficient coordination in the economy cannot occur unless the various agents involved (that is virtually everybody) speak the same monetary language. The institution that allows them to do so is money, but more specifically the unit-of-account function of money. The decentralised plans of hundreds of millions of consumers and millions of producers cannot mesh harmoniously in the aggregate if this common financial language [...] is missing. The efficiency of this language in performing this vital coordination role depends crucially on whether the unit of account always means the same thing to different individuals both at one and the same moment in time and over time" (Issing 1999a: 10).

[5]   Cf. Schumpeter 1934, Hayek 1968, Luhmann 1988: 31.

[6]   Cf. Steuart 1767a: 214, Hawtrey 1923: 1, Schumpeter 1970: 33.

come a *debtor*. Possibly he could "pay off" his debt by offering his own goods and services. Because of the probable lack of a double coincidence of wants, the creditor, i.e. the seller of the goods, will not – as a rule – be interested in an immediate delivery of any of the debtor's commodities. At most he may accept a promissory note, an *entitlement to resources* which can be asserted at will on any later date. By such an arrangement the creditor gains the flexibility of making use of the goods offered by the debtor if he feels any need for them. In particular, a promissory note could be accepted if the creditor expects to use it to settle his own debt when purchasing goods from some third party. If privately issued I.O.U.s circulate and are not (immediately) returned for redemption in goods, they evolve into *means of payment*.

The little known classical economist Henry Dunning Macleod regarded these promissory notes as the basic form of *money*. According to Macleod money is "nothing more than the evidence of services having been rendered for which an equivalent has not been received, but can at any time be demanded".[7] He interpreted the emergence of *coins* as a further financial innovation which renders the I.O.U. divisible and enhances its negotiability. The circulation and acceptance of coins emphasize the evolution of money from a claim against some particular debtor, to a general, socially established asset, which entitles anyone to an acquisition of all goods and services supplied in the market, or, to put it shortly: "Money must be defined in terms of debt".[8]

The conversion of an initially bilateral obligation into a social arrangement which endows the creditor with a *marketable* claim – i.e. which imposes the liability of delivering goods on to the market as a whole – can be taken as the evolutionary answer to a basic problem: the lack of information and low trust. The potential creditor of a bilateral contract cannot take for granted that the debtor will make his delivery and cannot anticipate the terms on which an I.O.U. will be accepted by third parties. He runs the risk that the debtor will not be willing or able to fulfil his liability. The law may help to enforce the claim in the first case but hardly in the second. Macleod recognized that the quality of promissory notes as means of payment depend on the expected solvency and delivery power on the part of the issuer. Excessive issues of notes would launch doubts as to their future redemption.[9]

The problem of low reciprocal trust, which impedes the realization of economic transactions and thus hampers social welfare, is less serious in cases of pure bilateral relations which both parties wish to perpetuate given their own long-term economic interests. The state of information will then be rather high and reneging

---

[7] Macleod 1855 (quoted from Skaggs 1997: 111).

[8] Hawtrey 1930: 545, cf. Schumpeter 1954: 320-1, Ingham 2000. This line of thought is also taken up by Riese (1995: 56, 59): "Money is not a credit, but emerges from credit." [All quotations from German texts have been translated by the author.]

[9] Cf. Skaggs 1997: 111-2.

on one's liabilities will be detrimental to the debtor also, as this would, in all probability, put an end to business relations. The problem of maintaining the credibility of promissory notes is far more pressing in the case of many-sided market relations. "The issue of confidence is chiefly one of multilateral trading."[10]

But it is just the existence of a multitude of market participants which enables a
solution of the problems of thin information and low trust: two-party agreements
can be extended to three-party arrangements. "All money is best understood as
credit. [...] Monetary relations are trilateral. Monetary exchange [...] involves a
third party of those authorities that may legitimately produce money".[11] If the potential buyer has at his disposal a generally accepted asset, he can acquire goods
more easily as the seller receives a marketable claim. The role of this asset can be
performed, for example, by precious metal coins, or by the pledge or promissory
note of a renowned, well respected wealth owner (only very few market agents
will enjoy the privilege of being able to issue notes which circulate as *money*).
Coins or notes then fulfil the role of a fiduciary agency.

Because coins and notes are denominated in simple accounting units they serve
both as standard of value and means of payment. As the ability of any asset to settle debts has far-reaching, practical significance for individual market agents, it
can be argued that serving as a means of payment is the essential function of any
money: using it as a yardstick in economic calculations then is merely a convenient behaviour once supply prices have to be denoted in units of this money.[12] It
might be interesting to note that even John Law, one of the founders of monetary
economics, still tended to think in terms of barter when he wrote that it was one of
the advantages of money to exhibit everywhere the same value – instead of recog-
nizing that competition made the *money prices of goods* to converge; he measured
money in terms of goods instead of measuring goods in units of money.[13]

Promissory notes initially represent claims to some units of real economic services. Because market agents are expected to minimize information and transaction
costs, these notes have to promise to deliver widely known, standardized goods,

---

[10] Hicks 1989: 47.

[11] Ingham 2000: 23, cf. Coleman 1990: 119, 186, Heering 1999.

[12] Keynes (1930: 3), on the other hand, emphasized the importance of a standard of account as opposed to a bare medium of exchange. "A money of account comes into existence along with debts, which are contracts for deferred payment, and price lists, which
are offers of contracts for sale or purchase. [...] Money itself, namely that by delivery of
which debt contracts and price contracts are discharged, and in shape of which a store of
general purchasing power is held, derives its character from its relationship to the money of account, since the debts and price lists must first have been expressed in terms of
the latter. Something which is merely used as a convenient medium of exchange on the
spot may approach to being money, inasmuch as it may represent a means of holding
general purchasing power. But if this is all, we have scarcely emerged from the stage of
barter. Money proper in the full sense of the term can only exist in relation to a money
of account."

[13] Cf. Law 1720: 4-6.

which are then used as accounting units. The crucial point is however, that the money function of a marketable promissory note does not hinge on its "real" backing but on the reputation of the issuer. Money is a substitute for the hypothetical system of a social organization where perfect information and unspoiled reciprocal confidence prevail. If perfect foresight could be assumed, in particular with respect to the fulfilment of bilateral contracts, a pure credit economy would be appropriate − and not a monetary economy. But as these preconditions cannot be met in an evolutionary setting, a market system with decentralized decision making will almost inevitably evolve as a monetary economy. Admittedly, a money payment in the case of incomplete information and low trust merely means shifting the confidential problem on to the standing of the money asset itself. But solving this reputation problem should be relatively easy; compared to the alternative way of forcing each market agent to convince market partners of his integrity and solvency in each and every market transaction.

The general acceptance of a promissory note circulating as money reveals that a claim against a particular debtor has turned into a claim against the market society as a whole − as each of its members is willing to deliver goods in return for a money payment. From a sociological point of view, Simmel held it to be "the core of truth in the theory that money is only a claim upon society. Money appears [...] as a bill of exchange from which the name of the drawee is lacking; [...] the liquidation of every private obligation by money means that the community now assumes this obligation towards the creditor." Simmel also emphasized that the acceptance of a money asset in market transactions is a prerequisite for the attitude of *holding* money; but he did not grasp clearly that money acts as a *substitute* for interpersonal confidence: "Without the general trust that people have in each other, society itself would deintegrate, [...] in the same way, money transactions would collapse without trust."[14] But the specific achievement of a monetary system is that communication and business relations are enabled even in a "low-trust society".

---

[14] Simmel 1907: 177-9. For a review of his "Philosophy of Money" see Laidler/Rowe (1980) and Deutschmann (1995).

1.2   The Organization of Society as a Payment Economy

> The feeling of personal security that the possession of money gives is perhaps the most concentrated and pointed form and manifestation of confidence in the socio-political organization and order.
>
> *Georg Simmel*[15]

> Dangerous human proclivities can be canalised into comparatively harmless channels by the existence of opportunities for money-making and private wealth [...]. It is better that a man should tyrannise over his bank balance than over his fellow citizens.
>
> *John Maynard Keynes*[16]

> The problem of scarcity [...] arises if someone for the sake of his own future excludes others from an access to resources. The question is: on what condition and how is he allowed to do so? [...] The answer made possible by the communicative medium money is: *if he pays.*
>
> *Niklas Luhmann*[17]

Any economic system needs a social agreement on the procedures which regulate the acquisition of goods and services. As there is no barter exchange in a market economy, the scarcity of resources – the key economic problem – appears to be mirrored in the scarcity of money. Not only is the distribution of income governed by a varying pattern of money prices and payments; Luhmann interprets money as a "communicative medium" which – by means of payment processes – *creates* a rather complex economic subsystem within the society. This approach overcomes the naive conception (which is rather common in economic theory) of a social system consisting mainly of agents and resources; to a large extent however social systems are characterized by patterns and processes of communication. Thus, money as a communicative medium enables the exchange of information between market agents by using a specific economic "language" (function of money as a standard of value); and it accomplishes the definite transfer of entitlements to available resources (function of money as a means of payment). "Money has no 'intrinsic value', its essence is limited to a reference to the system which enables and conditions its use. [...] The 'unit act' of the economy is the payment."[18]

Hence money is not a good, but derives its very function from its position opposite to the variety of goods and services. This is not at variance with the fact that the *function of money* in some periods of economic history was fulfilled by goods

---

[15] Simmel 1907: 179.
[16] Keynes 1936: 374.
[17] Luhmann 1988: 252 (with additional emphasized parts).
[18] Luhmann 1988: 16, 52, cf. 14, 46-7, 196-7, 230, 246-7, 252, Riese 1995.

and resources. Contract-based relations between the members of the market society are fixed in monetary units and have to be dissolved by money payments. Thus
the economic system exhibits a formal structure marked by the nominal-money
standard; this order corresponds to the also formally defined rule of law in a private-property society. Formal rules, for example the equality before the law, the
parliamentary (not imperative) way of political decision making, and the norm of
formal (not necessarily material) justice are of great significance.

Executing the economic process in a monetary framework shapes the social behaviour of the members of a market society; because the acquisition of money
counts as the overall criterion for success. Instead of just lowering transaction
costs compared to a hypothetical barter economy the use of money thus has a
formative, qualitative influence on the social order in a market system. Handling
economic transactions within a nominal, monetary framework increases the com-
plexity of society. The tension between the "real" economy and the "symbolic"
level of monetary relations may give rise to efficiency enhancing, but also to dis-
turbing effects.

The rule which links any acquisition of goods to a money payment creates a moti-
vation for "moneymaking" and thus standardizes social and individual behaviour.
The predominance of one-dimensional monetary aims has often been criticized.
Early theorists of civil societies however, regarded the orientation of human behaviour towards a desire for money income as a precondition for maintaining
stability in a free society which was no longer governed by authoritarian, religious
or ideological constraints. They argued that chaos, driven by the concurrence of
divergent patterns of conduct and ways of living, could only be prevented if a uniform, money-oriented style of behaviour should emerge.[19]

In a free, rule-based society, the results of evolutionary and competitive processes
– for example with respect to interpersonal distribution of welfare and income –
are legitimized by the way in which they came about, not by their substance.
Luhmann further assumes that distributing resources by means of money payments helps to calm down the struggle for relative income positions, inasmuch as
market agents are convinced that this pattern of allocation is objective and "fair":
goods can be acquired by paying prices and not by resorting to personal relations.
Thus there is no need to permanently make all efforts, including even violent
means, to strive for resources, because market agents can be sure that they will be
able to *buy* them later. "Money is the triumph of scarcity over violence."[20] The

---

[19] For an instructive study of these ideas see Hirschman (1977); he coined the phrase of
"money-making as a calm passion". The civilizing property of a predominance of money interest has also been emphasized by Keynes (see the quotation at the beginning of
this chapter).

[20] Luhmann 1988: 253, cf. 19, 69, 255. Simmel (1889: 60) commented critically on the
distinctive feature of a monetary society which forces all its members on an equal foot-
ing with respect to the assessment executed by the money standard of value. "The lack
of quality on the part of money implies [...] a lack of quality on the part of men who of-

idea that monetary patterns of income allocation enhance peace and consensus within the society can be contested however: it is just the formal uniformity of this procedure and mere quantity of money income which disclose and thus emphasize the different economic ability and power of society members. If wealthy and poor countries form a currency union, the extent of discontent with regard to the state of inequality of incomes may well increase.

Payments and non-payments tend to produce a structural hierarchy in the market position of economic agents. "The payment act establishes a very high *certainty of any use* of the money received on the part of the seller (i.e. the money owner) and at the same time a very high *uncertainty of the money's particular use* for all other agents."[21] The use of money comprises purchasing as well as the holding of money. Just as buyers gain on flexibility (being able to postpone definite decisions), sellers, on the other hand, face the problem of adapting their production to an uncertain future goods demand. Generally, the constellation of a "buyer's market" prevails where resources are offered in excess supply. "Since there is money, everyone, more or less, is more inclined to sell instead of to buy."[22]

Because of this asymmetry the microeconomic function of money as a means of payment may favour money owners. On the other hand, on the macroeconomic level, a constant real value of money is not guaranteed. By using monetary exchange instead of barter the scarcity of resources is in a way "transformed" in the form of scarce money, but not on a one-by-one basis; there is no single claim to each good. Rather, the effective quantity of money is determined independently from goods supply. As a consequence, the scarcity of *all* resources can increase compared to money – which is ruled out in a barter system.

The realization that the existence of money can cause a shortage of goods can be traced back to Locke. He regarded money, "some lasting thing that men might keep without spoiling", as the precondition for men's willingness to work more than it was necessary to satisfy immediate, basic wants. The seemingly unbounded striving for accumulation and wealth can only arise if there is some *store of value*; but money is not the only, or even the most suitable, asset which serves that purpose. Each money-financed demand for goods seems to aggravate the shortage of goods. "The access to resources produces scarcity, whereas at the same time scarcity is the motive for the access. [...] The access creates what it intends to surmount."[23] Luhmann's "paradox of scarcity" undermines his own above mentioned idea that the struggle concerning the distribution of income can be smoothed by

---

fer and demand money. [...] The only reason for one person having the same value as any other in a monetary-circulation system is that no one has any value, but only money. [...] Money is the absolutely objective standard which denies all personal characteristics."

[21] Luhmann 1988: 21.

[22] Simmel 1901: 722.

[23] Luhmann 1988: 179, cf. 98, 195, 252, Locke 1690: 25.

shifting the allocation procedure on to a level of money payments. In the case of rising prices people experience a real devaluation of their money holdings which will kindle the quarrel about the quantity of money income.

The economic reason for this type of macroeconomic disequilibrium is a stock-flow-problem: goods are supplied to the market from current production whereas money is being hold as a stock. Changes in the propensity to hold money can bring about marked fluctuations in goods demand and, thus, money prices. The instability of the price level is, therefore, a systemic risk in a monetary economy. From that two main tasks of monetary policy can be derived: the creation of money has to be controlled and economic incentives have to be maintained in order to stabilize money demand. "Money has to be kept scarce, even if we know that it – as a mere communicative symbol – it is not scarce."[24]

1.3 Money as a Public Good

> The demand for money is an imperfect substitute for the more intensive desire for unification, for the state.
> *Adam H. Müller*[25]

> Money was not established by law; with respect to its origin it is not a state-controlled, but rather a social phenomenon. [...] The institution of money, nevertheless, [...] has been improved by means of governmental recognition and regulation, and adapted to the manifold and varying needs of developing business transactions, in a similar way as common law by legislation.
> *Carl Menger*[26]

The social process concerning the search for, and agreement on, some money asset is characterized by the public-good features of money. Both criteria of non-exclusion and non-rivalry in its use are obviously fulfilled with respect to money as a *standard of value*. In a way, the use of money resembles the use of language: participants in interactive processes save information costs if they can communicate on a common level. The same logic applies to the existence of generally accepted rules of law.

A somewhat different pictures emerges when considering money as a *means of payment*. With respect to the problem of market acceptance we find not only a non-rivalry but also increasing returns in the use of money. The value of money holdings grows in line with the number of market agents who are willing to accept

---

[24] Luhmann 1988: 70, cf. Schumpeter 1970: 219, 224-5.
[25] Müller 1816: 139.
[26] Menger 1909: 574.

that money in return for their offered goods and services. Given increasing returns it is to be expected that any money asset will "conquer" the market very rapidly. Most probably the process of search, selection and (implicit) collective agreement on a money asset will lead to a monopoly solution where a market society will use only one currency. Such an outcome does not necessarily also represent a first best solution. The evolutionary process may come to a halt at some local optimum, which then persists even despite of obvious shortcomings. This may be due to a lock-in effect: market agents cling to that currency because its brand name would have to be written off if they should decide to make a transition to a new one. Thus sunk costs can bring about path-dependent equilibria in the market position of alternative currencies.[27]

The determination and the value of some medium of payment according to Locke rests on a "consent of men". Even gold drew its high market valuation not from the mere value of some precious metal, but rather from the (sometimes only implicit) agreement to use it as money. The acceptance of some money does not depend on physical properties of that medium but from a social convention, derived from the collective expectation that it will perform its function as a means of payment *in the future*. This highlights the potential allocative inefficiency and global instability of such an expectation ("sunspot") equilibrium. "The value of money [...] rests on fiction. [...] For maintaining that fiction social conventions are required which stabilize the confidence in the value of money, or better, the fiction of that value."[28]

Because competitive forces do not necessarily induce a welfare optimum, with respect to the selection of a money asset, the intervention of a public institution may be useful which could shorten the duration of search or correct occurring market failures. Government itself could define and supply a legal tender. In this spirit Knapp regarded money as a creation of the legal system. His approach has been criticized particularly because it mainly concentrates upon the idea that the validity of money rests on a convention (which in turn may be mediated by a governmental institution) and that it neglects the problem of protecting the real value of money.[29]

What should not been ignored however, is that Knapp's theory at the period of its origin was a very modern and path breaking one as it opposed the contemporary theory of metallic money. Simmel, too, at that time argued that the distinction be-

---

[27] Cf. Kindleberger 1967, Kindleberger 1984: 20, Grantham et al. 1977, De Grauwe 1996: 1-2. For a general treatment of path dependence see Setterfield (1997).

[28] Pierenkämper 1999: 229, cf. Locke 1690: 26, Hawtrey 1923: 177-8, 417, Kiyotaki/ Wright 1992. The idea of a social convention can also be found in Macleod (1882): "In the process of time all nations hit upon this plan: they fixed upon some *material* substance, which they agreed to make always exchangeable among themselves to represent the amount of *debt*" (quoted from Skaggs 1997: 112).

[29] Cf. Knapp 1909, Weber 1956: 75-80, 184-93, Schumpeter 1970: 82-3.

tween "backed" and fiduciary notes was "totally irrelevant" as even metallic money was nothing but a promise that the society would concede to the money holder the right to lay claim to resources. Simmel intimated that it was the duty of government to protect the purchasing power of money.[30]

A public good however, has not necessarily to be supplied by the state. As governmental agencies pursue their own interests, society could well end up with some "bad money", market failure only having been substituted by government failure. Even the political regulation of a currency system which has originated from a market process of search and agreement needs to rest on a proper knowledge of the type of market failure which may arise.

The individual decisions to use any money asset depend on economic costs and returns. Some technical features such as durability and divisibility enhance the convenience of its use. The far more important question is, which of the alternative money media allows the most favourable terms of trade when acquiring goods and services on the market. If private promissory notes are used as money, agents have the incentive to get hold of highly ranked notes; as their undisputed acceptance as a means of payment shows in relatively lower prices. This implies that only a few persons, who are supposed to be wealthy and reliable, will acquire the privilege to issue promissory notes which then find a ready market. As – in the case of success – these notes on average are not presented for redemption but circulate as money, the issuer himself enjoys the advantage of "buying" goods by means of self-produced money. Accordingly, many market agents may try to earn this "seigniorage" by issuing notes. Whereas, in general a public good is not supplied by private entrepreneurs at all, things are different in the case of money.

From this it follows that government should restrict the production of money, which proves to be an ambivalent task as this regulation may create and safeguard a private monopoly. As typical suppliers of money, *banks* often originated by way of a state-controlled foundation when the privilege to issue bank notes was granted to renowned and wealthy persons. By this act private and public interests were equally served: the public announcement helped to solve the "threshold" problem of the introduction, advertisement and acceptance of the new currency; the banking firm was protected against unwelcome competitors and the governmental agency got the assurance of low-interest credits in return.[31]

Thus we arrive at the most important deviation of money from the concept of a public good: the *use* of money shows the criteria of non-exclusion and non-rivalry, but its *procurement* indicates the private-good character of money. The disposition of means of payment requires the willingness to pay interest (or to bear opportunity costs, respectively). This is why the private supply of money is a profitable business.

---

[30] Simmel 1907: 177-8.
[31] Cf. Stadermann 1987: 53, De Grauwe 1996: 2-5.

2. Money, Interest and Capital

2.1 Neutrality of Money versus Nominal-Standard Economy

> In the end, individuals are only interested in the consumption of goods. This has always to be kept in mind when dealing with monetary theory.
>
> *Rudolf Richter*[1]

> A debt is fundamentally an obligation to give not money but *wealth.*
>
> *Ralf G. Hawtrey*[2]

> An economy where money is created by banking processes that finance the acquisition of capital assets and the production of investment outputs has essentially a nominal core.
>
> *Hyman P. Minsky*[3]

Up to now there has been no comprehensive and widely accepted *theory* of a monetary economy. Maybe this can be explained by the prevailing doubts within the profession of economists whether there is a *monetary economy* at all. The majority of economists believe that a monetary economy is merely a money *using* economy which however, in its basic nature, functions as a barter system. Therefore, in addition to real economic theories on production, consumption, trade and growth, a theory of money was put forward dealing, on the one hand, with the demand for money on the part of individual agents and, on the other, with the supply of money by the banking sector (including the central bank).

The existence of a theory of money however, may not be interpreted as to imply that the economic process is regarded as a monetary phenomenon. Rather, the theory of money is supposed to protect the core of the barter-theoretic approach against the widespread everyday impression of a dominance of monetary transactions. The popular saying of a supposed "uncoupling" of financial markets from the production process confirms the picture of a "real" economy which, if necessary, should be protected from the stubbornness and exaggeration prevailing on financial markets. "The theory of money is a theory of exchange involving the use of money. Both exchange and the use of money are social phenomena. Both can only be explained within the framework of a social model."[4] The announced

---

[1] Richter 1989: 31.

[2] Hawtrey 1923: 14.

[3] Minsky 1984: 454.

[4] Richter 1989: vii. The expression "exchange involving the use of money" goes back to Max Weber (1956: 636) who, contrary to modern mainstream economic theory, was

"social model" however is seldom being explored; rather, the usual practice is to fade out the level of monetary relations when essential economic questions are at issue.

The hypothesis of a neutrality of money provides the main justification for the mainstream habit, in the traditional research business, of downgrading monetary market contracts compared to the alleged fundamental real economic interrelations. The notion of neutrality did not come into fashion until the era of neoclassical economics[5] and refers to the independence of the goods and labour market equilibrium from the (exogenously given) quantity of money. The existence of money undoubtedly enhances the efficiency of transactions (thereby exerting a one-time effect on productivity) but its continuing expansion only causes the price level to increase in a proportional way, leaving the equilibrium value of real magnitudes untouched. The centre of gravity is determined by the supply of resources and their productivity, by a "natural" rate of unemployment and/or a "natural" rate of growth.

Box 1: General Equilibrium Theory and Money

From its very beginning neoclassical economics assumed that a market system could be organized without money at all. The famous example is Walras' idea of an auction where all (actual, contingent and intertemporal) supply and demand schedules are registered, followed by a physical exchange of goods and services after the equilibrium exchange ratios have been computed. Economic transactions therefore were seen as a direct trading of *stocks* (without any means of exchange). Thus, there seems to be no need for money in neoclassical exchange models. "The most serious challenge that the existence of money poses to the theorist is this: the best developed model of the economy cannot find room for it. The best developed model is, of course, the Arrow-Debreu version of a Walrasian general equilibrium."[6] Critics raised the objection that selling goods from a continuing *flow* of production bears more resemblance to a market economy; this principle then formed the Marshallian branch of neo-

---

well aware of the particular features of a monetary economy: "Any act of exchange involving the use of money (sale) is a social action simply because the money used derives its value from its relation to the potential action of others. Its acceptability rests exclusively on the expectation that it will continue to be desirable and can be further used as a means of payment. Group formation (*Vergemeinschaftung*) through the use of money is the exact counterpart to any consociation through rationally agreed or imposed norms. Money creates a group by virtue of material interest relations between actual and potential participants in the market and its payments. At the fully developed stage, the so-called money economy, the resulting situation looks as if it had been created by a set of norms established for the very purpose of bringing it into being."

5 Patinkin/Steiger (1989) note that the concept was put forward firstly by Hayek (1931: 27-8). As the predominant metallic money in the *classical* era was a produced good, it was impossible to separate the vector of relative prices from the level of absolute money prices as strictly as in the neoclassical approach (cf. Mill 1871: 488, 501-2, Laidler 1991: 10-1).

6 Hahn 1982: 1.

classical theory, which later became the platform of the Keynesian revolution. Interestingly enough, Marshall too may have drawn some of its economic insights from visiting a stock exchange; but the London market then showed continuous trading as opposed to the Paris bourse where spot trading was the rule.[7]

In the Walrasian tradition, actual (as opposed to hypothetical) market societies are considered as an imperfect variant of an ideal spot-barter system. It is imperfect because a *society* contains more than just the *economic* system; social norms and institutions may cause rigidities and frictions, i.e. divergences from the hypothetical barter solution, attainable free of charge. Lacking a centralized system of information and exchange, a continuing sequence of (bilateral and multilateral) barter transactions obviously is a longwinded and inefficient procedure. Because of prohibiting information and transaction costs many possible market may not even open up.

Embedding the economic system into a social environment however, will not block economizing behaviour, but rather create a device for lowering all sorts of transaction costs: that is money, which can be regarded as a substitute for the working of an auctioneer. In this spirit neoclassical theory holds that money acts as a lubricant without however interfering with the basic mechanisms and economic "truths" of a barter system. "The inefficiency of barter was often attributed to friction, and money was compared to the lubricant that would reduce that friction. In a frictionless economy, therefore, monetary exchange would have no advantage over barter."[8] Pigou already hinted at the inconsistency of that idea: "The conception of a neutral money, which shall allow everything to proceed as it would do if there were no money at all is parallel to that of a 'neutral' lubricant, whose presence shall make no difference to anything. The only lubricant which 'makes no difference' is a non-existent lubricant. A perfect lubricant generates no frictions and is thus, in a sense, passive. But nobody imagines that the search for a perfect lubricant will lead to the discovery of a 'neutral' one!"[9]

Obviously it is at odds with epistemological principles to consider a monetary economy as an improved version of an imperfect variant of some hypothetical way of organizing economic relations. Objecting to this strategy of research already Hayek emphasized that "money always exerts a determining influence on the development of the economy, [and] that the principles derived for an economy without money can be applied to an economy with money only with substantial qualifications".[10] The "introduction" of money into a market society does not move the system in the direction toward the analytical origin but rather away from it (*figure 2.1*).

This way of reasoning poses a difficulty for General Equilibrium Theory as money is not linked to the "first principles" and thus is left as "the last puzzle of economics".[11] The need for money arises because of some social and institutional peculiarities of economic behaviour, which look like market imperfections as seen from a barter-economic point of view. This setting then attaches a positive value even to (paper) money as market agents subject to imperfect information, in the passage of historical time, encounter randomly distributed opportunities to advantageous transactions. Holding

---

[7] Cf. Davidson 1978: 405-8, Kregel 1995, De Vroey 1999.
[8] Niehans 1978: 3.
[9] Pigou 1933: 188n.
[10] Hayek 1928: 218.
[11] Riese 1995.

money then is a rational behaviour, since these events cannot be predicted. A demand for liquidity arises because of asynchronous sales and purchases when agents move through historical time.

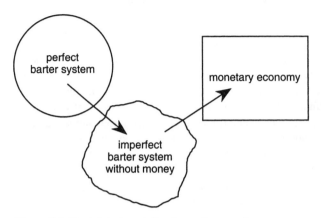

Figure 2.1: Postulated evolution toward a monetary economy

Following this approach (which bears some resemblance to the precautionary demand for money balances in Keynes) there is not much to be learned about the character of money itself. "One must assume [!] that money has certain unique properties which make it more suitable than other assets or goods as a medium of exchange in at least some transactions."[12] Moreover, the features of this sequential-trading economy are only negatively defined – as *departures* from the Walrasian market. Fundamental truths of a competitive equilibrium approach thus do not apply: there is no law of one price, market agents behave as price setter. Accordingly, it is hard to show why and how an evolutionary sequence economy should "converge" to an auction-type market system. Therefore we do not know whether market clearing and full employment will prevail in the long run.[13]

The axiom of a neutrality of money is violated in two ways:

• Information and adjustment problems may cause departures from general equilibrium in the short and medium run.[14]

• Of more importance, and more interest, from an analytical point of view, is the possibility that the long-term equilibrium position of real variables may change

---

[12] Hellwig 1993: 238, cf. Davidson 1981, Laidler 1988.

[13] Cf. Hahn 1982, Hahn/Solow 1995.

[14] "Mark I" monetarists thus believe in some temporary real impacts of monetary shocks (cf. Meltzer 1995). Similar views were held in classical economics. As the choice-theoretic foundations of a labour supply curve were yet not developed the labour market, equilibrium did not serve as a centre of gravity. Moreover, rational expectations were unknown; for a private lesson on that issue given to David Hume see Lucas (1996).

just because of these before-mentioned deviations. Fluctuations in the degree of the use of resources (capital and human) have repercussions – controlled by decay functions and economic incentives – on the stock and the growth rate of resources. In an extreme case the fundamental equilibrium value of a real variable is no longer unique but follows the history of its past movements (*hysteresis*).[15]

This, however, is a somewhat superficial way of reasoning. It is recognized that the existence and the growth rate of money may have an impact on the activity level and the dynamics of the economic system, but the basic relationships between the economic fundamentals – work, production, consumption – seem to remain unaffected. These economic, technical or even physical interrelations are universal, i.e. they are to be found in many economic and social systems, in primitive tribe societies as well as in former socialist planned economies. In all these systems decisions are based on real economic variables and technical means are employed in order to enhance the efficiency of production. These means are called "capital" in neoclassical economics[16]; which makes even the apes to live in capitalism as they use sticks to reap bananas more easily.

The characteristic of capitalism however, is not to be found in the fact that it has outperformed other systems in terms of economic efficiency and prosperity, but rather in its organizational feature: that market agents' calculation and interaction of economic activities are executed in *nominal* terms and contracts (of course, there are some reasons to believe that the second feature explains the first). Goods, services and assets are sold against payment of money, a pure symbol, which then allows the distinction between sales and purchases. Payment proceedings in a way constitute an hierarchical ranking of the spheres of goods and money.

One may guess that this is why early neoclassical economists insisted on money being not a means of *payment* but only a medium of *exchange* (thereby alluding to barter): "If we bear in mind the function of money of mediating goods and asset transactions [...]: there is no need and no justification to deal specifically with a preferred use, or even a function of money as a *means of payment*."[17] The exis-

---

[15] Formally we have

$$x^* = \bar{x} + \lambda\left(x_{-1} - \bar{x}\right) = \left(1 - \lambda\right)\bar{x} + \lambda\, x_{-1}$$

where the equilibrium value of some variable x^* (a level or a rate of change) depends on fundamental forces (determining $\bar{x}$) and on the difference between last period's actual value and $\bar{x}$. The parameter λ ($0 \le \lambda \le 1$) measures the degree of hysteresis. If $\lambda = 1$, the "natural" rate of unemployment, for example, only depends on the path of demand-determined employment. "High unemployment is even worse than we thought, because it raises the NAIRU, and lower unemployment is even better than we thought because it reduces the NAIRU" (Stiglitz 1997: 8).

[16] Cf. Richter 1989: 38. Looking at classical economists, at least Marx (1890: 379) knew that *capital* represents a specific social organization of production and not just an efficiency-enhancing tool.

[17] Menger 1909: 579, cf. by contrast Luhmann 1988: 196-7, Riese 1995.

tence of money-denominated contracts thus is generally interpreted, in line with the supposed fundamental principles of economics, "that agents negotiate nominal contracts, but care only about real values".[18] This is considered to be an indisputable dogma as its rejection seems to involve an assumption of *money illusion*.

But if market agents are said to be interested in "real values" we may ask why they do not demand bundles of goods in return for their market supply. Instead, they insist upon being paid in money, a medium which allows them to circumvent many problems with regard to information and trust, inevitably bound to a barter system. In addition, by selling against money, agents gain the advantage of acquiring an *option*: having money, the "universal equivalent"[19], at their disposal they are free to choose between any use of it on goods and asset markets, including the non-use. Money as an option grants flexibility and solvency to its holder and thus strengthens his market position as opposed to the owner of resources. Note that this *liquidity premium attached to money* depends on the inflexibility of money prices; or, to put it differently, it is the very essence of money prices to show at least some degree of rigidity in order to enable individual economic planning and a decentralized pattern of resource allocation. Therefore, the fact that contracts are denominated in money indeed has a far reaching bearing on the order of society.[20]

Insisting on money contracts does not at all (necessarily) imply some sort of money illusion. Of course, agents form expectations on the real equivalent of stipulated money payments (measured by the general price level) and its evolution through time (measured by the rate of inflation). *Workers* prefer being paid in money instead of receiving some share in the produce of their firm. This however is by no means a "natural" agreement. Pushing through the demand for money payment involves that the risk of realizing this produce on the goods market is passed on to the *firm* (which then is burdened with the liquidity problem of paying money wages). This arrangement is chosen by both parties nevertheless, because a central marketing of output by the firm is more efficient and increases the distributive margins. As the nominal wage then is fixed for some time span, both parties – before signing the contract – have to build expectations on its future real equivalent in order to compute the consumer's and the producer's real wage.

The credit contract represents a transfer of claims to resources. The real equivalent of these claims is particularly important for the *borrower*[21], whereas the price

---

[18] Goodhart (1994: 103) in a critical review of the modern theory of monetary policy.

[19] Marx 1890: 30.

[20] "The terms in which contracts are made matter. In particular, if money is the good in term of which contracts are made, then the prices of goods in terms of money are of special significance. This is not the case if we consider an economy without a past and without a future. [...] If a serious monetary theory comes to be written, the fact that contracts are indeed made in terms of money will be of considerable importance" (Arrow/ Hahn 1971: 357).

[21] This has been emphasized especially in classical economics: "Almost all loans at interest are made in money, either of paper, or of gold and silver. But what the borrower

level is irrelevant to the *lender* because his choice is not between holding money or purchasing goods, but rather between holding money or the bill of credit (granting a credit means to reallocate a stock of wealth which is to be distinguished from the saving decision). Both parties again have to take into account the expected rate of inflation during the repayment period as the borrower faces the threat of a real increase of his debt burden, and the creditor a loss of his financial wealth in real terms. The appropriate "Fisher modification" of the stipulated rate of interest is designed to compensate for the expected transfer of wealth, but this in no way reconstitutes the loan contract as a direct intertemporal transfer of resources: the creditor parts with money, not with resources, and the debt is settled by refunding money and not by delivering goods; his former status of wealth is only restored by getting back money as an "option asset".

As a consequence, the process of production too is integrated in a monetary framework. Its yield has to show in *money flows* as the entrepreneur is obliged to repay his debt in money terms. This simple fact was expressed by Marx' formula *M(oney)–C(ommodity)–M(oney)'* which later was taken up by Keynes: "An entrepreneur is interested, not in the amount of product, but in the amount of *money* which will fall to his share. He will increase his output if by so doing he expects to increase his money profit, even though this profit represents a smaller quantity of product than before".[22] The economic circulation in capitalism does not start and end up with commodities where money represents only an intermediate step, rather the production of commodities is but a transitional stage in the process of safeguarding and augmenting a stock of money wealth. Thus the process of production is subordinated to the logic of the asset market. "The market system needs a uniform category, in which all contracts are denominated, in order to enable competition between contracting parties. This uniform category is given by money. Competition of capital forms the basis of (the theory of) a monetary economy."[23]

---

really wants, and what the lender really supplies him with, is not the money, but the money's worth, or the goods which it can purchase. [...] By means of the loan, the lender, as it were, assigns to the borrower his right to a certain portion of the annual produce of the land and labour of the country to be employed as the borrower pleases" (Smith 1786: 152).

[22] Keynes 1933: 82, cf. 81, Marx 1890: 69-73, Luhmann 1988: 196-7.

[23] Riese 1987: 172.

2.2 Time, Interest and Money: The Myth of an Intertemporal Economy

> For money was intended to be used in exchange, but not to increase at interest. [...] That is why of all modes of getting wealth this is the most unnatural.
>
> *Aristoteles*[24]

> The element of Time [...] is the centre of the chief difficulty of almost every economic problem.
>
> *Alfred Marshall*[25]

> Interest on money *means* precisely what the books on arithmetic say that it means; [...] it is simply the premium obtainable on current cash over deferred cash, so that it measures the marginal preference (for the community as a whole) for holding cash in hand over cash for deferred delivery. No one would pay this premium unless the possession of cash served some purpose, i.e. had some efficiency. Thus we can conveniently say that interest on money measures the marginal efficiency of money measured in terms of itself as a unit.
>
> *John Maynard Keynes*[26]

In pre-classical economics "capital" was meant to be a sum of money invested in a business, where interest was a share of profit left to the creditor. Rigorous foundations for the existence of capital income were lacking. Indeed, some hints to an economic explanation of a positive rate of interest can be found in the study of the exceptions of the clerical ban on taking interest, which caught on from the 12th century onwards. Above all, these exceptions referred to the *risks* in the credit market: the case of "periculum sortis" applied to the fear that a repayment would be called off; "damnum emergens" was related to a late refunding; and "ratio incertudinis" covered the general uncertainty involved in credit relations. In addition, following a *opportunity-cost* approach, taking interest was permitted in the case of "lucrum cessans" where extending credit to somebody implied a profit foregone, which would have accrued from some other investment. Finally the case of "stipendium laboris" justified interest as a kind of *entrepreneurial income*.[27]

Classical economists then got down to "lift the monetary veil". They interpreted *capital as a means of production*, which came up as an obvious idea in an era of transition from trade to industrial capitalism, bringing about an unprecedented rise of prosperity within the establishing national economies. *Labour* was considered to be the root cause of value creation (whereas this function had been attributed to *land* in the physiocratic school), but only by using machines it appeared feasible

---

[24] Aristoteles 1996: 25.
[25] Marshall 1920: vii.
[26] Keynes 1937a: 101.
[27] Cf. Priddat 1993: 25-6.

to draw a "surplus" from employing labour which resulted from the difference between its average productivity and the real wage.

Via this way of reasoning the socialists were inspired to argue that the working
class were cheated out of their "right" to earn the whole yield of their work. On
the other hand, the neoclassical school, led by Böhm-Bawerk, complained about
the confusion of physical and value productivity: any surplus product cannot provide the entrepreneur with a lasting profit income because – in the absence of
other restrictions – competitive forces will induce further market entries and an
expansion of output, until the owners of *scarce* factors of production attract the
whole surplus, by means of rising factor prices. In the famous stagnation scenario
outlined by Ricardo the surplus income was reaped by the landowners, in the case
of scarce labour, with full employment, it would flow to wage earners. In equilibrium, only *rents* are left, i.e. incomes stemming from a *physical* scarcity of factors,
but no profits or interests, i.e. incomes related to the *value* of assets.

Thus it was the task of capital theory to put forward a particular scarcity on the
supply side, which prevents production to be extended to a point of zero profits.
The classical attitude of simply assuming a scarcity of physical capital obviously
offered no solution, but at best an illustration of that problem. "The real theoretical difficulty is rather to explain how, under stationary conditions, the possession
of capital can remain a permanent source of income."[28]

At this point *time* was brought into play. Jevons drew upon the fact that some,
particularly agricultural, processes need time for the ripening of the product and
thus took capital as a proxy for time. Output Y then could be modelled as a function of the passing of time t: $Y = f(t)$, the increase of production as $f(t + \Delta t) -
f(t)$. Relating this to the amount of product which is left in the process of ripen-
ing for one additional unit of time, i.e. which is withdrawn from a direct use, gives
the marginal product of capital (the marginal product of time). This is the real rate
of interest r, the physical yield of the time-consuming process of production:

$$r = \frac{f(t + \Delta t) - f(t)}{\Delta t\, f(t)} \quad \Rightarrow \quad r = \frac{df(t)}{dt}\, \frac{1}{f(t)} = \frac{f'(t)}{f(t)} \qquad [2.1]$$

A physiocratic writer would most probably have regarded this approach as a pla-
giarism (in a mathematical disguise) rather than a piece of evidence of scientific
progress. Nobody had denied that production processes embodied a dimension of
time (which perhaps may not had been appreciated in economic terms). Starting
from the physiocratic theory of rents Jevons substituted the power of time for the
power of nature and therefore offered an elegant variation of old-fashioned pro-
ductivity-based theories of interest. But of course it is an improper generalization
of functional relations valid in agriculture to assume that the passing of time will

---

28 Wicksell 1901: 154, cf. Bliss 1975: 3-4.

always increase the quantity or quality of some product (in chemical procedures the reverse can be true). Later it also became evident that the seeming unambiguousness of the above formula vanishes in cases of a more complicated term structure of employment of "capital" and labour; in general, an exogenously given rate of interest is the precondition for determining the length of production processes.[29]

Although Böhm-Bawerk still believed in the general productivity of "roundabout" production he shifted the attention to the demand side and thus pointed the way ahead for the future discussion by introducing the aspect of *time preference* on the part of consumers: resources are in limited supply for the purpose of capital accumulation if the owners of resources prefer an immediate use. The indulgence of human beings, their dislike to "wait" and to abstain temporarily from consumption, keeps factors of production in short supply, so that the saturation point with respect to the capital stock is never reached.

The crucial departure from the classical approach is that the gain of physical efficiency by using capital (i.e. machines) is no longer regarded as the basic reason for a positive rate of interest; rather, the crucial factor is the impatience on the part of consumers. They can only be induced to place resources at the investors' disposal by receiving interest which makes up for their time preference. Hence, for all firms an additional cost element is introduced: a minimum rate of profit (covering interest costs) which cannot be eroded by competition.[30] This equilibrium rate of profit is independent from productivity and is finally paid – as a deduction from the real wage – by the consumers.

Schumpeter stuck to the classical belief that interest was "paid" out of profits although he rejected the concept of a surplus. Thus he was forced to lay much emphasis on (temporary) monopoly profits – analyzed in a framework of a monetary theory of competition and evolution – which let the entrepreneurs accept the burden of interest payments. Very clearly he argued "that interest attaches to money and not to goods. [...] *Interest is an element in the price of purchasing power regarded as a means of control over production goods.*"[31] But in spite of this understanding Schumpeter shrank from attributing a liquidity premium to money holdings. As a consequence, his theory of interest was left – at best – incomplete on the supply side; contrary to his broadly presented theory of credit demand, the opportunity costs on the part of the lenders remain rather dim. At a more general lev-

---

[29] Cf. Jevons 1879: 240-1, Böhm-Bawerk 1884: 400-4, Hayek 1927. Critical opinions are expressed in Knight 1934, Schumpeter 1954: 322-34, 645-62, Riese 1988, Kurz 1998.

[30] The break between classical and neoclassical theories of capital, i.e. the contradiction between the idea of granting interest out of a surplus which originates from the productivity of capital, on the one hand, and the opposite conception of linking the rate of profit to the rate of interest, on the other, can best be studied in the work of John Stuart Mill (cf. Spahn 2000).

[31] Schumpeter 1934: 158, 184, cf. 190.

el, Schumpeter's almost tragical role in the history of economic thought is related to his attitude to present his monetary theory of capital and interest as a *disequilibrium* approach. This methodological "choice" labelled him as an heretic of neo-classical equilibrium theory who was pushed onto the sidelines of paradigmatic debates.

The neoclassical model of intertemporal equilibrium distinguishes between material, spatial and time dimensions of goods. On the "future" market, goods for present use are traded for entitlements to *specific* goods, to be delivered on some *definite* future date (contracts however can be designed to be dependent on contingencies). The relative price of present and future goods shows the degree of time preference and defines the real rate of interest. If in addition monetary contracts are allowed, the nominal rate of interest, to be paid for money loans, is derived from the real rate and the expected rate of change of money prices.

Box 2: Time Preference and Intertemporal Prices

Trading goods which only differ by their date of delivery is governed by time preference of individuals expressed by a rate discount δ assumed to be positive. Giving up one unit of a good today has to be compensated by the promise to get hold of $1 + \delta$ units tomorrow. There are three alternative ways of that exchange, arbitrage guarantees that the terms of trade will be equivalent (*figure 2.2*):

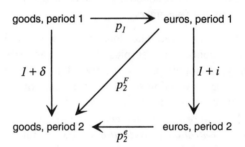

Figure 2.2: Alternative ways of transactions[32]

• In the most simple case present goods are exchanged for a claim to a larger amount of future goods which is redeemed tomorrow.

• Present goods are sold on the current spot market at a money price p_1 and the proceeds are used in the same period on the future market to buy claims to future delivery. The price of that claim today is:

$$p_2^F = \frac{1}{1+\delta} p_1 \qquad\qquad [2.2]$$

---

[32] Cf. Richter 1989: 154.

• Again the good is sold at p_1, but the money now is used to buy a financial asset which yields a nominal rate of interest i. This asset will be sold tomorrow and the funds are used to buy goods at the expected price p_2^e on the next period's spot market. Taking price expectations as exogenous and using the definition of the expected rate of inflation $\hat{p}^e = p_2^e/p_1 - 1$ gives the *intertemporal equilibrium condition* (proposed by Fisher) where a real rate of interest, represented by the discount rate $\delta = p_1 / p_2^F - 1$, and the expected rate of inflation determine the nominal money rate of interest as an endogenous variable:

$$1 + i = (1 + \delta)(1 + \hat{p}^e)$$ [2.3]

Equations [2.2] and [2.3] finally imply a relation between the money rate, the expected spot price and the current future price:

$$p_2^F = \frac{p_2^e}{1+i}$$ [2.4]

Time preference and expected inflation are independently given. An *increase of time preference* means a higher real rate of interest by definition. At the same time p_1 obviously will rise because of the growing demand in the current period. The effect on the nominal rate of interest can be studied by differentiating [2.3].

$$di = \frac{p_2^e}{p_1}\left[d\delta + (1 + \delta)\left(\frac{dp_2^e}{p_2^e} - \frac{dp_1}{p_1} \right) \right]$$ [2.5]

Three cases emerge:

• If $dp_2^e = 0$, two countervailing forces act on the nominal rate of interest, a positive effect because of the enlarged time preference, and a negative effect resulting from expected deflation. In a special case i will remain constant.

• The change of preferences is most clearly shown by $dp_2^e = - dp_1$ as the increased demand today will dampen demand tomorrow. Accordingly, the impact of expected deflation will increase and the nominal rate of interest might fall.

• If however future spot prices follow current prices in a random-walk pattern (each period's price level builds on the level prevailing in the previous period), rising prices today do not necessarily imply that they will come down tomorrow. The *relative* price level may stay unchanged ($dp_2^e = dp_1$). Then a special case, where $p_2^e / p_1 = 1$, yields the result that the nominal rate rises in line with time preference, i.e. with the real rate of interest r.

$$di = d\delta = dr$$ [2.6]

The stepwise determination of prices in each period (i.e. abolishing the market relevance of equation [2.4]) however contradicts the fundamental idea of intertemporal equilibrium theory which holds that all possible future events are already captured in the contracts of the "first" period. "The assumption that all intertemporal and all contingent markets exist has the effect of collapsing the future into the present."[33]

---

[33] Hahn 1980: 132.

The validity of this model of intertemporal transactions is questionable for several reasons:

In the *case of many goods* we have only a vector of intertemporal relative prices, but not *the* real rate of interest as the unique rate of return of capital.[34] Some critics therefore argued that neoclassical theory was not able to offer an analytical explanation of the rate of profit.[35] After the classical school failed in its attempt to found the rate of profit on physical productivity, the neoclassical school proved to be unsuccessful by resorting to intertemporal consumer preferences. This state of affairs – as will be elaborated in detail below – leaves the money rate of interest as the only candidate for explaining a positive rate of return on capital.

Irrespective of the variety of goods it can be disputed *whether the rate of discount inevitably is positive*. Vague presumptions about some "typical" human behaviour of discounting future needs are surely not sufficient as a foundation of an economic capital theory. A positive rate of time preference as such does not necessarily indicate a rational choice on behalf of market agents; continually they would have to regret tomorrow, the decisions made today.[36] In the framework of a pure barter system, the sign of the real of interest – computed from intertemporal prices – is more or less insignificant. If monetary transactions are permitted however, the problem arises that the money rate of interest, for obvious reasons, is always non-negative and that, therefore, the intertemporal equilibrium condition [2.3], in the case of a negative real rate, can only be fulfilled if the rate of inflation is sufficiently high. Thus the monetary sphere appears as a source of disturbances.

Money loans, in a system of intertemporal exchange, provide borrowers with monetary claims to resources without – if banks keep fractional reserves only – forcing other agents to declare an equivalent abstention from demand. Moreover, the liquidity of the banking system is practically independent from the saving decision (which merely implies a restructuring among the deposit items in the banks' balance sheets). As a consequence, the analytical and chronological "order" of saving and investment can be reversed, in comparison to a pure barter economy. "Forced" saving, by way of a general rise of money prices, can no longer be excluded. At this point, the quantity of money (which serves as an endogenously determined pure accounting medium in a perfect system of future markets) has to

---

[34] Cf. Hicks 1946: 154, Bliss 1975: 10, Richter 1989: 43-5.

[35] Cf. Robinson 1971: 8, Schefold 1976: 182, Milgate 1982: 22, 129-39.

[36] "There is literally no 'sense' in the notion of an inherent reluctance to postpone, or preference to future enjoyment, as a general principle embedded in human nature, rational or sentimental. Jevons saw this clearly. [...] The permanent and cumulative saving and investment we actually and typically find in the world cannot be explained in any degree through comparison between present and future enjoyment, or 'waiting' and being paid for waiting. [...] Wealth, viewed socially and objectively, is perpetual income capitalised, but what it means psychologically to the individual accumulator is a problem outside the sphere of the price theorist" (Knight 1934: 272n, cf. Friedman 1969: 21-2, Lutz/Niehans 1980, Richter 1989: 46)

be controlled by monetary authorities[37] – and thus we have finally arrived in the model of a monetary economy.

The more general issue is *why monetary contracts are permitted at all* or are even necessary in a system of intertemporal exchange. Their existence arouses suspicion that this system is flawed in some respects. For either agents are able to run their business by entering in direct barter contracts – then money is not needed; or the use of money indicates the inconvenience, or impossibility, of these exchange relations – then it remains an open question how many economic "truths", which have been discovered by studying the intertemporal equilibrium model, apply in a monetary economy as well. Here intertemporal transactions are almost exclusively carried out by establishing monetary creditor-borrower relations; and preferences with regard to future goods demand are *not* signalled to the producers today in a definite form. Thus they are forced to base investment decisions on *expected* sales and profits. Time preference of households shows in their propensity to consume, which has no bearing on intertemporal relative prices but on effective demand and, thus, income in the current period. It is very likely therefore, that changes in time preference will convey "wrong" messages to investors.[38]

The impact of these changes on the rate of interest in a monetary economy can hardly be compared to the results obtained in a barter model because of the different organizational logic of both systems. If future markets prevail, credit and labour supply can be integrated: households refrain from an immediate use of their endowments and provide the firms with goods and services. Their income – i.e. the amount of resources valued at market equilibrium prices – remain essentially unaffected; all endowments are supposed to yield utility to their owners (leisure can be substituted for working time). In a monetary economy, on the other hand, the labour market contract constitutes the workers' income, saving implies a loss of profits and the extension of credit represents a form of restructuring of wealth.

A strengthening of time preference may, in a monetary economy, also increase the nominal money rate of interest caused by an enlarged demand for transaction balances. This effect however, cannot be found in a pure intertemporal barter model where a fixed money supply does not exist. Even if the additional goods demand

---

[37] The central bank has to fix a price level target and – being an "foreign body" in a market economy – should be controlled by government (cf. Richter 1989: 137-80, 322).

[38] "An act of individual saving means – so to speak – a decision not to have dinner to-day. But it does *not* necessitate a decision to have dinner or to buy a pair of boots a week hence or a year hence or to consume any specified thing at any specified date. Thus it depresses the business of preparing to-day's dinner without stimulating the business of making ready for some future act of consumption. [...] Moreover, the expectation of future consumption is so largely based on current experience of present consumption that a reduction in the latter is likely to depress the former, with the result that the act of saving will not merely depress the price of consumption-goods and leave the marginal efficiency of existing capital unaffected, but may actually tend to depress the latter also" (Keynes 1936: 210, cf. 192-3, Kregel 1980).

leads to higher prices the path of inflation and of the real rate of interest remains undetermined.

The real rate of interest is a purely statistical variable which can be computed by deducting the expected rate of inflation from the nominal money rate, but, conversely, the real rate cannot be utilized to derive the money rate. *A real rate of return to which the money rate of interest can adjust does not exist in a monetary economy.* On the contrary, the nominal rate of interest is the only market variable which is assigned to an intertemporal debt relation. It imposes on the firms, being debtors in money terms, an obligation which converts the production process into an object on the asset market.

2.3   Capital as Cash Advance: The Monetary Theory of the Rate of Interest

> The question why capital is scarce is [...] best regarded as being, in the long run, the same question as why the rate of interest exceeds zero.
>
> *John Maynard Keynes*[39]

> Capital is a money advance which is necessary for the execution of production. Accordingly, the rate of profit too is a price for parting with liquidity, it is monetary rate of interest emerging on the goods market.
>
> *Hajo Riese*[40]

> Each payment involves the loss of the option of an alternative use of the financial means. Each non-payment involves the loss of the opportunity of satisfying wants here and now.
>
> *Niklas Luhmann*[41]

The neoclassical approach of explaining a uniform rate of return of capital not failed for two reasons: first, given heterogeneous capital goods, only a *vector* of yields can be derived. Second, as the elements of a production function should consist of physical quantities, the concept of marginal productivity merely determines *rents*, but no rate of interest as a yield of an asset. Wicksell therefore found himself compelled to a "analytical wrongness" which destroyed the uniformity in the theory of income distribution: the endowments of labour and land were introduced as physical quantities, capital however as a sum of money. As in Marx, capital was conceived as a *cash advance*, a financial constraint of the production process. "All these requisites [i.e. produced capital goods] have only one quality in common, namely that they represent certain quantities of exchange value, so that

---

[39] Keynes 1934: 456.
[40] Riese 1987: 163.
[41] Luhmann 1988: 224-5.

Box 3: The Marginal Productivity of Capital and the Rate of Interest

A production function $Y = Y(N,X)$ only contains *physical* factors, for example working time of labour N and capital goods X. The *value* of capital has to bear interest. If we ignore depreciation and inflation, profit maximization yields the first order conditions

$$Y_N' \left[= \frac{QU}{TU} \right] = \frac{w}{P} \left[= \frac{MU/TU}{MU/QU} \right] \qquad [2.7]$$

$$Y_X' \left[= \frac{QU}{TU} \right] = \frac{p_X}{P} \, i \left[= \frac{MU}{MU/QU} \frac{1}{TU} \right] \qquad [2.8]$$

where w denotes the nominal wage, i the nominal rate of interest, P the level of output prices and p_X the price of homogenous capital goods. For reason of clarification, the explicit notation of the variables' dimensions has been added where QU, TU and MU denote units of quantity, time and money, respectively.

From a production-function perspective, the marginal productivity of labour and "machines", Y_N' and Y_X', respectively, act upon factor prices (relative to the general price level) expressing the optimizing behaviour of entrepreneurs who compare the marginal return from using any factor with its cost. In the case of capital goods these costs consist of their market price and the cost of financing the *value* of capital equipment. The last mentioned item is a cost element originating in the asset market, it has no roots in the production process. Note that – unlike the real wage in [2.7] – the expression p_X/P in [2.8] is not a relative price: p_X indicates a *pure sum of money* which is charged with a rate of interest because the capital good has to perform as a capital asset. The concept of a physical marginal productivity of capital in no way offers a clue to the question why the *money value* of some factor of production has to yield interest as a (minimum) rate of profit. This becomes particularly evident in case of heterogeneous capital goods X_i, employed in different lines of production, where in each case their prices have to conform to their, most probably, diverging marginal products, although of course all processes have to yield the same rate of interest in a competitive equilibrium.

The textbook literature often refers to the simple case where Y and X represent qualitatively identical goods and thus $p_X/P = 1$. Here the physical marginal productivity of capital seems to determine the rate of interest. But a simple inspection of the dimensions of the variables on both sides of the equation $Y_X' = i$ reveals that they are not commensurable, taken at their face value: on the left we have a flow of quantities per unit of time, on the right a pure number, a percentage rate per unit of time. A closer look at [2.8] shows that, even when $p_X = P$, the price of the factor enters the equation as a *value* which leaves the dimension of the r.h.s. as QU/TU. Again, the employed factor performs as a capital asset on the part of his proprietor, irrespective of its physical homogeneity with regard to the output of the production process. The marginal product of "capital", narrowly defined, in that case should be seen to be equal to unity, not to the rate of interest.

collectively they may be regarded as a single sum of value, a certain amount of the medium of exchange, money".[42]

The rate of profit then is determined – contrary to Marx though – by the money rate of interest. It does not measure the scarcity of capital goods, but rather represents the cost of finance to be passed on in goods prices. A particular efficiency or differential rents of capital goods are reflected in their prices but not in the rate of interest; this is confused in the theory of the marginal productivity of capital.

The crucial problem is how to explain a non-temporary shortage of cash advances or, which comes down to the same thing, to give an explanation for a positive money rate of interest. If we ignore the banking system, private financial asset portfolios then consist of cash (for example gold coins) and securities. An extension of credit requires a restructuring of portfolios. We can hardly assume that agents are indifferent as to the choice between holding money and holding credit claims. In general, only a payment of interest will induce them to place a money loan at the debtor's disposal. "The rate of interest [...] has to be established at the level which, in the opinion of those who have the opportunity of choice – i.e. of wealth-holders – equalises the attractions of holding idle cash and of holding the loan."[43]

With respect to *risk*, it is a choice between a general entitlement to resources, guaranteed by the market's acceptance of money, and a specific claim on some particular debtor. The risk of default will show in a market price. The probability attached to refunding inversely establishes interest as a risk premium. "If there is any doubt about repayment, there must be interest; for no one will voluntarily part with money [...] in return for anything less than a 100 per cent probability of the principle being repaid. [...] The greater the risk of default, the higher (other things being equal) will be the rate of interest."[44] Even if the default risk should be fully insurable (which is questionable as the events are connected in a cumulative way just like unemployment in depressions) this would not affect the character of interest as a cost element located outside the sphere of production.

The argument of *time* picks up the thread of the neoclassical model of intertemporal exchange. As there is no real rate of return to which the money rate adjusts by means of arbitrage however, time preference cannot account for a positive rate of interest on money loans. Already holding money implies an abstention from using resources just like holding securities. At most, time preference acts as a (negative) motive for asset accumulation as such; but the prospect of earning some interest income can hardly be regarded as a compelling precondition for saving, given the

---

[42] Wicksell 1901: 145, cf. 149, Keynes 1933/34, Kurz 1998. Hicks (1974) noted that classical economists in general stuck to the "business man's concept" of capital as a fund, with an eye on the debt side of balance sheets, whereas the neoclassicals after 1871 adopted the view of capital essentially consisting of goods.

[43] Keynes 1937b: 213, cf. Hicks 1989: 64-71.

[44] Hicks 1969: 73-4, cf. Riese 1988: 383.

general advantages and convenience of possessing wealth in a private-property economy where individuals fear for their economic livelihood.

The *macroeconomic* stock of financial wealth is not affected by households' saving anyway because – all other items of effective demand remaining constant – the saving of firms (i.e. undistributed profits) reacts inversely which can be seen from basic circular-flow identities. Gross financial wealth can only increase if either additional credits launch the process of income creation, resulting in additional saving[45], or in case of a capitalization of newly arisen streams of expected profits: "Capitalist fortunes do not typically arise from saving income dollars and piling them up neatly, but by the creation of sources of returns, the capitalized value of which then constitutes a 'fortune'."[46]

Returning to the aspect of time, credit supply forces the wealth owner (given his general willingness to keep his wealth) to restrain from money holding for a certain period of time. Independently from the risk aspect this sacrifice has to be compensated by an interest payment, because only money bears a *liquidity premium* indicating an agent's *ability to pay*. The borrower agrees on his obligation to pay interest, as he can get resources only by paying money and not by offering his promissory note (these circumstances are modified, but not abolished, if bank deposits are taken into the picture). On the other hand, the owner of money demands interest because during the term of the credit contract he will be unable to make use of the option to restructure his portfolio in response to new information or a shift of preferences. "There is thus a probability that a portfolio choice, once made, is not optimal in light of what will be learned. This consideration, when combined with transaction costs, leads to a premium on 'liquid' or low-transaction-cost assets. This premium is in nature of an option purchase."[47]

---

[45] Here history of economic thought for a long time has resisted to recognize the importance of banks as creators of credits, not least because this threatened to undermine the traditional belief in the virtue of saving. In order to escape from this cognitive conflict holders of banking deposits later were regarded as *savers* although they just supply the banks with liquidity (cf. Schumpeter 1954: 1114, Chick 1983: 239).

[46] Schumpeter 1954: 573-4. This way of creating wealth "out of nothing" has also been emphasized by Knight (1934: 277): "The amount of capital is always the capitalised value of an expected future stream of services. When conditions change, capital simply appears or/and disappears, and is written up or written down without reference to 'production'."

[47] Hahn/Solow 1995: 144, cf. Riese 1995. Kregel (1998: 123) links the interpretation of money holdings as an option with Keynes' concept of "user costs": "Buying investment goods, or consumption goods, or buying financial assets [...] or repaying debt means that money will no longer be available to be 'used' at a future date when the prices of the assets or goods will be different. The 'user cost' of expending money today can than be defined as the present value of the potential future gain or loss that has been foregone or avoided by parting with money today. [...] The user cost of money could thus be defined as the equivalent of a call option on a deposit at the current interest rate. Alternatively, holding money uninvested in a portfolio allows you to avoid the sale of an investment asset to meet an unanticipated need for liquid funds."

Thus we may conclude that *the money rate of interest is an option price*. It expresses an illiquidity discount of all other assets. Interest is paid for the right to dispose of money *within the current period*. Correspondingly, firms have to earn interest by sales proceeds in each period to pay for the service of a continuing cash advance provided by capitalists. Whereas amortization represents the time aspect of the credit contract, *interest essentially is not related to the passing of time*; equally the rate of profit is not related to the time-consuming character of production. Liquidity premium is not an intertemporal category: it is no issue to be solvent "today rather than tomorrow", although the demand for liquidity may be felt to vary; which then influences the term structure of interest rates. Interest is a non-temporal price to be paid from current income in order to curb the agents' liquidity preference, i.e. to make them willing to part with money and stay illiquid in the current period. "Liquidity preference is the reason why ready money commands a premium over bills or bonds − is the cause, therefore, of the existence of a rate of interest."[48]

Wealth owners tend to be indifferent between money and other financial assets which serve as a means of payment. Therefore particular bank deposits yield low or zero interest. In the case of negotiable securities the creditor can only obtain the option of restoring his liquidity by taking the risk of capital losses. In general, the rate of interest controls the decision to hold cash and/or securities (which in most cases will not be a zero-one choice). Liquidity preference theory is superior to the loanable funds theory, as changes of the rate of interest do not (necessarily) depend on changes in the *flows* of saving and investment, but result from new valuations of the *stock* of financial assets.[49]

Keynesian views on the theory of the rate of interest are not fully convincing. Two years after the publication of his "General Theory" Keynes agreed with his disciple Townshend who had argued that interest is not a price covering the risk of default at the *end* of a repayment period, but rather a price compensating for the loss of liquidity *during* that period.[50] The explanations, though, given for this liquidity preference in the Keynesian literature are a bit ambiguous. The common departure from the neoclassical approach is that interest is not understood as a premium paid for non-spending of one's income, i.e. for the non-use of resources. But Keynes himself kept up the neoclassical tradition of emphasizing the inter-

---

[48] Hicks 1982: 240, cf. Hicks 1989: 52.

[49] Cf. Keynes 1937b, Townshend 1937.

[50] "A liquidity premium [...] is a payment, not for the expectation of increased tangible income at the end of the period, but for an increased sense of comfort and confidence during the period" (Keynes 1938: 294). Townshend had written: "The reluctance to part with liquid money − the property of liquidity which gives it exchange value and enables people to obtain interest by parting with money under contract − has its origin in the doubts of wealth-owners as to what may happen to values *before the end of any interval, however short*; and I suggest that the basic cause of interest is bound up with this" (1938: 291, cf. Heinsohn/Steiger 1996: 183).

temporal aspects of interest and money when he wrote that "*the importance of money essentially flows from its being a link between the present and the future*".[51]

This misses the point, as this link is given by intertemporal (debt) contracts in money terms whereas money is kept precisely because of its convenience in the current period. Keynes' phrase should even be turned upside down: *money helps to eliminate time from the economy*! Without money and a mutually matching coincidence of wants, barter transactions, almost inevitably, would involve some type of a credit contract; as the seller of goods would have to accept the buyer's promissory note which entitles the bearer to take a certain amount of the debtor's goods and services at some future date. It is just the use of money which makes it possible to avoid the imponderables of intertemporal credit contracts, by introducing the possibility of a direct *purchase*: handing over a generally accepted claim which immediately settles the sale contract and pays off the buyer's debt.

The choice between holding money and a money-denominated debt contract, i.e. the credit supply decision, involves the above mentioned balancing of interest income on the one hand, and the convenience of solvency and flexibility on the other. Obviously, the option of staying liquid is particularly valuable in a state of imperfect information.[52] In an economy which evolves through historical time, the subjective perception of the uncertain future will have an impact on liquidity preference and, thus, on the rate of interest. This effect is captured in Keynes' famous remark: "Our desire to hold money as a store of wealth is a barometer of the degree of our distrust of our own calculations and conventions concerning the future. [...] The possession of actual money lulls our disquietude; and the premium which we require to make us part with money is the measure of the degree of our disquietude."[53]

But it should be noted that the – rather trivial – finding that the future is uncertain concerns all economic decisions and may not be taken as an *explanation* of a positive rate of interest. And the "fundamentalist" branch of Post Keynesians was surely wrong in propagating the argument that because of uncertainty the tools of equilibrium theory no longer apply.[54] Hence, in some respect, even the Keynesian

---

[51] Keynes 1936: 293.

[52] "Expenditures on goods, services and assets involve commitments of an agent's resources to illiquid ends. But if the future is uncertain, agents may prefer *not* to make such commitments, and instead remain liquid. Exercising this 'option to wait' by remaining liquid enhances the agent's flexibility in the face of an uncertain future" (Setterfield 1999: 482).

[53] Keynes 1937c: 116.

[54] See e.g. Davidson 1978: 10-32, 140-158, Robinson 1980, Shackle 1982. Kregel (1976) however had already pointed out that in Keynes' methodological concept of a shifting equilibrium, different expected states of the world would simply appear as shift variables in choice-theoretic market functions and thus would not preclude even a long-run analysis.

school in its battle against the neoclassicals, adhered to the traditional belief that the roots of the rate of interest are to be found in the phenomenon of time.

Finally, we can take up the question of Wicksell again. He linked the concept of a monetary notion of capital to the widespread idea that the scarcity of this (value of) capital could be overcome by means of saving. Although the connection of time preference, interest and saving appeared to him as rather complicated, he believed that a continuing accumulation would tend to render capital abundant and to lower the rate of interest.[55] This way of reasoning however is inappropriate in a monetary economy, because market agents do not (as they do in a barter model) choose between consumption and investment: credit-financed investment may take up resources by way of forced saving (i.e. rising prices). But we may not expect lower interest rates from capital accumulation, as the rate of interest – contrary to a widely held myth – does not express the relative scarcity of some physical factor of production but rather the relative scarcity of means of payments.[56]

Keynes himself also succumbed to this confusion. Whereas, on the one hand, he argued that liquidity preference is the reason why "the world after several millenia of steady individual saving, is so poor as it is in accumulated capital-assets", he also, on the other hand, hoped for a continuing process of investment to bring down the marginal efficiency of capital, which then should lead to an "euthanasia of the rentier". Obviously, on this occasion, he forgot his own analysis which had yielded the result that the money rate of interest is determined *independently* from the rate of profit.[57] We may surmise that it was Keynes in his role of a public-spirited reformer, wanting to get rid of the "objectionable features of capitalism" (for example high capital incomes), who put forward the argument that "interest to-day rewards no genuine sacrifice"[58]; thus he lapsed back into the old way of thinking.

---

[55] Cf. Wicksell 1901: 209, Marshall 1920: 483, Kurz 1988.

[56] The liquidity theory of the rate of interest in no way implies that the relative scarcity of means of payments may be overcome by monetary policy actions. Attempts to increase the quantity of money without limit will simply erode the notes' reputation as a means of payment.

[57] "It is much preferable to speak of capital as having a yield over the course of its life in excess of its original cost, than as being *productive*. For the only reason why an asset offers a prospect of yielding during its life services having an aggregate value greater than its initial supply price is because it is *scarce*; and it is kept scarce because of the competition of the rate of interest on money. If capital becomes less scarce, the excess yield will diminish, without its having become less productive – at least in the physical sense" (Keynes 1936: 213, 242, 375-6, cf. Keynes 1933/34).

[58] Keynes 1936: 221, 376.

2.4 Equilibrium and Employment in a Monetary Economy

> Money as a store of wealth stands as a barrier of full pro-
> duction, that is, unemployment is caused by money.
>
> *Dudley Dillard*[59]

> In a certain world, there would be no reason for holding
> money, nor would there be any involuntary unemployment.
>
> *Paul Davidson*[60]

> The market-analytic contents of a monetary theory of pro-
> duction can be summarized as follows: money constitutes
> the general budget constraint of the market system which
> makes *interest* into a *monetary* phenomenon.
>
> *Hajo Riese*[61]

If the function of money is no longer performed by generally accepted promissory
notes of some renowned wealth owner but by notes issued by a central bank, it
may appear that the rate of interest could be fixed at will by monetary authorities.
But although central banks are able to provide financial markets with some guid-
ance, they have to adjust their interest rate policies according to the prevailing
market conditions.[62] The *art of central banking* consists of continuously mastering
the threefold task of maintaining the solvency of the banking system; of safeguarding the value of the currency; and of taking into account the demands for interest income on the part of the owners of financial wealth.

Of course, satisfying these demands is no functional precondition in a monetary
economy; but given the liberty of free capital movements in an open economy,
market agents can play national central banks off against each other by withdraw-
ing funds from low-interest currency areas. With fixed exchange rates, this problem leads to the constraints of key currency systems. If exchange rates are allowed
to fluctuate, central banks may tolerate or even promote (in order to enhance exports end employment) some depreciation, as long as there are no signs of a
"flight from the currency". The crucial question is whether the efficiency of a
monetary economy depends on a particular degree of price stability. The scarcity
of money can only be defined relative to the price level. If prices were perfectly

---

[59] Dillard 1955: 12.

[60] Davidson 1978: 12.

[61] Riese 1988: 381-2.

[62] In former times prominent central bankers felt even stronger than today that the rate of
interest was a market variable, not a policy instrument. The president of the German
Reichsbank Havenstein stated in 1908: "The policy of a central bank does not create the
discount rate, rather, it is essentially determined by the economic circumstances of a
country [...]. Therefore the central bank's interest rates, in principle, [...] have to adjust
to the money-market's rate, the bank [...] can influence that rate only within moderate
limits" (quoted from Borchardt/Schötz 1991: 181n).

flexible the control of the monetary strain would require a marked volatility of interest rate policies. Thus, the stability of financial markets requires some *rigidity of nominal prices*.

In *deflation*, the central bank loses its control over the money market. As long as commercial banks are able to maintain their liquidity they may opt to reduce their indebtedness to the central bank, which then contributes further to the shrinkage of the money supply. If however, the firms cannot pay off bank credits because of insufficient cash flow, the banking system runs into a liquidity crisis. A collapse threatens when (because of pecuniary returns of holding cash) the money demand increases, whereas (for fear of real debt overload) the demand for credit vanishes; so that the banks are confronted at the same time with rising cash withdrawals and a loss of assets which are eligible for refinancing. The rate of interest then can be low in absolute terms, but overall economic recovery may be blocked by bankruptcies and the lack of profit expectations. What is needed then is a reflation driven by fiscal and/or open-market policy, which does not hesitate to monetize even bad loans.

On the other hand, the existence of macroeconomic supply constraints is not necessarily detrimental to profits or profit expectations. Bottlenecks on goods markets may even signal profit opportunities and foster general economic activity. Many investment projects prove to be profitable, particularly in an *inflationary* environment, as the criterion of success consists of a comparison of monetary values. The process gathers momentum if expected inflation feeds back on goods demand, i.e. if market agents aim to evade losses in the real value of their financial wealth. The displacement of the home currency, as a medium of wealth formation, indicates a progressive loss of money functions which tends to spill over on goods and labour markets until finally contracts are being denominated in some other money standard.[63] The key problem here is a *non-neutrality* emanating from money as a nominal standard (to be distinguished from the ordinary debate on the existence of real impacts of monetary expansions): market agents attribute real effects to the use of money which should be no part of its essential services. The spreading of real-value considerations in the use of a currency points to its decline.

The stability of a monetary economy requires stability of nominal values. Already at the end of the 19th century when he designed his vision of a future pure paper money standard, Wicksell became the founder of monetary macro theory, as he recognized that in an economy propelled by bank credits the stability of money as a standard of value would not be ensured by endogenous market forces; there is no guarantee that, in case of excess demand on goods and labour markets, economic activities – measured in nominal values – is checked by means of the real balance effect. Maintaining price stability thus had to be the primary task of monetary policy. Wicksell's research program represents the transition from a theory

---

[63] Cf. Schumpeter 1970: 219, 224-5, Robinson 1938.

of intertemporal trade to a theory of a monetary economy: the main topic changed from the analysis of the intertemporal use of resources to the problem of stabilizing money prices – an issue which does not come up in "pure future economies".[64] The money rate of interest develops into a policy instrument controlling the macroeconomic activity in the current period.

Of course, a state of excess demand is not the rule, but neither is general excess supply. Despite the seemingly empirical evidence in recent years there is no convincing argument why unemployment should be an inescapable feature of a monetary economy. Profit expectations and the creation of credit are the two cornerstones of the system's mode of operation. For various reasons, which have been extensively discussed in the previous decades, there are only weak and ambiguous links from the degree of utilization of factor supply to investment-driven macroeconomic activity.

The general equilibrium in a monetary economy essentially has a *nominal* character, notwithstanding the practice of central banks to use (estimated) real variables, like the production potential, or "natural" rates of growth or unemployment as benchmarks for their monetary policy decisions. In former times they used the money price of gold for that purpose with little consideration for trade and commerce. The evolution of monetary policy targets from internal and external exchange rates (i.e. prices of reserve assets or foreign currencies, respectively) to the goods-market price level will be analyzed in subsequent chapters.

Box 4: Money and Unemployment

In the Keynesian literature three lines of thought have been propagated which aim to prove that unemployment for systematic reasons is an inevitable feature of a monetary economy.

(1) The "fundamentalist" branch of Post Keynesian theory starts from the observation that unemployment appears only in monetary market economies and thus concludes that therefore it must be "caused by money" (which is an odd reasoning as there are no non-monetary market economies and there was hidden unemployment in planned economies). The core of the argument seems to be that uncertainty keeps interest rates high via liquidity preference. Already Keynes argued that the long-term rate of interest for decades could be too high for maintaining full employment. This was said to be due to two peculiarities of money:

• A *zero elasticity of production* indicates that Say's Law is violated. An increased demand for money as a store of value proves to be a "bottomless sink for purchasing power" as money cannot be privately produced.

---

[64] Cf. Wicksell 1898: 178-96, Hawtrey 1923: 420, Hicks 1989: 102-11, Holtfrerich 1989. Hayek (1928, 1931) on the other hand continued to believe in the necessity of intertemporal changes of the price level. In particular, a "balanced evolution" was said to require falling prices due to improvements in technology. Hayek did not think of distributing productivity gains through nominal wage increases.

• A *zero elasticity of substitution* then prevents that the price effect of an increased demand for money induces a demand to other, reproducible assets. A falling price level due to lower goods demand equals a higher value of money which in turn makes holding money to appear even more profitable.

The conclusion seems straightforward: "Unemployment develops [...] because people want the moon; – men cannot be employed when the object of desire (i.e. money) is something which cannot be produced and the demand for which cannot be readily choked off."[65]

But the second argument knocks the bottom out of the first: falling prices increase *real* money supply even if its nominal stock should be invariant. Therefore the rate of interest should fall which in principle should exert a stabilizing impact. In order to rule out a return to full employment Keynes resorts to wage and price rigidities and adverse expectations. This only means that the adjustment processes in the case of unemployment are *indeterminate*, there is however no logically compelling reason to believe that unemployment is *inevitable*.

(2) The rationing or disequilibrium approach seems to work on the assumption that there can be no involuntary unemployment in a pure barter-model economy: with all payments in kind, market agents can negotiate on the real contents of the employment contract which also comprises a contract for the sale of consumption goods. Virtually labour and goods markets are integrated, labour services being exchanged for a delivery of commodities. Hence, we should expect a market clearing real wage to emerge. Moreover, it is often assumed that households can make their own use of potential working hours (leisure or self-employment) so that the possibility of an excess supply of labour cannot arise.

The introduction of money in such a system according to classical economists does not preclude a full employment equilibrium. "Goods can serve many other purposes besides purchasing money, but money can serve no other purpose besides purchasing goods. Money, therefore, necessarily runs after goods, but goods do not always or necessarily run after money. The man who buys does not always mean to sell again, but frequently to use or to consume; whereas he who sells always means to buy again."[66] In Clower's rationing model, however, the existence of money causes a separation of labour and goods markets. "Money buys goods and goods buy money; but goods do not buy goods."[67] Now money seems to give rise to a *coordination failure*: unemployed persons are not hired, not because the expected real wage would be too high, but rather because the market does not signal the consumption demand of additional workers *after* the wage payment has been made.

This approach to explain the existence of unemployment by the monetary constitution of a market systems proves to be unsatisfactory for various reasons:

• In no way can it be taken for granted that in the case of an arbitrarily given vector of endowments all resources and services will yield a positive equilibrium price. Hence, unemployment cannot be ruled out even in a hypothetical barter world.

---

[65] Keynes 1936: 231, 235, cf. 203-4, 210-21, Dillard 1955, Dillard 1987, Davidson 1978: 145, Davidson 1981, Chick 1983: 293-311.

[66] Smith 1786: 186.

[67] Clower 1967: 207-8.

• Moreover, a coordination failure of the above described type could be avoided in a barter world only in the trivial few-goods case. In general, workers do not consume the goods which they help to produce. The problem of coordinating factor demand, product supply and goods demand would thus be huge – and it is just in order to solve this coordination problem that the market has invented money! Therefore, it is inappropriate to blame money for unemployment, without money things would be even worse.

• Finally, the rationing approach ignores a temporary financing of goods demand by means of transfers, credit or sales of assets. "If Clower wants to buy champagne he can convey this signal to champagne producers by means of a consumer credit, followed by additional wage-earning work in order to pay off his debt."[68]

(3) If only "money buys goods" and if scarceness is one of its essential peculiarities one might by led to conclude that the stock of money should be interpreted as a kind of budget constraint which necessarily – compared to the vector of physical endowments – imposes a narrower restriction on economic activities. Excess supply of resources then appears as a characteristic feature of a monetary economy.[69]

From a theoretical point of view this reasoning seems flawed; first, because it is not the stock of money but the volume of credit which limits the employment of resources; second, because fixed prices and a given technique of production have to be assumed to establish a link between the volume of credit and the amount of employment; and third, because single market agents will not restrict their credit supply in order to aim at a state of excess supply. Just as unemployment is a precondition for a positive rate of profit in classical theory, it might appear likewise necessary for maintaining price stability in a Keynesian world. Hence, the prevention of a wage-price spiral is the duty of monetary policy, unemployment may be a by-product, or even a means of that policy, but it is not necessarily the basic state of a market economy.

---

[68] Streißler 1983: 464, cf. Robinson 1971: 12-3, Hahn 1977, Hellwig 1993.
[69] Cf. Riese 1987: 158, Riese 1988: 386, Riese 1995: 49, 57, and – for a critical review – Heering 1991: 99-102.

Summary of Part I

A private-ownership economy, taking advantage of the division of labour, can only be efficiently organized by the existence of a standard of value. It serves as a benchmark in economic calculations and as a denomination standard of private contracts. On a variety of markets goods, services and assets are bought and sold in exchange for money, which acts as a decentralized information, ranking and selection device with regard to the social value of individual market supply. The economic process of a market system thus is mirrored in a continuum of payment acts, which establish an economic (and in part also social) connection between market agents and bring about the compatibility of individually planned market behaviour.

Sequential trading on different markets confronts economic agents with the problem of imperfect information as to their future needs and the economic capability and potentially reneging behaviour of their contract partners. Thus agents offering goods and services do not likewise want particular goods and services in return, which can be offered by their clients immediately or which are promised to be delivered in the future. Instead they prefer being paid in units of marketable claims to any goods, which can be held as an option, but also be executed at any time.

The sought-after medium of payment exhibits some features of a public good, serving as a "language" of economic communication, but it also manages a definite and exclusive transfer of private property rights. Even in "low-trust societies", this institutional set-up of monetary exchange allows a pattern of the distribution of resources and income, which as a formal procedure is socially accepted (although it might be corrected by governmental distribution policies). Problems related to a lack of information on the trustworthiness of market agents are being projected onto the qualitative features of money; individual market agents thus are relieved of behavioural standards − but this enforces the monetary medium to meet an outstanding demand for reputation.

A theory of a monetary economy cannot make use of all of the conventional wisdom which has been elaborated from the analysis of a barter economy, i.e. from the neoclassical model of intertemporal exchange. This is not because these theories are wrong, but because they refer to an economic order which is substantially different from the market system. The latter can be characterized as a payment society or a nominal-standard economy, where market agents try to assess the real contents of nominal contracts, but nevertheless insist on payments to be made in monetary units. Adjusting money prices for expected inflation in no way justifies the use of barter-type economic theories.

A peculiar feature of a monetary economy therefore is the demand for solvency. This can be met by paying interest, which is the price compensating the liquidity premium of money. The idea, prevalent in the history of economic thought, that the rate of interest (and thus, in equilibrium, the rates of return on other capital assets) ought to be explained by the interplay of time-consuming, but productive "roundabout" production and intertemporal preferences should be assessed as a wrong track of economic theory. This neoclassical approach of interpreting the rate of interest as an intertemporal price might be analytically well founded for a simple barter system, but not for a monetary economy. Capital has to be envisaged in money value terms; accordingly, it yields a rate of profit which in equilibrium is given by the money rate of interest. The contradictory opinion, put forward in classical (and partly in neoclassical) economics, that the basis of profit and interest is to be found in the productive power of nature, industry and/or labour, or time, is flawed for analytical reasons: following that line of reasoning only rents, i.e. an income of physically scarce factors, can be derived; the approach fails to give an understanding of interest as an income accruing to the money value of assets.

Time preference can neither be envisaged as a generally valid trait of rational human behaviour, nor be used as a factor unambiguously determining the nominal or real rate of interest in a monetary economy. Here, the rate of interest does not express an intertemporal demand or use of resources, but represents an "entry fee" to be paid by market agents allowing them to participate in the monetary process of resource allocation. It is determined by individual decisions as to the allocation of portfolios of financial wealth (and monetary policy in an open economy with liberalized capital markets has little scope for pursuing interest policies which for longer time spans diverge from world market trends). Keynes also maintained an intertemporal approach and interpreted money as a link of the present and the future, which finally made the rate of interest an indicator of the uncertainty of the future. Actually however, money serves to eliminate the time dimension from economic transactions, allowing the substitution of cash payments (with lower demands on the agents' reputation) for intertemporal credit contracts which would have to stipulate mutual deliveries of goods and services.

The traditional view also overrated industrial capitalism in terms of economic history because the monetary economy which unfolded (anew) around the 12th century in Western Europe is much older. Interest income already existed when the surging process of production had to offer an equivalent capital income. As interest thus is no measure of the scarcity of capital, it will not be brought down by the process of accumulation and saturation. A by-product of the organization of a market system as a monetary economy is that the creation of income, on a micro as on a macro level, primarily depends on the ability and willingness to spend money, which implies that market agents are confronted with the risk that their endowments of resources may lack marketability. In a market economy, goods tend to be plentiful, labour in excess supply, and money is scarce – whereas in a socialist planned economy resources always were in short supply and its "money" was no money at all.

PART II
BANKING AND THE RISE
OF MONETARY POLICY

3. Banks as Creators of Money

3.1 Money as a Regulated Medium

> Token money always is the genuine money, because of its
> highest degree of abstraction and its lowest degree of direct
> utility; then gold and silver follow as substitutes; if these are
> not available, even corn can take over the money's role.
>
> *Karl Polanyi*[1]

> The issue of paper as a substitute for coin is not a branch of
> productive industry; it is a thing which ought to be regulated
> by the State and be included in the department of admini-
> stration.
>
> *Thomas Tooke*[2]

The *theory* of money has established the supposition that its functions can be fulfilled only by assets, or media, which are distinguished by some particular reputation. But it is still an open issue which market agent or social institution will provide such an asset. This question invites a look at the *history* of money. For epistemological reasons, however, there is little hope that the historical beginnings
will reveal the "true" and "genuine" essentials of any economic phenomenon. On
the contrary, primitive forms of money may prove the most complicated ones: because the evolutionary market process may not yet have discovered the efficient
and functionally appropriate elements of a monetary order[3] – and in addition we
have to keep in mind that the efficiency-enhancing property of market evolution is
but an axiom.

Traditional monetary theory holds that goods bearing the lowest transaction costs
grow into media of exchange. Smith, Menger and Schumpeter – to name but three

---

[1] Polanyi 1957: 319.
[2] Quoted from Andréadès 1909: 270n, Lutz 1936: 40-1.
[3] Cf. Schumpeter 1970: 16-8, Heering 1999.

famous economists – seemed to have believed in a gradual transition from a barter to a monetary economy; the idea was that the initial bilateral exchange of commodities had been facilitated step-by-step, by using the most marketable commodity with the lowest transaction costs as a medium of exchange which then evolved into money.[4] Economic history research however, did not confirm the hypothesis of an emergence of money from barter. "Monetary exchange systems have not evolved out of non-monetary exchange ('barter') systems but out of non-exchange systems."[5] Accordingly, modern neoclassical theory no longer identifies the analytical and historical foundation of money. The transaction-cost approach only claims to explain the *use* of money, considering the inconvenience of barter exchange, not its historical *origin*.[6]

Although the discovery of historical "truth" is not the focus of attention in this study, it should be noted that a cursory look into the history of money conveys the impression that media serving as money often have been regulated in particular ways. These media showed low transaction costs in their use, but they were not easily available for everyone. Money does not seem to be a cheap medium of exchange, but rather a regulated and supervised medium of payment.[7]

In ancient Greece, temples in return for delivered sacrificial animals issued receipts, which then took over the function of money. Thus money had its origin in a sacrifice; this is the core of Laum's theory of "holy money", an idea which undoubtedly can be reconciled with the traditional view of money arising from barter, as the sacrifice can be interpreted as an exchange contract between man and god. The crucial point however, is that ancient coins stamped with animal heads do not prove that, for example, cattle served as money; it was not the *substance* but the *sign* of the sacrifice which became money. The scarcity of these signs rested on the abstention from consumption which was the prerequisite for the sacrifice, and the high reputation of the issuing institution provided a widespread acceptance for that money.[8] The possession of a reserve of commodities and the ability to issue certificates, which gave evidence for a depositing of goods and circulated as a means of payment, turned the temple into a bank and enabled it to grant credit.

The once popular view of regarding commodities, or precious metal coins, as the "true" money, and paper money as a mere substitute, should be rejected against the background of historical research. Simple economic reasoning enables one to understand that goods, which are easily obtainable or reproducible at low costs, at most can serve as a *standard of value*; their common use may have been promoted

[4]   Cf. Smith 1786: 10-3, Menger 1909, Schumpeter 1970: 20-3, Niehans 1978: 103.
[5]   Leijonhufvud 1977: 229, cf. Polanyi 1957, Kindleberger 1984: 21, Heinsohn/Steiger 1996: 81-2.
[6]   Cf. Richter 1989: 112, Dowd 2000.
[7]   Cf. Grantham et al. 1977.
[8]   Laum (1924) explicitly made reference to the nominalism in Knapp's theory of money.

by means of low information costs as they were well known. These commodities might even have served as a *medium of exchange* in cases where the problem of an insufficient coincidence of wants impeded in bilateral barter transactions. But they are not suitable for serving as *means of payment* because otherwise market agents would concentrate on producing these "money" goods. After a while, being in excess supply, they would lose their value and would no longer be accepted as payment. The American "tobacco money" in the 17th and 18th century therefore rested on a limited production; later it was substituted by certificates which promised a delivery of tobacco, precisely specified in quantitative and qualitative terms. Keynes summarized the basic issue: "It is unlikely that an asset, of which the supply can be easily increased [...], will possess the attitude of 'liquidity' in the minds of owners of wealth. Money itself rapidly loses the attitude of 'liquidity' if its future supply is expected to undergo sharp changes."[9]

Money cannot properly be understood by means of its ability to save transaction costs; and marketable goods cannot serve as a means of payment. Monetary economies therefore typically develop a payment technology in order to create and preserve the standards which are necessary to execute economic interaction and exchange in imperfect-information and low-trust circumstances. That is why the commercial banking system forms the core of a monetary economy.

Box 5: Banking Business and the Liquidity Problem

The classical example of a credit based on a privately owned stock of resources (goods, precious metals, assets) is given by a contract which grants an entitlement to the creditor's wealth to a borrower, who in turn hands over his bill of debt. Actually, the credit contract represents a creation and exchange of two liabilities (*table 3.1*):

• Immediately the wealth owner becomes a debtor as he is faced with the claim to his resources. The borrower can use up the claim at once or pass it on when purchasing from third parties if they accept the wealth owner's promissory note as a means of payment.

• In the long run, when the term of the bill of debt expires, the borrower has to refund the note or the resources to the creditor – including interest which also has to paid in kind or in notes. In the latter case an excess demand for notes arises in the market which gives them a premium. On a macroeconomic level, the payment of interest is feasible if wealth owners increase the issue of notes by means of their own (consump-

---

9 Keynes 1936: 241n, cf. Galbraith 1975: 579. It is revealing that Smith (1786: 10-3) attributed the transition from cattle (sic!) to metal coins as means of exchange to "irresistible reasons", but then only mentioned durability and divisibility, and not the scarcity as the merits of metal coins. He regarded the stamping of coins as a quality certificate which helped to lower information costs on the part of money users; the physical substance of metallic money should be easily verified. But Smith did not recognize that the stamp of some well respected institution could confer market acceptance even to a money asset without intrinsic value.

tion) purchases. This is the basic variant of "seigniorage", i.e. earning real income by issuing worthless paper money.

Table 3.1: Balance sheets in the case of resource-based credit

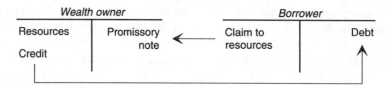

If the notes circulate as money the wealth owner becomes a *bank*. The profitability of founding a bank is obvious: by issuing non-interest bearing, but fully backed promissory notes the interest-bearing quantity of assets can be doubled (assume that the initial stocks of resources consists of assets). Often, market acceptance of notes only rested on their small-units denomination where relatively high transaction costs prevented a redemption ("Zettelbanken"). Reputable banks possessed an asset reserve consisting of precious metals (for example gold). Their *business of attracting deposits* is taking in coins and bullion which then is acknowledged by credit entry or issue of notes (*table 3.2*).

Table 3.2: Changes in balance sheets in case of attracting deposits

The *business of granting credits* has a similar formal structure: again, the bank purchases an asset – a bill of debt – and pays in return by credit entry or notes. The crucial difference to the case above is the appearance of a liquidity problem on the part of the banks as they commit themselves to the redemption of notes and deposits into gold, an asset which they are unable to produce (*table 3.3*).

Table 3.3: Changes in balance sheets in case of credit extension

Bank		Customer	
+ Credit	+ Deposits/ notes	+ Deposits/ notes	+ Debt

If both types of transactions are integrated the consolidated balance sheet reveals that the credit borrower, when he executes his option to redeem notes or deposits, receives the gold coins deposited by other customers. Market agents cannot discern whether circulating bank notes originate from depositing gold or from taking out a bank loan. In case of notes issued by competing private banks the information problems on the part of the public multiply. Business practices and solidity of banks can hardly be assessed by individual clients and users of bank notes.

Moreover, the high reputation of some banks can easily be exploited by an over-issue of competing banks. "Reputation [...] has a public good element, externalities relating to the reputation of others in the same field, that can easily misused by free riders."[10] According to Bagehot the business of granting credit precedes the attraction of deposits, because the latter requires voluntary decisions on the part of non-banks which can only be expected after a bank has earned some reputation.[11] This reputation however is likewise the precondition for the market acceptance of bank notes originating from an extension of credit; otherwise they cannot perform a function of money.

In order to expand the profitable lending business commercial banks – if the reserve ratio is to be kept constant – have to obtain additional deposits. Therefore banks have to pay higher interest rates on deposits or improve their functional characteristics (enabling transfer payments, drawing cheques etc.). The external effects in the use of a currency may also increase the demand for bank deposits without additional pecuniary or non-pecuniary yields. "The supplier issues a liability, which is used as money, and purchases an asset (extends credit). The source of the profit of the issuer of money (the bank) is the margin between the interest rate earned on the asset and the interest paid on the liability. When the liability of the bank gains increasing acceptance as money, the users are willing to pay more for the service. [...] In this sense the issuer of money profits from increasing returns to scale."[12]

The crucial dilemma of a commercial bank – and the systemic risk of the bank business – however, is that the stock held as reserve is simultaneously both too large *and* to small:

• It is too large because it bears (usually) no interest and is useless in "good times"; this reasoning will induce a further expansion of the lending business.

• Each stock of reserves below 100 % of issued notes and deposits is too small because the bank is illiquid in case of a "run"; thus a "lender of last resort" should exist which in principle is able to supply additional reserves.

Apart from this basic *risk of illiquidity* the bank's balance sheet reveals the *problem of solvency*: acting as an intermediary between borrowers and depositors the bank holds assets the value of which may vary whereas deposits are nominally fixed in terms of reserve units. The contract between the bank and the depositors is "incomplete" as they have no control on the choice of the bank's assets and, accordingly, do not participate in their risk. Although value and yields of the bank's assets may fluctuate, the depositors' claims to the bank's reserves remain unaffected. This obvious tension could be relieved by letting depositors share the market risks of the banks' business of acquiring and holding financial assets – but of course this would at the same time deprive bank deposits of their money functions.[13]

---

[10] Goodhart 1988: 64, cf. Hawtrey 1923: 9, Hicks 1989: 55-63.

[11] Cf. Bagehot 1873: 37-45.

[12] De Grauwe 1996: 3-4.

[13] Cf. Goodhart 1988: 85-95, Hellwig 1998.

3.2   Metallic Money, Bank Deposits and Government Money

> Symbolical or paper money is but a species of credit: it is no
> more than the measure by which credit is reckoned.
> The use of paper money is to keep reckonings of value be-
> tween people who have property; the use of coin is to avoid
> giving credit to people who have none.
>
> *James Steuart*[14]

> In God we trust, all others pay cash.
>
> *Modern saying*

> Lend not to him who is mightier than thou; or if thou len-
> dest, look upon thy loan as lost.
>
> *Ancient saying*[15]

In the classical gold-standard currency system, according to a widespread opinion, the function of money was performed by gold (coins). A cursory inspection might confirm the view that gold is much more suitable than promissory notes of renowned wealth owners: a scarce medium which could not easily be manipulated by the parties involved in market transactions and which therefore seemed made to be a neutral intermediary in the process of private contracting. In actual fact however, metallic money was a "bad" money as its elasticity of production (i.e. the possibility to obtain money by employing resources) was not at all zero, but positive and, above all, volatile.

The European feudal economy in the 14th century got caught in a crisis. The pest reduced labour supply; farmer riots and rising wages ruined the landowners; a trade deficit with Eastern countries had resulted in an outflow of gold and silver – the "money of the world" – and price deflation induced a hoarding of coins. Because of its wool exports, it was only England that did not suffer from a shortage of precious metals. Thereupon private and public (financially distressed) investors began to search, mine and rob gold all over the world; depending on the price level, this proved to be an outstanding investment strategy. "Gold was in the 15th and 16th centuries the most lucrative as well as the most symbolic of all commodities. [...] Gold and silver, while they were not themselves wealth, were the objects, or rather the indication, of profitable economic activity. To attract them one had to produce [...]. It was necessary to import a little, export a lot, and attract foreign silver in exchange for merchandise."[16]

Whereas Spain sent out Columbus and later on undertook periodical expeditions to Central and South America, the English concentrated upon catching the Spa-

---

[14]   Steuart 1767a: 212, Steuart 1767c: 265.

[15]   Quoted from Ehrenberg 1896a: 22.

[16]   Vilar 1960: 65, 185, cf. 191-2, Steuart 1767b: 126-7, Ehrenberg 1896a: 407, Wallerstein
       1974: 21-42, Kindleberger 1984: 24-7, North 1994: 40, 66-9, 76-86.

nish ships before their arrival in Europe. Francis Drake's piracy in the second half of the 16th century turned out to be extremely profitable and laid the foundations of the British gold reserves. "He repaid Elizabeth 47 times the value of her initial investment, and the Queen knighted him on his flagship."[17]

On a macroeconomic level, the "money production" supported goods demand, particularly in those countries where wages lagged behind prices and thus facilitated a "profit inflation". The flow of gold to Europe helped to finance the excessive public consumption in Spain, but could not prevent national bankruptcy in the end. Other countries, above all England, profited by the expansion of demand starting from Spain as increasing exports stimulated home income and industrial development. The mining of gold was equivalent to a procedure of monetary expansion which later was – somewhat ironically – suggested by Keynes: private firms should be permitted to dig up bottles filled with bank notes which previously had been buried by the Treasury.[18]

But apart from the geographic discoveries, it was an extremely expensive and inefficient way of money creation, which also could not be controlled and thus led to considerable fluctuations of the price level. During the "big inflation" in the 16th century (which however only amounted to an annual inflation rate of less than 2 %) the Spanish were the first to hit upon the connection of the gold inflow and the rise in prices, which later became known as the quantity theory of money.[19]

Moreover, the circulating gold coins in no way met the qualitative standard of a sound metallic money: they did *not* show high costs of imitation and low costs of verification; because of manifold attempts to counterfeit (at the mint and by way of "clipping") money, users could never be sure with regard to the metallic value of the coins. Therefore, businessmen paid each other by issuing and passing on bills of exchange; balances were settled by bill brokers. Since 1550, on the Genoa bill fair, an artificial clearing currency was used which had a fixed exchange rate vis-à-vis a basket of gold coins originating from the best five coinages.[20]

---

[17] Vilar 1960: 142-3, cf. 32, 62-8.

[18] Cf. Keynes 1930: 135-45, Keynes 1936: 129-30, 220, Ehrenberg 1896b: 63, 150, 156, 200, Vilar 1960: 37, 149-54, Wallerstein 1974: 76-86, 165-71.

[19] "The Spanish of the 1600s understood perfectly well that because they had too much gold, and later silver, these metals had been drained from the country; that despite this loss the metals had a major influence on the domestic economy through the credits, guarantees, and interest payments to which the precious metals were committed; and that 'inflation' in the monetary circulation had compromised domestic and foreign expenditure, driven up prices and encouraged idleness and unproductive occupations. Moreover, they saw that rising prices had been fatal to Spanish production, which could not compete with foreign goods" (Vilar 1960: 166, cf. 161-2, Wallerstein 1974: 69-76, Galbraith 1975: 21-5).

[20] Cf. Ehrenberg 1896b: 233-41, Grantham et al. 1977, Hicks 1989: 48-9.

Box 6: Financing International Trade

Commercial banks facilitated a nearly cashless financing of international trade which tended to abolish the need for cross-border gold movements (*figure 3.1*)[21]: if a Hamburg merchant A exports commodities to Amsterdam, the Dutch importer B pays by forwarding a bill denominated in guilder. The bill represents an order given to his Amsterdam bank to hand out cash to the bearer at the date of maturity (or to credit his account). A sells the bill to his Hamburg bank and receives a cash payment (or a credit entry) in mark. At the same time, other transactions may take place: an agent C has to settle an invoice due to his imports from D. He can do that by making out an own bill or – as it is assumed here – by purchasing a suitable bill to be paid in guilder. C instructs his Hamburg bank to acquire this bill against debiting his account. The bill is sent to agent D who passes it on to his Amsterdam bank which in turn debits the account of the initial issuer B.

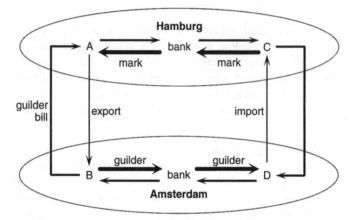

Figure 3.1: Trade and payment flows

In the above example, only the Hamburg bank is dealing with guilder bills which are bought and sold against mark (actually, all banks are active in this business). The price clearing the market is the exchange rate (fixing the price for the purchase of a bill allowed to circumvent the clerical interdiction to take interest). Obviously, the banks had to take into account exchange rate expectations and they made wide use of innovative financial techniques in order to avoid losses. For stabilizing the market, Dutch authorities felt compelled to prohibit speculative exchange rate bets already in 1541.

The bad quality of coins made "bank money", i.e. deposits, occasionally to show a premium as it was preferred by market agents. The 1609 founded Amsterdam Bill Bank (like the Hamburg Bank which was established in 1619) successfully intro-

---

[21] Cf. Mill 1871: 612-8, Ehrenberg 1896b: 19-20, Kindleberger 1984: 35-41, Stadermann 1994: 40-1, North 1994: 31-4.

duced a stable deposit currency, fully backed by a no longer minted guilder coin, which above certain limits could only be used for clearing purposes. "A florin banco has a more determinate value than a pound of fine gold, or silver; it is a unit which the invention of men, instructed in the arts if commerce, have found out. This bank money stands invariable like a rock in the sea."[22]

The history of modern banking started in the 12th century in Italy where the Medici became the dominating financial power in the 14th and 15th century. In Germany, Fugger's wealthy trading company developed into a leading banking firm. Considering the large risks prevalent in world trade, a gradual shift towards granting large-scale credit to governmental dynasties promised a simple and profitable business, particularly as this business held out the prospect of participating in the courtly way of life. Deposits of coins were acknowledged by the issue of promissory notes which were assessed to be as safe as gold. European royal dynasties were provided with credits, which however had to be renewed time and again because the debtors were unable to refund. Due to the still low developed economy there were no private large-scale borrowers; therefore Fugger and other European banking firms remained dependent on the business relations with public debtors. Thus they earned lucrative interest margins – but finally failed as a result of various national bankruptcies.[23]

Suffering from permanent financial distress, the royal dynasties were open-minded with regard to the foundation of banks from which they hoped to gain advantage. In 1716, John Law was invited to the French royal court and was charged with the task of solving the urgent problem of public debt. He persuaded the authorities that issuing paper money was a far more elegant way of financing public spending compared to the usual debasement of coinage (or compared to futile hope for a success of the alchemist experiments, pursued at the court, of a synthetic production of gold). The notes of his newly founded Banque Générale de France, which for the most part came into circulation by way of government credit, found a ready market.

Astonishingly, they kept their reputation for a while after the king took over the bank, undermined the terms for the redemption of notes, and set out to pay off the public debt by means of an ever increasing note issue. This practice was coupled with the project of a joint-stock company which promised high profits from trade and the mining of gold in Louisiana. The seeming soundness of this project, the prosperity supported by monetary expansion and the fact that Law still was held in great esteem made share prices to rise very rapidly. More and more shares were sold, the proceeds however did not flow into the mining company but were pump-

---

[22] Steuart 1767a: 218, cf. Steuart 1767b: 313-31, Smith 1786: 205-09, Ehrenberg 1909, Vilar 1960: 204-10, Kindleberger 1984: 47, Stadermann 1994: 45-54, North 1994: 112-3.

[23] Cf. Ehrenberg 1896a: 18-22, 41-50, 119-39, 148, 175, 186, 351, 375-80, 408, Kindleberger 1984: 42-4, Hicks 1989: 53, North 1994: 56-69, 90-1.

ed into the royal budget. The money then was "recycled" into the economy by public spending and finally fuelled share prices again. Occasional attempts to redeem notes into gold made the speculative bubble burst in 1720 which ended in a complete collapse of the paper currency system.[24]

For a long time already, financial markets had known how to distinguish between private and governmental money. In his "Discourse upon coin" Davanzati in 1588 aimed at a reconciliation of a money emerging from spontaneous market transactions, which varied in its value, and a money created by the state, which should exhibit a constant value. The sovereign should be allowed to issue token money of whatever substance, but he should not have the right to alter its metal content by fraud.[25]

In principle, government could maintain the market acceptance of state-issued money, even in case of a bad reputation, by prescribing that tax payments have to be made in that currency. Public expenditure then would be limited by the balanced-budget restriction. Additional finance could – if at all – only be obtained by incurring debt in foreign (or market) currencies. On the contrary, in the American literature money for a long time has been defined as a non-interest bearing (!) bill of debt which is "issued by the government to finance its budget deficits".[26] The historical background of this view is that the American government in the 18th century – for lack of an efficient tax and banking system – in fact printed notes, which afterwards were devalued by strong attacks of inflation. It is true that government itself will be affected by a destruction of the monetary system, which implies that the authorities – as a "big" agent – should be able to internalize negative feedbacks of their own inflationary macroeconomic mismanagement. But it would take some centuries until politicians began to implement this finding by means of institutional reform.[27]

---

[24] In the French nation, this episode caused a vague "love for gold" in currency matters which had a lasting effect until the 1970s (cf. Steuart 1767b: 256-310, Steuart 1767c: 268-73, Galbraith 1975: 32-7, Binswanger 1982, North 1994: 129-34).

[25] Cf. Vilar 1960: 189-90.

[26] Tobin 1969: 19.

[27] Cf. Knapp 1909, Galbraith 1975: 54-76, Stadermann 1987: 132-3, Ritter 1995.

3.3 The "Backing" of Money in the Banking Doctrine

> The profit of the bank is to receive interest for what they lend, and to pay none for what they owe. What they owe is the paper they issue. They owe this to the public; and the security which the public has, is the security which the bank received from the person who borrowed from them.
>
> *James Steuart*[28]

> This plan of making debts payable in gold is merely a device for keeping the variations in the value of the monetary unit within bounds.
>
> *Ralph G. Hawtrey*[29]

> Money is a fiction, after all, worthless paper that acquires value only because large numbers of people choose to give it value. The system runs on faith. Not truth or reality, but collective belief.
>
> *Paul Auster*[30]

French budget and monetary policies have also been criticized by Macleod. The glut of Law's paper money was said to be the result of the fact that it had not been based on the debt of a wealthy person possessing net assets, but rather on the liability of a heavily indebted, insolvent agent. "Only currency that signified debt, of an individual or of society in general, was limited in quantity by the nature of its process of creation."[31] By *public debt*, in this respect, Macleod understood the foundation of money on metallic coins. These coins were seen to represent a liability of the whole market society vis-à-vis their bearer. On the other hand, a promissory note circulating in the market could serve as money which was based on *private debt*.

This last-mentioned case plays a role in the history of economic thought and stresses the origin of money from a debt relation. And as the more traditional theory of metallic money had "solved" the key problem of explaining and preserving the scarcity of money by resorting to the "natural" argument of a limited physical supply, the credit theory of money aimed likewise to ensure that the stock of private property – and the willingness to consent to an encumbrance of that property by issuing money notes – would serve as a restriction against the evil of an excess supply of money; at the same time, establishing a link between circulating notes and some private property, supported the belief in a "real equivalent" of token money, which seemed to be necessary in order to maintain the market acceptance of that money in a setting of imperfect information and low trust.

---

[28] Steuart 1767c: 257.
[29] Hawtrey 1923: 414.
[30] Auster 1997: 39.
[31] Skaggs 1997: 121, cf. Macleod 1889.

For Mill, however, it was a fallacy to believe "that a paper currency cannot be issued in excess so long as every note issued *represents* property, or has a *foundation* of actual property to rest on".[32] The idea that private-property based money will obtain and keep its market value by way of its construction suffers from an intractable trade-off:

• For private promissory notes to be accepted as general means of payment, they ought to be issued by some already *renowned* wealth owner. But just these persons might be tempted to exploit the market confidence by over-issuing notes.

• On the other hand, it is hard to see how any small proprietor, even if issuing only limited amounts of I.O.U.s, will reach a position at all where his promissory notes are held as means of payment.

The second point was made plain – more or less involuntarily – by the "last mercantilist" James Steuart (his magnum opus was published a few years before Smith's "Wealth of Nations"). Steuart aimed at a stimulation of trade and commerce by means of lowering the rate of interest which in turn required a monetary expansion. His proposal thus was the "melting down of property": The quantity of money should be increased, "by converting land into paper money. [...] This is no more than a contrivance for turning into *circulating value*, which is the principal characteristic of *money*, the obligations of private men, which in all countries are considered to be of an equal value with any coin."[33]

In no way should the quantity of money be limited by the stock of gold reserves. In order to diminish the power of gold owners over the determination of the rate of interest, he argued that "money can be made of paper, to the value of all the solid property of a nation". In principle, there were no reasons why landowners should not have the right to issue their own notes. Steuart regarded it as an evil that instead a landowner was forced, when demanding a bank credit, to offer his landed property as collateral and in addition to pay interest. "And for what does he pay this interest? Not because he has gratuitously any value from the bank, since in his obligation he has given a full equivalent for the notes; but the obligation he has given carries interest, and the notes carry none. Why? Because the one circulates as money, the other does not. For this advantage, therefore, of circulation, not for any additional value, does the landed man pay interest to the bank."[34]

In this passage Steuart has made clear – thus involuntarily defeating his own policy proposal – that the *backing* of any promissory note in no way is sufficient to establish it as money. The crucial aspect rather, is the "advantage of circulation", i.e. the peculiarity of perfect *liquidity* which defines the money function of a means of payment, whereas other financial assets just by their pecuniary yield re-

---

[32] Mill 1871: 547.
[33] Steuart 1767c: 248, 252.
[34] Steuart 1767b: 147, 149.

veal their lower degree of liquidity. Market agents are willing to pay interest in order to dispose of money because money yields a *liquidity premium*. Steuart finally arrives at a Keynesian understanding of interest rate theory: "Money, while it is employed in circulation, can carry no interest; the moment it lies idle to one man, were it but for a day, it may be worth interest to another, who willingly pays for the use of it, when he has occasion either to buy what he wants, or to pay what he owes."[35]

Although Steuart finally acknowledges that backing is no *sufficient* condition for a promissory note to become money, he strongly recommends that it should be a *necessary* condition for issuing bank notes. He distinguishes between three types of bank credit:

• The precondition for *private market agents* to obtain credit is to offer sufficient security;

• *commercial credits* rest on the banks' confidence in the ability and success of the enterprise;

• in case of a *public credit* banks assume that the sovereign's funds are large enough to finance periodic interest payments.

Steuart regarded bank notes stemming from commercial credit to be the most insecure. Therefore, banks should discount commercial bills, but issue notes only against best securities, mortgages in particular. A bank's credit was said to be "precarious, unless the value of the securities upon which they lend, be equal to all the notes in circulation".[36]

Steuart thus reveals the roots of the "Banking Doctrine" the weakness of which is to be found in the application of microeconomic principles of "sound banking" to a macroeconomic analysis. The approach tends to overlook the fact that the *value* of securities becomes an endogenous variable, not least depending on the volume of credit and the quantity of money. It makes no fundamental difference whether the securities "backing" a note issue consisted of trade bills or durable assets:

• In the first case, the level of *commodity prices* becomes indeterminate as each nominal trade volume is being financed. The path of prices, whether driven from the supply or the demand side, can no longer be controlled although banks confine themselves to discounting "solid" trade bills ("real-bills fallacy").

• In the second case, a speculative bubble of rising *asset prices* may emerge which finally is bound to burst, thus stabilizing the monetary system through a "regulation by panic" (Lord Overstone).[37]

---

[35] Steuart 1767c: 248, cf. Hicks 1989: 62-71.

[36] Steuart 1767c: 257, cf. 256-8, Steuart 1767b: 160, 173-4.

[37] Cf. Lutz 1936: 37-8. John Law also propagated to issue money against the security of land the *value* of which he regarded particularly stable because of its limited supply!

Thus the important finding is that encumbered property cannot guarantee the scarcity and stability of money. Even if the stock of pledgeable assets would serve as the upper limit of credit – and thus money – creation, some additional measures have to be taken in order to preclude that limit from being reached. Demanding a security when granting a credit may be seen as a risk-reducing device, albeit an imperfect one, on the part of commercial banks, but it is neither necessary nor sufficient in order to render a currency trustworthy. It is true that market forces, during their evolutionary process of search, have conferred a money function on promissory notes of wealthy proprietors; but from this it does not follow by way of logical inversion that money essentially is an entitlement to private property.

Already Macleod had realized that creditors in a barter exchange prefer to receive marketable *claims* to resources, not resources as such. Linking bank notes to gold or assets served as a makeshift to keep money in short supply and to solicit market acceptance. The demand for a backing of a currency is but a device for preserving its scarcity, as the production of money then will entail *costs*. The promise of redemption is a commitment of the bank, which aims at giving rise to the expectation on the part of money users that there will be no over-issue of notes. "In order to prevent such abuses, then, commodity convertibility was, for classical monetary economics, a *sine qua non* of a sound monetary system."[38] Crises of confidence caused bank runs; this did not mean however that the "true" agents' preference was for gold, but simply that one institutional device for maintaining a currency's reputation had collapsed and some other confidence-building measure had to be invented. According to Luhmann it "makes no sense to search for a final 'backing' of money's value beyond money itself. Neither gold nor solid foreign reserves nor tangible assets nor the authority of the state guarantee the value of money. This guarantee rather is given by the money's scarcity."[39]

Box 7: The Property Theory of Money and Interest

The idea that money should be based on private property has recently been put forward anew. "True money is a claim to the property of market agents and it can exist only and exactly in an amount determined by the willingness of proprietors to enter

---

The failure of Law's bank is but one example of the fundamentally flawed idea of an asset-backed money. Another famous case is the episode of the "assignats", a currency supposed to be backed by land during the time after the French revolution. The expectation held by the authorities that these notes would flow back to the issuer through sales of plots of land did not materialize. Therefore ever increasing amounts of notes had to be issued, which then lost their value in the same way as the land prices would have dropped if the whole stock would have been offered for sale in the market in one go (cf. Law 1720: 83-92, Mill 1871: 547-8, Hawtrey 1923: 240-61, Schumpeter 1970: 56-7, Sargent/Velde 1995).

[38] Laidler 1991: 34.

[39] Luhmann 1988: 201.

into a debt contract encumbering their wealth."[40] The theory of property-based money succumbs to the fallacy of taking some historical solution of the problem of how some money asset might gain acceptance in the market as the *essential* institutional background of money in general. The approach however may have some merits in explaining the economics of a low-developed one-tier banking system. It is obvious that the credit-supply decision of a mercantilist trading company or banking house will be affected not only by the borrower's ability to offer securities, but also by the stock of wealth and the propensity to take risks on the part of the creditor. After all, he issues entitlements to his private property and thus loses the *property premium* which – as a non-pecuniary yield – can be envisaged to measure the convenience to dispose of unencumbered wealth (it does not comprise the risk of default in a narrower sense as the borrower is obliged to offer security).

The classical root of the property-money approach shows in its *explanation of the rate of interest* which follows the lines of a production-cost-of-money theory, rather than a money-demand portfolio theory: the rate of interest is seen to be the price compensating the loss of the property premium, in the very act of money creation. It is not conceived as a return making up for the loss of liquidity when choosing between money and bills of debt in a creditor's portfolio, because money is supposed not to exist before the act of granting credit. "The crucial point was that bank notes did not enter circulation through the exchange of produced commodities, as believed by classical and neoclassical theory, but rather by lending and charged with interest. Moreover, the rate of interest was not derived from the yields of production, but itself determined the terms of production."[41]

Owning property is assumed to be necessary on the part of both agents entering a credit contract: the claims to the creditor's assets or resources circulate as money (which is destroyed at the end of the contract period), the borrower is forced to give security and likewise loses a property premium. Hence, one is led to ask why the creditor's property represents a kind of a reserve asset, whereas the borrower's property serves as a pledge only, or, to put it differently, why the creditor's I.O.U. is accepted on the market as money, whereas the borrower's bill of debt is a bill of debt. Two points can be raised:

• First it can be noted that the property-money approach involuntarily confirms the liquidity theory of interest: if both parties involved in the credit contract lose their property premium, but only one of them is rewarded by receiving an interest payment, the rate of interest exactly is a measure of the degree of liquidity the market attaches to the creditor's promissory notes.

• Second, it seems that, in principle, each wealthy market agent could issue his own "money". Why should he opt for an indebtedness instead? The answer given is hardly convincing: some (most) proprietors *choose* not to issue own money notes as they dislike that bearers might *at any time* demand the issuer to hand over his resources, whereas a bank is only allowed to do so in case of the debtor's default.[42] The more simple truth however is that the market would not accept *any* proprietor's promissory notes as money.

---

[40] Stadermann 1994: 15.
[41] Stadermann 1994: 89, cf. Heinsohn/Steiger 1996: 163-201.
[42] Cf. Heinsohn/Steiger 1996: 239-40, Heinsohn/Steiger 2000.

The property approach not only ignores the public-good problem inherent in the use of any money (thereby retreating even behind Steuart) but also overlooks the fact that even in a property-money setting, market agents cannot avoid a choice between various assets, which in turn will give rise to a liquidity-based rate of interest: just because some wealth owner's notes circulate as means of payment they will get into the hands of persons who are not in debt vis-à-vis their issuer. These agents might decide to *lend* these notes or to keep them as a store of value. This choice between holding money or a specified claim denominated in the very money units will induce the money owner – for various liquidity-preference reasons analyzed above[43] – to demand interest for granting a credit in money terms.

Steuart also had already noticed that particularly commercial credits sometimes were granted without any collateral demanded by the bank. Later, the pound sterling as the leading currency of the financial world, came off the gold backing for some period of time without losing its reputation, and today nearly all currencies of the world are issued without granting the right of redemption to their bearers. In view of the contra-factual evidence therefore, it is questionable to what extent the property approach may claim to offer a *positive* theory of money and interest. It is conspicuous that the authors occasionally speak of "true", "genuine" or "good" money if it is backed by private property; if it is not, the money system is even named "despotic".[44] The reader might conclude that a *normative* intention of establishing and preserving monetary stability drives – and misleads – the analytical reasoning (for backing money by property is neither necessary nor sufficient for attaining that goal).

For some time, the Bundesbank's practice of executing its repurchase transactions with the banking system, by making use of titles of public debt, was condemned as the beginning of the mark's decline; now bills of public debt are being re-interpreted as representing an entitlement to the property of the country's taxpayers, and thus might advance to a particularly well-suited collateral when creating central-bank money.[45] But apart from these contradictions, the property approach dodges an answer to the question how monetary policy should preserve monetary stability. The belief that "property which can be encumbered [...] determines the quantity of money and ensures its scarcity", is absurd, as the *value* of private-property assets in turn depends on the quantity of money: the fact that property as such is scarce "because it is ascribed to proprietors and does not represent a so-called free good"[46] in no way ensures a short supply of money relative to the commodities sold on the market.

In order to control macroeconomic dynamics by means of a *price* (which indirectly contains activities on the goods market by establishing some minimum standard of profitability), the central bank, in a two-tier banking system, when issuing central-bank money quotes a rate of interest, which of course is no longer the compensation for the loss of some property premium. The quality of the central bank's assets matter however: the property-money theory is right to stress the advice that any central bank should dispose of marketable assets which can easily be sold if the home currency is in need of a rapid stabilization.

---

[43] See above ch. 2.3.
[44] Stadermann 1994: 15, 139, Heinsohn/Steiger 1996: 225-9.
[45] Cf. Heinsohn/Steiger 1996: 230-1, 275, Heinsohn/Steiger 2000.
[46] Heinsohn/Steiger 1996: 287, 259, cf. 275, 308.

3.4 The Monetary Logic of Mercantilism

> If money be wanting, credit will die.
>
> *James Steuart*[47]

> At a time when the authorities had no direct control over the domestic rate of interest or the other inducements to home investment, measures to increase the favourable balance of trade were the only *direct* means at their disposal for increasing foreign investment; and, at the same time, the effect of a favourable balance of trade on the influx of the precious metals was their only *indirect* means of reducing the domestic rate of interest and so increasing the inducement to home investment.
>
> *John Maynard Keynes*[48]

> Mercantilists are fascinated by money serving the acquisition of more money, i.e. the earning of a rent or a profit. Money is wealth or contributes to wealth as it is being capitalized, i.e. lent against interest.
>
> *Hans Christoph Binswanger*[49]

The opening of commercial banks in the mercantilist era not only resulted from the courts' financial plight, but also in great degree from the widely held view that the economic development in general was impeded by monetary factors. Three arguments can be distinguished:

• The vast number of coins exhibiting different or unknown quality involved prohibiting transaction costs and represented an obstacle for trade and commerce. Accordingly, merchants pressed for more uniform monetary conditions which appeared to be attainable by an increased use of bank notes and deposits.

• The banking business, on the other hand, was limited by their gold reserves which reproduced the monetary restriction on a higher level. Thus measures had to be taken in order to strengthen the banks' liquidity. The stock of gold and silver reserves, in a way, served as an assurance against the risk of a breakdown of the banking system.[50]

• Finally, the macroeconomic importance of the banking business was emphasized by the mercantilist view that the (bank) credit was regarded to be the logical starting point of the economic process. In terms of capital theory an advance of a sum of money marks the first step of all trading and producing activities, which then are expected to prove profitable in terms of money. The capability and willingness

---

[47] Steuart 1767c: 248.
[48] Keynes 1936: 336.
[49] Binswanger 1982: 102.
[50] Cf. Wallerstein 1974: 45-6.

of (wealthy) market agents to accomplish this money advance appeared as a potential impediment of economic development.

Classical economic theory did not show much understanding of these problems. Only the first point mentioned was not contentious. Because money was regarded as a means for facilitating the exchange of goods, a welfare gain could be expected if technical imperfections of any money medium were repaired. Ricardo therefore recommended the establishment of a paper money system which should exhibit low costs in its production and a high degree of transparency in its use; in order to prevent over-issue the notes ought to be fully backed by precious metals.[51]

The second point triggered off a basic debate on the alleged confusion of money and credit in the works of mercantilist writers: it was said that they erroneously attributed an interest effect to a change in the quantity of money which in fact stemmed from a change of credit-market conditions. But this criticism overlooks that credit and money creation actually coincided in the simple mercantilist setting: if Fugger granted a credit to some client, his promissory note, an entitlement to Fugger's wealth, would circulate as money. Moreover the reproach is unfounded analytically, as the mercantilists knew how to differentiate between the price of money on the goods market, i.e. the inverse of the price level, and the price of money on the credit market, i.e. the rate of interest.[52]

With regard to the credit extended by commercial banks, it must not be ignored that the imminent short supply of reserves had a bearing on the national balance of payments: a trade deficit obliged domestic banks to make up for the balance in the clearing of export and import bills by paying ready cash to the foreign country which implied a continuing loss of their gold reserves (if borrowing from abroad did not ensure a sufficient compensation).[53] The understandable interest in the avoidance of bank failures, and in the maintenance of domestic credit, thus led to the political goal of a positive trade balance which was implemented by resorting to a support and protection of domestic companies. With respect to currency matters, in order to turn the foreign exchanges favourable for the domestic country, the target was a positive *balance* of the valued transactions; this strategy was coupled with a policy of general economic promotion aiming to increase the overall *level* of business activities.

This "typical mercantilist" policy of supporting exports has later been heavily criticized. From a microeconomic point of view, protectionism proves to be detrimental to the competitive order, bringing about welfare losses in the long run. With regard to macroeconomics, production and exports were said to be an end in itself, thus ignoring the fact that the final, true criterion of assessing the perform-

---

[51] Ricardo 1824, cf. Vilar 1960: 316-7f, Galbraith 1975: 47.

[52] Cf. Smith 1786: 182-92, Binswanger 1982: 102.

[53] "Bullion is the 'cash' of international trade; paper currencies are of no use there" (Bagehot 1873: 22, cf. Steuart 1767b: 180-98, Steuart 1767c: 258-9).

ance of an economic system is consumption. Krugman's verdict of old mercantilism and its modern variant, "strategic trade policy", is unequivocal: "The purpose of trade is imports, not exports. Exports are a cost."[54] Hindering free trade is said to give away gains in real income and consumption, which would otherwise accrue from the exploitation of international division of labour.

This line of reasoning however, adheres to a static theory of allocation, and takes no account of the fact that a strategy of export-led growth, up to now, seems to be the only successful model for developing market economies. Apart from the favourable effect of a trade *surplus* on the position of the home currency on world financial markets and the demand effect on employment, a high trade *share* implies an orientation of domestic industries towards the qualitative standards of world market, which in the long run will strengthen the "supply side" of the economy. The post war "economic miracle" in West Germany likewise rested on an export surplus, preserved by a monetary policy heading for an undervaluation of the mark.

Since the days of Adam Smith, the main criticism runs that mercantilism adhered to a static zero-sum conception of welfare, according to which one country could only gain at the expense of the welfare of another. "When two places trade with one another, this doctrine supposes that, if the balance be even, neither of them either loses or gains; but if it leans in any degree to one side, that one of them loses and the other gains in proportion to its declension from the exact equilibrium." Smith goes on to assure that, on the contrary, all involved trading countries would attain an advantage, and adds: "By advantage or gain, I understand not the increase of the quantity of gold and silver, but that of the exchangeable value of the annual produce of the land and labour of the country, or the increase of the annual revenue of its inhabitants."[55]

This passage reveals that Smith – and probably many writers on that subject – misunderstood the basic issue of the mercantilists: with respect to international trade they did not aim for efficiency and welfare gains, a topic to be analyzed in a barter-theoretic approach, rather they wanted to preserve the banks' and the national economies' *solvency*. Of course, on a world scale, wealth and income were not given, but the stock of reserves, consisting of precious metals (ignoring additional production which did not represent a short-term option for commercial banks). The change in the distribution of reserves, following a balance-of-payment disequilibrium, actually resembled a zero-sum game.

The corresponding liquidity problems have been played down by classical economics. Hume propagated an adjustment mechanism which was expected to "automatically" settle balance-of-payment disequilibria: an outflow of gold caused by a domestic trade deficit would trigger a monetary demand expansion abroad which

---

54 Krugman 1996: 19, cf. Mill 1871: 578-9.
55 Smith 1786: 209, cf. 213, 279-88.

Box 8: Free Trade and Welfare Gains

Consider two countries equipped with different production frontiers of the two goods x and y. Let country 1 have a *comparative advantage* in producing y: here one additional unit of y requires (under the condition of diminishing returns) the withdrawal of less units of x from other productive uses, if compared to the shape of the production frontier of country 2. On the other hand, the indifference curves expressing consumers' preferences also differ between both countries. If there is no trade between the countries both produce and consume in A. Because of the asymmetrical shape of the transformation and indifference curves the relative price of the two goods (shown by the slope of the dashed tangent) in country 1 does not match the corresponding price in country 2 (*figure 3.2*).

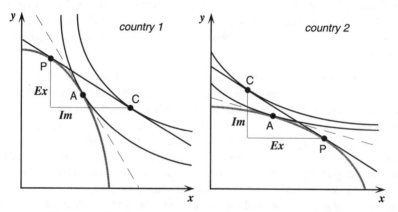

Figure 3.2: Foreign trade with two goods in a two-country case

If both countries start to trade with each other the relative prices of the two goods will converge to the uniform world market price (which is represented by the slope of the bold tangent). As thus prices change in both countries, production and consumption will adjust. In both economies it proves to be advantageous to let the consumption mix (C) differ from the relative quantities of domestic production (P). The corresponding surplus (deficit) of production with respect to domestic consumption is balanced by exports (imports), i.e. $Ex_1 = Im_2$, $Im_1 = Ex_2$. Because of the first country's comparative advantage with respect to y, we here find an increase of production; a corresponding shift can be observed in country 2.

The relative change of the product mix (A → P) differs from the relative change of the consumption mix (A → C) because of the specialization patterns in each country's production. The division of labour has been intensified on a world scale allowing both countries to reach a higher level of consumption, i.e. both gain from a welfare-theoretic point of view. Among the assumptions necessary for the validity of this plea for free trade is that capacities in both countries are fully utilized and the structure of production and employment can be easily adjusted.

in turn would bless the domestic economy with export demand and a gold inflow. In accordance with that approach Smith described a prohibition of gold exports as inefficient and harmful as this would restrict prices increases abroad and, hence, domestic exports. In case of an abolition of the prohibition the home country "only" had to fear a temporary decline of prices; but Smith ignored the noticeable connection of price level movements, on the one hand, and periods of prosperity and depression, on the other.[56]

Actually however, national price levels did not move inversely, but in line; and trade deficits were financed by way of international credits. Even in the mercantilist literature it is noted that profits earned from trade were in no way hoarded but (re-) directed towards those countries where interest rates were relatively high.[57] This means that countries suffering from trade deficits, gold outflows, and thus, high interest rates were able to balance the foreign exchanges, by means of capital imports, which at least in the short and medium term would replace the proceeds accruing from goods exports.

However, this link between trade deficits, rising rates of interest and capitals flows is not at all compelling. Only in a hypothetical two-country world model can banks be confident that capital inflows will – in the foreseeable future – level out reserve losses resulting from an unsuccessful trade performance. In fact, the adjustment process in the case of multilateral international relations is time-consuming; banks in a deficit country therefore will run into liquidity problems before – triggered off by their initial gold losses – the monetary expansion in the *world economy* enables that country to earn additional profits from a rise of exports.

Here it has been assumed that in each country, which is affected by this transmission process, the domestic quantity of money expands proportionately to the increase of gold reserves. But this basic assumption of Hume's theorem on the self-adjustment of the balance of payment was even not generally valid at his time; and it could no longer be maintained the more the national banking system developed and the more national banking policy started to take into consideration the economic situation of the home country when deciding on the stance of its credit policies. Large national banks then took care to uncouple the volume of credit, and thus the stock of money, from fluctuations of the stock of (gold) reserves. The *asymmetric character of international monetary relations* becomes apparent: if central banks in surplus countries aim to prevent a pro-cyclical policy of credit expansion and decide to dampen monetary expansion in times of export surpluses or reserve inflows, on a world level the demand expansion will fail to appear, which otherwise would have allowed deficit countries to solve their balance-of-payment problems.

---

[56] Cf. Smith 1786: 219-21, Hawtrey 1923: 89-91.
[57] Cf. Steuart 1767a: 107-8, McKinnon 1988.

The mercantilist concerns about the solvency of national banks thus were quite justifiable. They were also right in their – although vague – understanding of a monetary restraint of income formation on a macroeconomic level. This can be studied by looking at a modern economy in a system of fixed exchange rates: if a policy of increasing investment at home is dangerous, because of its negative impact on the trade balance given the risk of lagging capital imports, employing a bundle of industrial policies and protectionist measures is the only feasible strategy which allows an expansion of domestic income; either directly or indirectly by way of increased gold inflows from export proceeds, which in turn enables a further expansion of domestic credit. Perhaps it was not recognized that protectionist import restrictions would hamper foreign income formation, which thus caused a negative feedback on home exports; nevertheless, the net effect of the mercantilist policies for the national economy could be expected to be positive.

Under these market conditions also the hands of modern monetary policy would be tied. This was all the more true in an economic system where no proper central banks existed but only – more or less powerful – commercial banks. As a loyal mercantilist, Steuart propagated a low rate of interest which "is the soul of trade; the most active for promoting industry, and the improvement of land". But he also recognized the limits of an *administrative* lowering of interest rates: this would favour the landowners and encourage the demand for "unproductive" credit. The crucial point however, is that in case of a maximum rate fixed by the authorities the "purses of all monied people would [...] be fast shut": a refusal to grant credit and a capital flight being the consequence.[58]

The overriding interest in the distribution of gold reserves in the world economy showed that mercantilist economic policy aimed to enlarge *national*, not international welfare. The level of reserves determined the upper limit of the domestic volume of credit which was necessary to finance the process of production. Disposing of gold and money was regarded as a *means* to prosperity; but mercantilists did not identify money with wealth. Money funds were seen as a supply constraint of employment and production, particularly of export goods, thus closing the circle induced by the reserve flow effect of a trade surplus, measured in value terms. Therefore financiers and creditors ranked high in mercantilist theory.[59] The focus is on the supply-side aspect of finance, not Keynes' message that from a macroeconomic perspective income is created by monetary effective demand. Thus the mercantilists' understanding of the working of a monetary economy led to a kind of monetary supply-side policy.

---

[58] Steuart 1767b: 143, 146. The same view was held by Locke (cf. Eltis 1995).

[59] Cf. Law 1720: 10-3, 40, 56-9. This background helps to understand Steuart's (1767b: 182) statement that "the acquisition of coin, or of the precious metals, adds to the intrinsic value of a country, as much as if a portion of territory were added to it". For a defence of mercantilism against Heckscher's somewhat unjustified criticism see Keynes (1936: 335-51).

4. The Emergence of Central Banking in England

4.1 The Foundation of the Bank of England

> In England, the banking system of which has reached an extension and perfection unknown in other parts of Europe, [...] motives for keeping private *hoards* no longer exist, and they are all transferred to the banks, particularly to the Bank of England.
>
> *John Fullarton*[1]

> A good bank is one which does not pay out.
>
> *Mercantilist saying*[2]

Building up a domestic banking system and economizing the stock of gold reserves were among the main tasks of mercantilist economic policy, which aimed at the development of the national economy. The foundation of the Bank of England fitted well into that pattern of policy making. Not only commercial circles, but the population at large, demanded a standardization of the currency order; goldsmiths, who until then had run a profitable business of taking in coins for the issue of – as was argued – undervalued notes, ought to lose their market power; a lowering of interest rates was expected to support national prosperity.[3] Above all, it was felt that there was an urgent need to redress the fiscal gap, during a time of armed conflict. This last-mentioned point seemed to have been the driving force behind the bank-foundation project. "Had the country not been at war in 1694, the government would hardly been disposed to offer a favourable charter to a corporation which proposed to lend it money."[4]

A further motive was to take a first step towards a *nationalization of financial markets*. In the 16th century, Antwerp was the nerve centre of international capital, which used to ignore borders in its investment and lending activities.[5] The

---

1 Fullarton 1845: 94*.
2 Vilar 1960: 250.
3 The 1765 founded royal Prussian Bank likewise was assigned with the mercantilist mission, "to encourage the circulation of the Bank's notes, to utilize capital, to support trade and commerce and to guard against an immoderate rise of interest rates" (quoted from Ziegler 1993: 491, cf. Holtfrerich 1988).
4 Clapham 1944a: 1, cf. North 1994: 112-5.
5 This cosmopolitan behaviour of the financial powers met with (ideologically or religiously motivated) disapproval on the part of the German population. "Perhaps we might say that the Germans, people who preferred farming, compared to all other European nations, next to the Spaniards, always had the poorest understanding of the essence and

successful financial manager of the English court working at Antwerp, Sir Thomas Gresham, had in 1569 already recommended independence from foreign creditors to his principals. In order to tap domestic sources of finance it seemed necessary to loosen the prevailing restrictions on the free market movements of the rate of interest. England's public finance enjoyed a good reputation at that time, not least because Gresham admonished the king to redeem his obligations on time. The realization of such a bank foundation project however, still took up more than hundred years. Yet in 1640 King Charles, caught in heavy financial distress, confiscated the bullion of private businessmen – which induced wealthy citizen to place their precious-metal fortune in the goldsmiths' hands, rather than in vaults of a royal bank.

The Bank of England started to operate in 1694 as a private joint-stock company by granting a "foundation credit" to the king. "In the first place all the capital up to the last shilling had been lent to the Government. The only security the shareholders had was the good faith of the debtor."[6] At the same time, the Bank carried out a discount and credit business vis-à-vis private clients, accompanied by a note issue which was limited by the amount of the basic government credit. At first, the Bank did not hold an institutionally guaranteed monopoly; its notes were not declared legal tender before 1833. Unlike most of the banks on the continent, it did not work mainly as a deposit bank; the notes of which are fully backed. Although the Bank's notes formally represented a claim to gold or silver it was obvious that a fully fledged redemption was impossible. The Bank "never pretended to take the deposit for any other purpose than that of trading with it. [...] It coined [...] its own credit into paper money".[7]

In view of these circumstances the success of the Bank and the acceptance of its notes may appear astonishing. It overcame occasional critical stages, at times of political unrest and armed struggles, because the court, the proprietors, and the commercial world stood by the Bank. They were willing to put their own interests last for the benefit of the preservation of the collective interest in a stable banking system; at times an imminent bank run was cushioned by ostentatious deposits. This understanding of the importance of an efficient currency order, and the merchants' readiness to accept the notes as means of payment, on principle, for more than two centuries helped to keep the parlous balance between royal and private interests. The Bank charter (the permission to run a bank and issue notes) was granted for limited time, but always renewed in return for the prolongation of the governmental credit (at special rates). On the other hand the Bank was able to strengthen its privileged market position and was granted a monopoly for note is-

---

the importance of mobile big capital" (Ehrenberg 1896a: 406, cf. 411, Wallerstein 1974: 174-8).

[6] Andréadès 1909: 84, cf. 14-26, Ehrenberg 1896a: 412, Ehrenberg 1896b: 34-5, 59-60, 171-4, Kindleberger 1984: 50-3.

[7] Rogers 1887 (quoted from Andréadès 1909: 82).

sue in 1742. This market regulation was qualified by an exception in favour of small country banks, which of course increased the number of newly founded banks over the years and thus complicated the control of money market conditions on the part of the Bank of England.[8]

The fact that each government credit implied an increase of note circulation met with stubborn, although ineffective, criticism uttered by Macleod: "The way to *create* money is for the Government to *borrow* money. [...] There is nothing so wild or absurd in John Law's *Theory of Money* as this. His scheme of basing a paper currency upon land is sober compared to it."[9] We see again that the backing of money may be quite irrelevant if the reputation of the issuing bank and the acceptance of their notes can be preserved in another way. As a more pragmatic observer, compared to Macleod, Steuart explained the sound character of the Bank's notes by the government's right to collect taxes and duties; hence he judged: "No security, therefore, can be better than the notes of the Bank of England, while government subsists."[10]

Political and economic stabilization contributed to an easing of the capital market at the beginning of the 18th century, which can be seen from the rapid decrease of interest rates on newly issued government paper (*figure 4.1*). After 1740 until the end of the century, starting from a minimum of 3 %, there was rising trend of long-term interest rates, accompanied by slowly rising prices. The impact of government borrowing on the capital market yield had a substantial effect on private sector activities. Over the whole period, the Bank of England discount rate was kept constant at 5 %. This remarkable inverse term structure of interest rates may have stabilized the money market; the issue of notes was limited, but the Bank stood ready to act as a lender of last resort.[11]

In the 18th century the English gold reserves increased for two reasons. First, the economy took advantage – by means of additional exports – of the income effects of a general boom which had been induced and was propelled by a flow of gold emanating from South America and entering Europe via Portugal. Contrary to the way in which things developed in the 16th century, this process did not now lead mainly to price increases but rather – supported by population and rural productivity growth – to a sustained expansion of production, and thus marked the transition to industrial revolution. This radical structural change took place in England in only 40 years between 1770 and 1810. Through the expansion and improve-

---

[8] Cf. Andréadès 1909: 85-9, 121, 127, 171-2, Bagehot 1873: 45, Vilar 1960: 211-6, 281, Kindleberger 1984: 76, North 1994: 134.

[9] Quoted from Andréadès 1909: 124.

[10] Steuart 1767b: 249, cf. 242-56.

[11] Of course it can be doubted whether this interest policy followed some kind of strategy. According to Stadermann (1994: 66, 71-5) the true motive of the discount policy was the attempt – pursued in the interests of owners of financial wealth – to resist the tendency of falling capital yields, a widely discussed topic in the classical era.

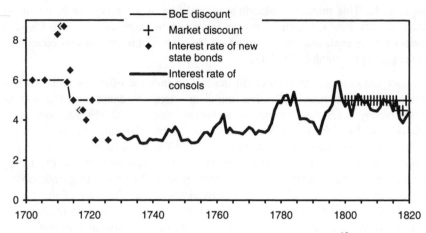

Figure 4.1: Interest rates in England in the 18th century[12]

ment of the banking system, a key obstacle for economic development – as seen by the mercantilists – was gradually removed. Savings were not hoarded but deposited with the banks, which in turn favoured financial conditions of investors.[13]

The second cause of the growth of gold stocks in England was the new fixing of the official gold-silver parity in 1717, which did not correspond to relative market prices. It implied an overvaluation of gold which according to "Gresham's Law" drove undervalued silver coins out of circulation. Arbitrage brought about an influx of gold as the English mint paid a relatively high price compared to world market conditions. "This surprising change made England, unwittingly and unintentionally, the home of the gold standard."[14]

---

[12] Data from Homer 1977.

[13] "The last school of economists who seriously feared that economic growth would fail because of lack of money and credit, or because of high costs of providing finance, the school of the mercantilists, died out around 1750. Not the arguments put forward by classical economists, but rather the facts made them fall silent. The mercantilists resigned because their problem had been settled: there was enough money and credit to finance all economically reasonable projects, due to the expansion, efficiency and integration of national and – later – international credit institutions. The new monetary topic of classical and neoclassical economics thus no longer was the lack but the abundance of money and credit: i.e. inflation" (Hankel 1993: 441, cf. Bagehot 1873: 65-8, Andréadès 1909: 161-2, Vilar 1960: 199, 225-31, 256-62, North 1994: 123).

[14] Vilar 1960: 220, cf. 172, 211-21, Ricardo 1810, Laidler 1991: 29-32, North 1994: 50. Kindleberger (1984: 55-60) noticed that Gresham's Law was ascribed wrongly to Gresham by Macleod since the understanding of the disequilibrium market position of currencies of divergent quality had been already expressed in 1360 by the French bishop Nicholas Oresme.

Box 9: Bimetallism and Gresham's Law

Assume that a country mints 4 gold coins ("guineas") out of one ounce of gold and 5 silver coins ("shilling") out of one ounce of silver. Let costs of production (i.e. world market prices) per oz. gold and silver be 80 shilling (sh) and 5 sh, respectively. The exchange ratio then is 1 oz. gold = 16 oz. silver. Ignore additional costs and profits ("seigniorage") which might accrue from minting. In equilibrium the official parity between silver and gold coins has to be fixed at 80/4 sh = 20 sh = 1 guinea.

Fixing a "wrong" parity which does not correspond to market prices causes a disequilibrium. In case of, say, 25 sh = 1 guinea, gold is overvalued. If the mint buys an ounce of gold (the equivalent of 4 guineas) at a rate of 100 sh it becomes profitable on the part of private market agents to withdraw silver coins from domestic circulation, using them to get (by means of production or barter) gold abroad, and finally offer it to the national mint. Investing 80 sh in the acquisition of foreign gold thus yields 100 sh. As a consequence, the country records an inflow of gold from all over the world.

A similar sequence occurs in case of a change of costs of production. If one ounce of gold can be mined by spending 60 sh, whereas the official parity remains at 20 sh = 1 guinea, gold again is overvalued. Hence, bad money drives good money out of circulation. Traders buy one ounce of gold for 60 sh on the world market and sell it to the mint at a price of 80 sh. Restoring equilibrium requires either to change parity to 15 sh = 1 guinea or to increase the weight of the guinea from 1/4 to 1/3 oz. gold.

4.2 Suspension and Resumption of the Gold Standard: The Bullion Controversy

> By passing the Restriction Act the English Government had discovered the philosopher's stone for which the alchemists of the Middle Ages had searched in vain. [...] The system of inconvertible paper money did good service in England.
> *André M. Andréadès*[15]

> I never should advise a government to restore a currency which was depreciated 30 per cent.
> *David Ricardo*[16]

In the wake of the European armed conflicts after the French revolution volatile gold flows with changing directions were to be observed between France and England. The Bank of England for political reasons felt obliged to expand its credit to the government. Note issue increased correspondingly, the pound sterling fell on the foreign exchange and gold reserves dwindled rapidly. The Bank's directors saw "that they had to choose between their own bankruptcy and that of the

---

[15] Andréadès 1909: 203-4.
[16] Ricardo in a letter of 1821 (quoted in Foxwell 1908: xxxvi).

Government".[17] A bank run in 1797 finally forced a formal suspension of the right
to cash in notes. Interestingly enough, this event at first did not set off negative repercussions on the markets; merchants and other commercial banks ostentatiously
agreed to continue to accept notes without limit. The state of affairs stabilized rapidly, gold flowed back to England; the resumption of cash payments would have
been possible, but was postponed.

In the following years budget policy deviated from the cautious stance which had
at first been chosen, when considering the awkward market position of a paper
currency. Private credits also surged in an inflationary boom (*figure 4.2*). Note issue accelerated and the market price of gold exceeded the fixed mint price. A continuing depreciation of the pound sterling resulted from trade deficits (due to rising prices, strong demand dynamics and an export embargo imposed on England
for a time) and subsidies paid to England's allies on the continent. Gold coins had
vanished from domestic circulation; they were smuggled and sold abroad at a
profit.[18]

This situation formed the background for a scientific inquiry which was executed
by the Bullion Committee in 1810. The point at issue was whether gold had become more valuable or notes had been depreciated. At that time, this question was
not at all trivial: in a gold standard system, a rise in the price of gold measured in
units of money could be explained, as a supply-side phenomenon, by a deterioration in the conditions of producing gold or, as a monetary demand effect, by the
consequences of new gold discoveries. According to widespread opinion however, these considerations were held to be irrelevant because they referred to a
metal-based currency; in a pure paper currency standard, which had in fact been
established since 1797, an excess supply of notes – which then would drive prices
– was believed to be impossible, as the circulating amount of notes would automatically be regulated by the real need felt for them on the part of market agents.

The directors of the Bank too assumed that there were different principles of note
issue in each regime: in the first case, it was a strict duty to maintain the price of
gold and the exchange rate, in the second case, note issue should be oriented according to the volume of "solid" bills of exchange which were seen to be "backed"
by real transactions so that money creation could not be inflationary: "A bank,
under prudent management, might issue notes in proportion to the demands made
on it, and without taking into account the rate of exchange and the price of guineas; always provided that the notes were issued in exchange for real and convertible assets, such as commercial bills of undoubted solidity [...] based on actual
commercial transactions."[19]

---

[17] Andréadès 1909: 193, cf. Clapham 1944a: 267-8.
[18] Cf. Andréadès 1909: 195-210, 218-25, Clapham 1944a: 268, Schumpeter 1954: 690-2,
    Vilar 1960: 309-14, Galbraith 1975: 44-5.
[19] Andréadès 1909: 216, cf. 220-9, Bagehot 1873: 54-5, 86-7, Clapham 1944b: 24-5,
    Schumpeter 1954: 706-17, Kindleberger 1984: 61. The Banking Doctrine according to

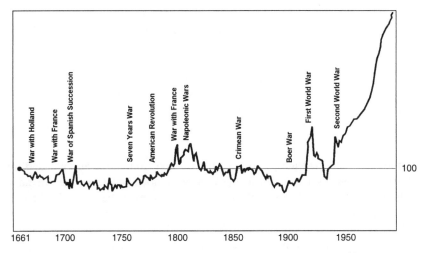

Figure 4.2: British consumer prices (1661 = 100, log scale)[20]

Thus the Bank of England had fallen in line with the Banking Doctrine, which met with harsh criticism from the majority of the Bullion Committee: this theory was said to confuse money and capital (or credit, respectively). It ignored the fact that an additional extension of credit not only provides finance to the newly in-debted investor, but also implies an increase of the circulating quantity of money, particularly if notes, being inconvertible, do not flow back to the issuing bank. In-convertibility means that the money function of a standard of value is no longer fulfilled by gold but by paper money, "a circulating medium whose value varied only in proportion to its quantity". The appropriate criterion to measure whether there is an over-issue of notes was said to be very simple and unambiguous: "*The only real test is to be found in the state of the foreign exchanges and the price of bullion.*"[21]

---

which a note issue not only was permitted but rather was required in case of a "real" demand on the part of the commercial circulation has a long-lasting tradition in the his-tory of central-bank theory and policy. Still a hundred years later the president of the German Reichsbank, Havenstein, argued that a central bank granting credits which were "justified and necessary as they served production and trade" would not create "artificial purchasing power". The Reichsbank firmly believed – drawing upon the alleged rele-vance of a distinction between pure financial bills and solid trade bills – in the real-bills doctrine, boasted about the efficiency of its 30 paper mills in the midst of German hy-perinflation, and justified its discount policy by its "duties vis-à-vis the German econ-omy" and the assurance that this policy stance represented "only" a reaction to the rising money demand (cf. James 1998: 46-51, Holtfrerich 1988). The Fed also asserted in 1923 that any volume of credit financing "productive uses" could not be excessive (cf. Fried-man/Schwartz 1963: 253).

[20] Data from: The Economist, 22.2.1992, 68.

[21] Andréadès 1909: 224, 227, cf. 212-3, 226-7, Clapham 1944b: 22. An exchange rate tar-get for guiding the note issue was also recommended by Tooke (cf. Rieter 1971: 169-

The fact that indicators and criteria for the issue of notes in a regime of paper currency are not that distinct from the rules and guidelines prevailing in a fully convertible gold standard currency was obviously not clear to many contemporaries. Backing the currency by a gold reserve in the practice of banking policy had probably led market agents, scientists and politicians astray; the misunderstanding was in the belief that the restraints imposed by this backing were seen as regime-specific: so that after the transition to a new monetary regime of inconvertible paper money, economic behaviour was seen to be relieved from the subordination to these restrictions.

Ricardo also supported the position of the Bullion Committee and pleaded for a reduction of note issue in order that – after some price and exchange rate adjustments – the former obligation of note redemption could be re-established. The government however, to give themselves greater room for manoeuvre in a period of armed conflicts, put off this step for a decade. Such a conflict between economic understanding and political constraints played an important part in the history of monetary policy. Clapham concedes that some directors of the Bank of England may have been bad economists, but many critics of the Bank were naive from a political point of view. "Ricardo, who had made a fine fortune by dealings in war issues, wrote as from an ivory tower in a time of untroubled peace."[22]

Only in 1819 did the government implement the necessary steps for the return to a fully fledged gold standard in 1821 (First Peel's Act). In the meantime however prices had risen further; the amount of deflation which was necessary for an orderly reintroduction of the former gold parity implied such a heavy real appreciation of government debt that Ricardo now dissociated himself from his former recommendation. Mill also recognized the increased burden of public debt, but considered the resumption of cash payments to be imperative in order not to disappoint the long-term confidence of private owners of financial wealth.[23]

The return to the gold standard proved to be the wrong answer to a properly posed question. Of course monetary policy should be concerned with safeguarding the stability of the currency. But in the preceding two decades the Bank of England had, at least temporarily, managed to attain that goal without an official commitment to convertibility. "And the proof is, that for more than ten years after the suspension of cash payments the Bank paper was undepreciated, and circulated at

---

73). It can perhaps be taken as evidence of the deeply rooted metal-based monetary thinking on the part of classical economists that Andréadès himself (1909: 223) reproached the adherents of the Banking Doctrine for believing that gold no longer served the function of a standard of value and "that the paper money was the real measure of all commodities and that gold was only one of those commodities whose value is determined by reference to this invariable and universal standard". In the light of the analysis of the Bullion Committee with respect to the change of the standard of value this criticized position however is absolutely correct.

[22] Clapham 1944b: 28.

[23] Cf. Ricardo 1810, Mill 1871: 553-5, Andréadès 1909: 235-42, Kindleberger 1984: 62-3.

no discount in comparison with gold."[24] The Bullion Committee had shown – at least implicitly – a way to a modern strategic concept of monetary policy which rested primarily upon keeping the quantity of money in short supply; this concept could have been employed in principle without tying the currency to gold. The renewed commitment to a guaranteed price of gold as such may have been reasonable as a confidence-building measure. But at the same time this marked a retrograde step in the understanding of banking and in the theory of monetary policy. This was to become evident in the ensuing passionate debates on the alleged metallic foundations of the monetary system.

4.3 From Palmer's Rule to Peel's Act: The Separation of Money and Credit

> It is the duty of every bank and most of all a central bank to be rich.
> *Richard S. Sayers*[25]

> The weapon for the defence of the gold reserve is a contraction of credit.
> *Ralph G. Hawtrey*[26]

> There was a lag in understanding the need to have the money supply inelastic in the long run but elastic in the short.
> *Charles P. Kindleberger*[27]

The obligation to resume cash payments left key questions regarding the amount of note issue and the reserve ratio unsettled. Moreover, the Bank of England seemed to have forgotten some of the practical knowledge it had acquired at the time when it was forced to actively defend its gold reserves. During the crisis of 1783 the feared "external drain" was countered for the first time by a quantitative reaction of credit extension. "The directors had noticed that if the issues could be restricted even for a short time, the coin, instead of being exported, flowed back even more quickly than it had been withdrawn; they had thus arrived at the following rule: 'That while a drain of specie is going on their issues should be contracted as much as possible, but that as soon as the tide has given signs of ceasing, and turning the other way, it was then safe to extend their issues freely'."[28]

Now the Bank seemed to have forgotten this lesson. After committing itself to gold again it was on the verge of bankruptcy almost every ten years. It was not

---

[24] Bagehot 1873: 86.
[25] Sayers 1936: 27.
[26] Hawtrey 1923: 110.
[27] Kindleberger 1984: 90.
[28] Andréadès 1909: 158, cf. Vilar 1960: 286.

victim but – according to Mill – the party responsible for financial instabilities. "For nearly half a century there never has been a commercial crisis which the Bank has not been strenuously accused either of producing or of aggravating."[29] Critics argued that the Bank tended to support booms for too long. In some cases it kindled speculation by means of low interest rates, thus driving the investors who were chasing after high yields into ever more risky projects; in financial circles the saying was "John Bull can stand many things but he cannot stand 2 per cent". Trade deficits and the breakdown of excessive expectations then typically launched a "run" on the Bank, after note issue had been maintained in spite of dwindling reserves. "A more miserable history can hardly be found than that of the attempts of the Bank [...] to keep a reserve and to manage a foreign drain between 1819 [...] and the year 1857."[30]

It has to be recognized however, that the position of the Bank of England in the financial market and its self-image was subject to substantial changes in the decades following 1820. Some critics may have ignored the fact that the Bank's business practice, initially, was marked by a vague feeling of being responsible for the stability of the monetary system. This was clearly expressed in a rule, put through by the Bank's director Palmer, according to which the gold reserve should make up one third and interest-bearing paper two thirds of the Bank's assets. The last-mentioned item should be kept fixed in absolute terms (thus stabilizing the flow of the Bank's profits), which implied that fluctuations of note circulation were accompanied by parallel changes of the gold reserve. Insofar it was the public, and not the Bank, which determined the amount of notes by choosing between notes and coins.

The crucial point of this concept was that the Bank did not employ any excess reserves for backing an additional expansion of credit, but rather kept it as an enlarged reserve. Therefore, the Bank did not feel compelled to practise a credit restraint if later gold should flow out. It was even possible to increase lending in times of a critical financial strain in the market, which relieved the pressure on other banks. The effect of gold losses on the quantity of money thus was sterilized in order to pursue the macroeconomic role of a lender of last resort.[31]

This well-meant concept suffered from some serious shortcomings:

• The Bank's shareholders opposed to the profits foregone by not entering into active competition with other banks in times of surplus reserves. This indicates that the Bank's behaviour was not at all dominated by a private profit motive; rather,

---

[29] Mill 1871: 648, cf. Andréadès 1909: 404.

[30] Bagehot 1873: 23, cf. Andréadès 1909: 248-53, 261-2, 267-8, 314, 331-6, Clapham 1944b: 200, Laidler 1991: 21. Stadermann (1994: 55) speaks of the "Bank's years of apprenticeship".

[31] Cf. Mill 1871: 661, Andréadès 1909: 257, 279, Schumpeter 1954: 697-8, Kindleberger 1984: 89.

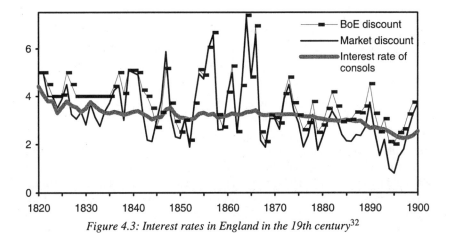

Figure 4.3: Interest rates in England in the 19th century[32]

the traces of an anti-cyclical credit policy rested upon the willingness to temporarily put this motive last.[33]

• In practice, it turned out to be difficult to judge whether a strain on financial markets was temporary in character, and could be overcome by a credit expansion on the part of the Bank, or heralded instead a fundamental weakness of pound sterling, which exposed the Bank itself to the danger of bankruptcy. Mostly, this risk was perceived too late; then the Bank – aiming to escape – stopped lending abruptly, which in turn aggravated the liquidity crisis.

• From 1833 onwards, when the legal ceiling for the discount rate of 5 % was abolished, the Bank was free to employ interest policies in order to stabilize the market. But this opportunity was at first only barely used; in times of crisis the rate was raised too late and too little. Interest rate policies did not become more flexible and volatile before the mid of the 19th century (*figure 4.3*).

After the crises of 1825-26 and 1836-39, political quarters initiated steps in order to safeguard monetary stability by means of an established *institutional rule*. Lord Overstone highlighted the double task of the Bank of England: to control the economy's money supply, on the one hand, and to run the profitable business of granting credit as any other private commercial bank, on the other. In terms of the Bank's balance sheet, this conflict means that in the first case the note issue varies

---

[32] Data from Homer 1977. The comparison with *figure 4.1* shows that in the 19th century short-term interest rates reflect the changing liquidity conditions in the market whereas long-term rates of consols also during times of crisis fluctuated less (this however does not apply to long-term rates of private paper). The decreasing trend of long rates should be seen in conjunction with a deflationary price trend which continued up to 1895 (cf. *figure 4.2*).

[33] Cf. Ziegler 1990: 81, Ziegler 1993.

with the gold reserve, and in the second case with the volume of credit. A bank could hardly be urged to refrain from entering into profitable credit contracts. Therefore, the conclusion was that Palmer's Rule could not be fulfilled by a single institution. Consequently the idea came up to divide the Bank of England into two departments.[34]

This proposal was then realized by Peel's Second Act of 1844. The *Issue Depart-ment* was charged with the task of preserving the currency order by issuing notes at a fixed gold parity. The primary goal was the maintenance of a sufficient re-serve with which to ensure England's balance-of-payment solvency. The basic quota of notes was determined by the amount of government debt which was ac-tually held by the Bank in 1844, and thus was seen to serve as a solid security (the status quo was simply declared as a norm!); any additional note issue had to be fully backed by newly acquired gold reserves. The *Banking Department*, on the other hand, was allowed to run the ordinary business of a private commercial bank. Its reserve consisted of notes which, above all, were to be obtained by sell-ing securities on the capital market, or by attracting deposits from abroad (fol-lowed by a refinancing transaction with the Issue Department where notes were exchanged for the cession of claims to foreign exchange). The note issue of the other commercial banks was severely restricted and disappeared hereafter; they held reserve and working balances with the Banking Department (*table 4.1*).

The project of separating money creation from credit supply was the most impor-tant practical innovation in the history of monetary economies (and was harshly criticized by Tooke). A uniform (monopolistic) currency allows a full realization of the positive returns to scale accruing from the use of money. At the same time the problem of preserving macroeconomic stability of that currency is being dis-engaged from the aggregate effects of the private business of granting credit. Commercial banks are free to pursue the goal of profit maximization, but are forced to operate under a liquidity constraint imposed by some independent agen-cy (a central bank). "The hierarchical structure of the banking system allows a combination of centralization and decentralization: a centralization of the money as a medium and a decentralization of decisions on economic operations."[35]

Lutz expresses the "key problem of a monetary order" as follows: the credit side of the banks' balance sheets can be exposed to the influence of competitive market forces, but the money side should be controlled by a supervisory agency accord-ing to macroeconomic criteria.[36] This assignment passes the responsibility for the

---

[34] Cf. Loyd 1844, Andréadès 1909: 273, 279-99, Clapham 1944b: 172-85.

[35] Luhmann 1988: 146-7, cf. Rieter 1971: 147, De Grauwe 1996: 6.

[36] Lutz (1936: 29-33) established this normative assignment by referring to the empirically distorted view that money would have been created by the state through many centuries; only in the 19th century an undesirable trend had evolved where money creation was an uncontrolled consequence of credit supply. For corresponding to the facts this view however ought rather be reversed.

Table 4.1: Balance sheet of the Bank of England (mill. pound)[37]

Issue Department

Assets	1844	1903	Liabilities	1844	1903
Gold coins and bullion	14,4	32,2	Notes	28,4	50,6
Government credit	11,0	11,0			
Other securities	3,0	7,4			

Banking Department

Assets	1844	1903	Liabilities	1844	1903
Gold coins and bullion	0,9	2,1	Deposits	13,3	44,4
Notes	8,2	22,0	Proprietors' capital / Rest	18,2	18,4
Government credit	14,6	17,0			
Other securities	7,8	21,7			

stability of the economic system onto the government or to a state-dependent central bank. Later, the authorities attempted to exploit the powerful market position of the central bank in order to pursue various macroeconomic targets.

The immediate problem in England however, was that the division of the Bank failed to create an efficient two-tier banking system. The passing of Peel's Act in 1844 obviously made the Bank of England believe that it was relieved from the burden of being responsible for safeguarding the stability of the financial system. The task of protecting the value of the currency seemed to be solved by a legal automatism; the Issue Department had totally lost its latitude and room for manoeuvre (which is why it degenerated to a mere counter in the following years). The Banking Department also did not take care of the macroeconomic aspects and consequences of its banking business, let alone the role of a lender of last resort, because all these topics – according to the letter and the intention of the law – were regarded as assigned to the Issue Department.

As a consequence, the Banking Department gave the goal of profitability special emphasis, rather than the goal of maintaining liquidity of the banking system. Immediately, it entered into competition with the other joint-stock commercial banks, which in the meantime had been founded, and reappeared – by markedly cutting its discount rate – as a powerful contestant on the money market (*figure 4.4*). Contrary to their well-meant intentions the monetary-policy reformer had not

---

[37] Cf. Andréadès 1909: 290, 296-310, Bagehot 1873: 12. Consolidation of both balance sheets reveals that the share of gold reserves in all assets increased from 30 % to 38 %. The backing ration of notes (and deposits) went up from 76 % (46 %) to 120 % (47 %); this indicates that the Bank of England, at the beginning of the 20th century, had become factually a deposit bank following the example of the Bank of Amsterdam.

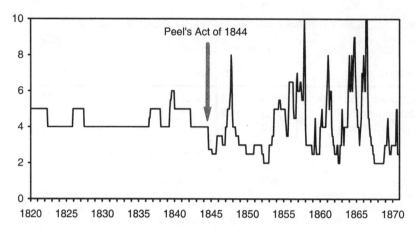

Figure 4.4: Monthly discount rates of the Bank of England[38]

established a central bank, but had *abolished* the existing beginnings of a central-bank behaviour on the part of the Bank of England.[39]

It does not come as a surprise therefore, that the English banking system was hit by further severe crises in 1847, 1857 and 1866. Their course was different though compared to the pattern of previous crises. After the notes of the Bank of England had been declared legal tender in 1833, and because their redemption was regarded as guaranteed, the liquidity preference of market agents in critical moments not longer aimed first of all at gold, but at these notes. The convertibility of notes in no way ensured the convertibility of deposits. Thus – as it happened in 1847 – a situation could occur where the Banking Department, for lack of its own reserves, ceased to pay out notes to its clients even though the vault of the Issue Department was filled up with gold. This revealed the paradoxical content of the Bank Law. For Hawtrey it was a platitude, "that gold reserves exist to be *used*. It is futile to establish a rule to secure the accumulation of a gold reserve in support of the legal tender note issue, unless, where urgent need arises, the gold can in the last resort be released."[40]

If on the other hand gold flowed abroad, the Banking Department's stock of note reserves was diminished because the public, as a rule, did not substitute notes but deposits for gold; thus a credit restriction was enforced which brought about a pro-cyclical monetary effect. In principle the reduction of note supply was in accordance with a basic idea of the Bank Act: the strict linkage of notes and gold reserves was expected to strengthen the self-adjusting market forces in the sense of

---

[38] Data from Clapham 1944b: 429-32.

[39] Cf. Ziegler 1990: 22-5, 39, 82-3, Ziegler 1993, Andréadès 1909: 314, Clapham 1944b: 190.

[40] Hawtrey 1923: 82, cf. Schumpeter 1954: 727n, Laidler 1991: 22-3, Ziegler 1993.

Hume's model. In the case of an outflow of gold, no compensating additional note issue should be allowed which might postpone the general decrease of the price level. This fall of prices promised to restore equilibrium by means of increasing exports. The bankers though knew that it would take too long until an initial loss of reserves would, via a reduction of nominal demand on the goods market, also lead to a lowering of money demand: "A drain might be sudden and a price fall slow."[41] Nevertheless, the "corset" given to the Bank of England can also be understood as a device for precluding any crisis at all; as the rigid limit imposed on the note issue was hoped to hinder the development of an excessive boom.[42]

4.4 The Currency-Banking Controversy on the Elasticity of Money Supply

> Let us have notes [...]. We don't mean, indeed, to take notes, because we shall not want them; only tell us that we can get them, and this will at once restore confidence.
>
> *From a debate in parliament 1847*[43]

> One depositor can get metal, but all cannot, therefore deposits are not money.
>
> *Lord Overstone*[44]

> Bank notes [...] were money paper that had illegitimately usurped the role of paper money and were now to be forced to behave as if they were legitimate gold money. This is the whole philosophy of Peel's Act.
>
> *Joseph A. Schumpeter*[45]

The proponents and adherents of Peel's Act (who also mostly had supported the majority position of the Bullion Committees) are counted among the "Currency School". Essentially, it drew upon the quantity theory, which explains the internal and the external value of money by the amount of circulating notes and coins. Among the indispensable preconditions for this approach to hold, is a clear-cut *definition of money* and a proper understanding of the *transmission process* between changes in the quantity of money and the movement of macroeconomic va-

---

[41] Clapham 1944b: 195, cf. Andréadès 1909: 274, 322.

[42] The idea of a preventive avoidance of crises, in the period following until today, became a topic of considerable importance in the theory and practice of monetary policy. The argument can be found in Hayek's "disproportion approach" of explaining economic crises and is at the root of the concept of monetary targeting. Today we do not seem to know how to conform to Keynes' (1936: 322) advice: "The right remedy for the trade cycle is not to be found in abolishing booms and thus keeping us permanently in a semi-slump; but in abolishing slumps and thus keeping us permanently in a quasi-boom."

[43] Quoted from Andréadès 1909: 336n.

[44] Lord Overstone 1857 (quoted from Kindleberger 1984: 85).

[45] Schumpeter 1954: 700.

riables. But with respect to both points the Currency School showed some weakness:

• Money was regarded to consist of coins and notes of the Bank of England; according to Ricardo and Lord Overstone these notes should not be paper money, i.e. a credit claim used as a means of payment, but rather should represent gold. Such an understanding of money for many observers seemed obsolete. In 1833 private joint-stock banks *without* the permission to issue notes had been licensed in London. It was just this kind of regulation, established in order to improve the efficiency of checking the money supply, which induced a vast and uncontrollable expansion of payments by means of checks and transfers[46] – this is the typical pattern of financial innovation, valid until today, which reacts to a restriction of the use of certain money assets: "Fix any M_i and the market will create new forms of money in periods of boom to get around the limit and create the necessity to fix a new variable M_j."[47]

• The hypothesis, that the dynamics of a market system (in nominal terms) can be stabilized by means of the control of a narrowly defined money aggregate, should have been supported by proving the constancy of a corresponding money velocity. But the Currency School had only offered some vague allusions to the connection between notes and deposits. The concept of a money multiplier was, as yet, unknown; empirically, it did not seem to have been constant either. The quantity theory was still presented as an analysis of flow variables. The beginnings of understanding the velocity of money as a stock-flow relation can only be found in John Stuart Mill. But even Mill thought it necessary to emphasize that the "hoarded" part of the quantity of money had no impact on goods demand and prices. The truly propelling force of spending, for him, was credit, whereas the quantity of money was seen as a more passive, endogenous entity.[48]

The Currency School thus was unable to grasp that a boom could develop even without an excessive issue of notes. Exactly this was the main objection made by the Banking School, where the critics of Peel's Act gathered: for controlling economic dynamics by a *quantitative* limitation of the means of payments, bank deposits (followed most probably by further money substitutes) ought to have been regulated as well. In principle however, the Banking School considered a surveillance and restriction of note circulation to be unnecessary – at least, if these notes were fully convertible. Notice that, contrary to the position held during the Bul-

---

[46] "It was only due to its naive definition of money that the practical execution of that abstruse [currency] theory did not immediately cause a collapse of the British currency system. As deposits with the commercial banks and thus circulation of checks (and bills) were not subject of any regulation, a growth of money supply which was oriented at the needs of payment circulation and credit creation was not precluded as a principle" (Ziegler 1993: 479, cf. Andréadès 1909: 275, 301, Lutz 1936: 39-42, Schumpeter 1954: 695, 700, Rieter 1971: 122-39, Kindleberger 1984: 85).

[47] Kindleberger 1978: 58.

[48] Cf. Mill 1871: 496, 524-32, 651-77, Schumpeter 1954: 704-5, 727, Laidler 1991: 14-7.

lion Controversy, it was no longer believed that backing notes by "good" bills of exchange would guarantee stable prices. The Banking School also stood by the gold standard and assessed irredeemable paper money as a risk to the stability of the currency.

Hence, both schools differed little with respect to the basic goals of monetary policy, but did differ in categorical and empirical questions as to the definition of money, and in their judgement on the kind of rule which was held necessary in order to preserve the value of the currency.[49] The Banking School played the more liberal part as the basic decision in favour of gold convertibility was held to be sufficient; moreover, it demanded that the Bank of England should admit its responsibility for its factual role as the "bankers' bank". The Currency School intended to impose a limit for the amount of notes, which was arbitrarily chosen and thus unfounded. Because of the shortcomings of *both* approaches there is no winner in the Currency-Banking debate:

The Bank of England's policy, bound to the Currency School, failed in practice because of the fact that a banking system – particularly in case of rampant uncertainty – needs a flexible money supply in the sense that the public is free to choose between deposits and notes, whereas the rate of interest controls the general liquidity tension on the money market. The supply-side guideline of a rigid connection of gold and notes is not efficient: it does not preserve monetary stability during a boom as the volume of credit and deposits then expand in line; it fuels perturbation and liquidity preference in the markets when, at times of crisis, portfolios are restructured favouring "solid" assets. Or, to put it differently: an absolute fixing of money supply destabilizes money demand. "Any notion that money is not to be had, or that it may not to be had at any price, only raises alarm to panic and enhances panic to madness."[50]

Currency *and* Banking School belong to the tradition of the quantity theory of money insofar as they postulate a parallel movement of the nominal variables: wages, prices and money. It is hard to accept the argument that the quantity-theoretic substance of the Currency School would show in its attempt to establish an exogenous money supply.[51] An *autonomous* management of the quantity of money was only enabled by the political decision to *deviate* from the Currency Doctrine: in order to prevent a breakdown of commercial banks on account of illiquidity, government was forced, several times, to pass a "Bill of Indemnity" authorizing the Bank to increase note issue beyond the statutory limit, provided that it kept the discount rate at a minimum of 8 %. This was intended to meet the money demand on the part of the banking system and the public. Interestingly, in some cases it turned out to be unnecessary actually to increase the note issue to that ex-

---

[49] Cf. Schumpeter 1954: 725-31, Laidler 1991: 36.

[50] Bagehot 1873: 28, cf. Ziegler 1993: 482n.

[51] Cf. Blaug 1995.

tent, as already a letter indicating that the limit be abolished calmed down liquidity preference on the part of market agents: "The publication of the Chancellor of the Exchequer's letter had a magical effect. The certainty that money could be got took away all desire to have it".[52]

As a consequence, the *government* became the actual lender of last resort – this had been, early on, predicted and acknowledged by Mill, Peel and Lord Overstone. The flexible handling of the commitment to the money-supply rule brought Peel's Act a long life (until 1928), because it was simply suspended in case of emergency. But this practice tempted the Bank of England for example in 1857, to continue its inappropriate business behaviour in anticipation of a coming Bill of Indemnity; and for a long time it left the onus of looking after macroeconomic and financial stability to the political authorities. The initial procedure of scrutinizing the necessity and efficiency of a Bill of Indemnity, by setting up an investigating committee, was however soon seen as superfluous. "The principle of having a rule but breaking it if one had to was so widely accepted that after the suspension in 1866 there was no demand for a new investigation. [...] Hard-and-fast rules were agreed not to be workable".[53]

As the Currency Doctrine had been institutionalized in practice, the Banking School on the other hand had had no possibility to gain the experience that the mere principle of guaranteeing the redemption of bank notes in no way preserves monetary and macroeconomic stability. The Banking School did not offer any practical criteria for the execution of monetary policy:

• Each commitment saying that notes are to be redeemed gives a signal to the market that there exists a "better" currency backing the circulating one. This knowledge induces market agents to switch over to the superior currency in times of crisis. Hence, the commitment to redeem, which is meant to be a confidence-building device, proves to be unsatisfactory as it gives rise to the occasion to check the seriousness and practicability of just that very commitment. Besides, even a hundred-percent backing (i.e. a currency board) does not necessarily suffice to stabilize the market, because bank deposits remain uncovered.

• If the redemption has to be practised in both directions a central bank is forced to monetize any excessive amount of gold (and foreign exchange) which will bring about undesirable effects on prices and the rate of interest (the well-known problem of importing inflation in case of fixed exchange rates). With regard to the domestic value of money it is irrelevant whether circulating notes are redeemable or not. Typically enough though, advocates of the Currency School – more than

---

[52] Andréadès 1909: 336, cf. 353-61, Hawtrey 1923: 87-8, Clapham 1944b: 209-10, Kindleberger 1984: 91-2, Laidler 1991: 22-3.

[53] Kindleberger 1978: 164, cf. 163, Mill 1871: 662-77, Andréadès 1909: 329, 343-52, Schumpeter 1954: 727n, Ziegler 1990: 118.

their antagonists – were able to recognize that the commitment of backing notes with gold would not in any case provide a stable nominal anchor.[54]

The broad definition of money developed by the Banking School is considered to be "modern" as it refers to the gradual differences in liquidity of the wide range of assets and thus takes into account the permanent innovative process of creating new financial titles in the money market.[55] The differentiation between cash, on the hand, and deposits, claims and securities, on the other, is levelled – and as a consequence the basic distinction between money and credit, which the Currency School had attempted to establish, and to institutionalize, by creating different types of banks, gets lost analytically in the Banking School. Schumpeter also later contested the fact that a somehow "given" quantity of money could be defined; he nicely argued that it was impossible to use a claim to a horse for riding, but claims to money could be used to buy.[56] The identification of "money" and "claims to money" however eliminates the rate of interest from economic theory.

The question whether money ought to be defined narrowly or broadly misses the peculiar feature of a two-tier banking system: here single monetary functions, to some extent, are performed by different money assets. Central-bank money alone is a standard of value *and* a means of payment in the sense of an ultimate discharge of contracts. Besides, certain bank deposits, i.e. claims denominated in units of central-bank money ("inside money"), can serve as a means of payment. The transfer of these claims are accepted instead of a definite payment because the promise of these claims being redeemable in central-bank money ("outside money") is taken as credible. The public here assumes that the commercial banks operate under a liquidity constraint imposed on the part of a controlling central bank. As and insofar as commercial banks do not issue notes on their own account and name ("Citibank dollar") they are not able to create money. The acceptance of "inside money" is being derived from the reputation of the central-bank money.[57]

---

[54] Cf. Andréadès 1909: 318, 386. The German Reichsbank only in 1927, in the aftermath of the turmoil of hyperinflation, reached a quantity-theoretic understanding: "A large increase of the circulating quantity of money, even if fully backed by gold, is bound to produce detrimental effects on price formation" (quoted from James 1998: 56).

[55] "The money-quality of assets is something imposed by the business habits of people; it is attached in varying degree to various assets [...]. To label something as 'money', the supply of which is to behave according to rules laid down by legal authority, is to build on shifting sand" (Sayers 1957: 5, cf. Laidler 1991: 13-4). This understanding of money had a lasting influence, not only on the new Banking School headed by Kaldor, but also is at the root of the popular saying of "plastic money" or "electronic cash" (credit cards and internet banking, respectively).

[56] Cf. Schumpeter 1954: 321, Schumpeter 1970: 233-5.

[57] Cf. Riese 1995, Issing 1999b.

4.5   Interest Rate Policy and the Two-Tiered Banking System

> As Lord Goschen has remarked, the thing needed above everything in a crisis is cash.
>
> *André Andréadès*[58]

> We must look first to the foreign drain, and raise the rate of interest as high as may be necessary. Unless you can stop the foreign export, you cannot allay the domestic alarm. The Bank will get poorer and poorer, and its poverty will protract or renew the apprehension. And at the rate of interest so raised, the holders [...] of the final Bank reserve must lend freely. Very high loans at very high rates are the best remedy for the worst malady of the money market when a foreign drain is added to a domestic drain. [...] What is wanted and what is necessary to stop a panic is to diffuse the impression, that though money may be dear, still money is to be had.
>
> *Walter Bagehot*[59]

> The essence of central banking is discretionary control of the monetary system. [...] Working to a rule is the antithesis of central banking. A central bank is necessary only when the community decides that a discretionary element is desirable.
>
> *Richard S. Sayers*[60]

Neither the Banking nor the Currency School were able to work out the high importance of interest rate policy for the theory and practice of central banking:

• According to the Banking Doctrine the amount and structure of the means of payment are determined by market forces; there is no norm which should be imposed on the public by monetary policy. If the banking system (including the central bank) adjusts to the market demand for financial assets (including money) the rate of interest is no longer influenced by market forces and degenerates to a purely institutional variable.[61]

• The Currency School proposed to link the quantity of notes to the central-bank reserve. The impact of this policy on the rate of interest was recognized, but there

---

[58] Andréadès 1909: 405.
[59] Bagehot 1873: 27-8, 31.
[60] Sayers 1957: 1.
[61] The modern Banking School builds on Keynes' remark on the rate of interest as a "highly conventional, rather than a highly psychological, phenomenon" (1936: 203) and, in general, regards an unlimited refinancing of commercial banks at a "given" rate of discount as the only appropriate behaviour on the part of the central bank. A restrictive interest rate policy for restoring price stability is being rejected by referring to the dominance of supply-side causes of price increases which renders a demand restriction an inefficient measure for fighting inflation (cf. Kaldor 1985, Moore 1988, Dow/Rodriguez-Fuentes 1998 and – expressing a critical opinion – Laidler 1989).

was yet no idea of controlling market agents' behaviour by means of price incentives. For some time, the discount rate could also not be employed as a flexible tool of monetary management.[62]

Not least because of the shortcomings of contemporary monetary *theory* the business policy of the Bank of England was developed as a reaction to *practical* challenges. Contrary to the intention of Peel's Act, not the Issue, but the Banking Department over the years and decades advanced to the position of a central bank. This should not be misinterpreted as a late victory of the Banking Doctrine; rather, it resulted from the experience that the rule-based management of the quantity of money which had been assigned to the Issue Department proved to be inadequate to stabilize the financial system. The initial attempts of varying the *quantity* of credit and note issue stepwise were replaced by a change of *price* conditions (*table 4.2*): Because a passive exploitation or confirmation of a current market constellation threatened to bring the Bank on the verge of bankruptcy (*case a*), already at the end of the 18th century the directors in critical stages practised a quantitative limitation of advances. Peel's Act then shifted this restriction on to the liability side of the Bank's balance sheet (*case b*).

This regulation however only directly concerned the Issue Department. On the other hand, it proved impossible to pursue the commercial business of the Bank of England following the same crude pattern of fixing a quota on the volume of credit. The aspect of having to serve the interests of its clients in a competitive surrounding induced the Banking Department not to set aside the need for liquidity on the part of the public, particular in times of financial strain, but rather to manage and contain the demand for liquidity by modifying the rate of interest. The discount rate was chosen both in accordance with the state of competition and with the stock of available reserves of the Banking Department. After the passing of Peel's Act the volatility of the Bank's discount rates increased markedly (*figure 4.4*). As long as interest rates remained in a moderate range and the market demand for cash continued to grow, the "open discount window" could only provide the liquidity until the stock of reserves was depleted (*table 4.2, case c*). Then the Bill of Indemnity had to come into effect, as the government shied away from the risk of a financial crisis on account of an absolute limitation of money supply.[63]

---

[62] Monetarism later separated note issue from the central bank's reserves and pleaded for flexible exchange rates which enables an autonomous money supply. The long-run rate of interest is regarded as being determined by the market. From the point of view of practical monetary policy though, the character of the quantity of money as an intermediate target is emphasized whereas the operative instrument is the short-term rate of interest (cf. Goodhart 1994, Issing 1997).

[63] This *case d* represents an exception also in today's monetary policy making. The additional quantitative restriction of the refinancing of commercial banks, besides raising interest rates, sometimes serves as a signalling device; it is imposed in order to demonstrate the seriousness of the central bank's intention to fight inflation, or to defend the currency on the foreign exchange.

*Table 4.2: Impact of alternative instruments of monetary policy
in a boom period threatened by internal and external drain*

Instruments of monetary policy		Volume of credit	
		endogenous (or following the market demand)	restrictive
Interest rate	fix (or following the market rate)	(a) unlimited satisfaction of money demand, loss of reserves, bankruptcy of the Bank	(b) micro destabilization (private bankruptcies) because of cash shortage, macro stabilization via (indirectly) increased interest rates
	restrictive	(c) macro stabilization through restriction of credit via the rate of interest, micro stabilization: available finance (at high rates)	(d) macro stabilization through restriction of credit via the rate of interest, no lender of last resort: micro destabilization

After 1860, Goschen and Bagehot proposed that in times of crisis, when gold was withdrawn from the Bank by domestic and foreign clients, a resolute policy of interest rate increases should be pursued; aiming to contain credit demand, strengthen capital import and, thus, defend England's reserves. Only the price reaction of credit supply and capital flows to interest rate changes mattered – which the Bank should push through if necessary *against* market forces – not looking at some reserve ratio of the circulating quantity of money. "What is almost a revolution in the policy of the Bank of England necessarily follows: no certain or fixed proportion of its liabilities can in the present times be laid down as that which the Bank ought to keep in reserve. [...] It has been said that the Bank of England should look to the market rate, and make its own rate conform to that. This rule was, indeed, always erroneous. The first duty of the Bank of England was to protect the ultimate cash of the country, and to raise the rate of interest so as to protect it." At the same time *additional* credit – at high rates – should be extended to market agents caught in financial distress (Bagehot's Rule), aiming to avoid bankruptcies which could easily bring about undesirable repercussions on the Bank's solvency. "This policy may not save the Bank; but if it do not, nothing will save it."[64]

---

[64] Bagehot 1873: 155, 97, cf. 22, 27-31, Mill 1871: 660-1, Andréadès 1909: 308-9, Clapham 1944b: 258, Kindleberger 1984: 90. Bagehot's Rule (*case c*) shows the reverse constellation of prices and quantities if compared to the former bank reaction to a liquidity crisis (*case b*). Somewhat exaggerating Schumpeter (1954: 729) argued that the theory of central banking had become a rigid "cult of the bank rate" after 1850.

In the following period, the interest policy of the Bank of England seemed to follow Goschen's proposal. Nevertheless this hardly indicates that the Bank now rapidly changed from a commercial-type to a true central bank, which was prepared to take on the responsibility for macroeconomic development; it is doubtful whether the relative stability of financial markets in the second half of the 19th century can be explained by a wise bank policy. The Bank directors disagreed on whether gold movements were induced by the rate of interest or the volume of credit. Bagehot complained that it took many years before they understood the analytical connection between interest rates, macro dynamics, trade and capital movements.[65]

The Bank tried (like all other commercial banks) occasionally to defend its liquidity status by means of interest rates increases. This behaviour had a far-reaching impact as London over the years had become an international money market, i.e. a clearing location where world-wide payment flows were settled; a bill drawn on London was rated as being practically equal to a gold transaction. Although the Bank of England had many foreign borrowers and depositors the volume of its business as such was too small to control the national level of interest rates and, thus, cross-border capital movements. But the Bank discovered that it could absorb liquidity from the market by selling securities, which then finally forced its private competitors to keep their discount rates in line with the rate charged by the Bank. Soon this policy worked smoothly: the commercial banks began to react with interest rate increases – even *ahead* of the Bank's own moves – if some supposed lower limit of the Banking Department's note reserve was expected to be reached.

But safeguarding the convertibility of pound sterling on the foreign exchange was *not* the "first and foremost motive of the Bank", rather it aimed to prevent that, in the case of a difference of interest rates, it would lose market shares to competing private banks.[66] The intention of the Bank's interest rate policy was of a more private nature, profit-oriented rather than of a macroeconomic character. Declarations by the Bank would suggest that it regarded its stock of gold as its *own*, and not as a *national* reserve; likewise market agents in the financial sector basically were seen as *competitors*, and not as protégés. The Bank rightly refused the Banking Principle of discounting good bills any time, but also sometimes let it be known that it did not see itself in the role of an institution, which alone is responsible for the smooth functioning of the money market. The primary reason was not to preclude the possibility that other banks might be tempted – considering the promise of receiving liquidity support if need be – to engage in profitable, but risky projects (this type of moral-hazard problem was discussed only later). The

---

[65] Cf. Bagehot 1873: 17, 23, 89, Clapham 1944b: 236, Ziegler 1990: 13, 24, 119, Stadermann 1994: 89.

[66] Sayers 1936: 116, cf. Andréadès 1909: 317-20, Lutz 1936: 46-59, Galbraith 1975: 49-50, Ziegler 1990: 18, 117-21.

key problem rather was the conflict between private profit interests and national tasks of a central bank. "The maintenance of the Banking Department's solvency and the convertibility of its deposits, which basically preserved the confidence in the national credit system, conflicted with the strategy of aiming at an adequate dividend."[67]

In 1858 the Bank of England had decided to restrict the rediscount facilities for discount houses and bill brokers; the motive was to induce these agents to keep their own reserve and to protect the Bank's reserve from "unauthorized" demands. The "Economist" under its new editor Bagehot consented to this decision in 1860: "As the bill-brokers are the rivals [sic!] of the Bank they cannot expect the Bank should act towards them with special and peculiar favour."[68] Thus it came as no surprise that the next crisis in 1866 was triggered off by the failure of a major and renowned discount company. Even then directors of the Bank protested against the claim to lend support to commercial banks in times of financial distress.[69]

From political quarters, there was also the demand to let commercial banks have a share in the costs of keeping reserves; not only because the Bank's stock of gold appeared insufficient as a *national* reserve, but also because this was regarded as "fair" with respect to the competitive order in the financial market. The idea, that the Bank of England alone ought to keep the reserve of the whole country, for Bank director Norman in 1866 was "impracticable and unsound in principle". The commercial banks were asked to deposit reserves with the Bank of England. But such an arrangement demanded that the Banking Department did not use these reserves for its own credit expansion. The necessary confidence of private agents however was shaken time and again because of the ambiguous behaviour on the part of the Bank of England; so that the commercial banks in part began to keep gold reserves on their own.[70]

This indicated a threat of lapsing back into a one-tier banking system without a central bank – which was basically favoured by Thornton and Bagehot. Decentralized reserve keeping though is inefficient compared to pooling or an insurance contract. Moreover, a competitive free-banking system will most probably be instable as, in the case of a liquidity crisis, no single bank has the incentive and resources to act as a lender of last resort. On the other hand, it was argued that a system of competing bank currencies would protect society from inflation: banks

---

[67] Ziegler 1990: 140, cf. 116, Andréadès 1909: 325, 365, Schumpeter 1954: 697.

[68] Clapham 1944b: 241. On the colourful personality of Bagehot see Rieter (1996).

[69] The failing company was Overend, Gurney & Co, which had interpreted the decision of 1858 as a "declaration of war" on the part of the Bank of England and had reacted in an appropriate manner: in order to demonstrate its market power the company drew large amounts of notes, thus threatening the liquidity of the Bank, and then generously deposited the notes at one stroke – each one cut into two halves (cf. Clapham 1944b: 234-50, 263, Ziegler 1993, Andréadès 1909: 326n, 353-61).

[70] Cf. Andréadès 1909: 340, Bagehot 1873: 19, 50, Clapham 1944b: 285, Ziegler 1990: 125-7.

running a relative expansive business could trigger off a rise in prices (as measured in their currency), but would be deterred from this policy by a demand for higher interest rates to be paid to their depositors.[71]

From a macroeconomic point of view, this case resembles a system of flexible exchange rates where different rates of national inflation can coexist. But for microeconomic reasons it is unlikely that different currencies will be simultaneously used in a uniform economic area because high information and transaction costs and economies of scale will favour the evolution of a monopoly solution. The notes of the English country banks were denominated in pound sterling, which implied that a rise of prices could not be attributed to the issue of single banks. In this case, it does not pay for each bank to restrain its credit supply: this is an unrewarded concession for achieving the public good "monetary stability", but a loss of business profit.[72]

The main shortcoming of the English monetary system was that the Bank of England – on account of its status as a private enterprise which could not easily put its profit motive last – until the end of the 19th century saw itself as a competitor of the other commercial banks; it thus took quite some time before the Bank got used to the role of the nation's central bank.[73] A precondition for efficiently executing surveillance and stabilization functions in financial markets is that operative agents accept the central bank as a trustee of their *general interests*. This in turn requires that the central bank does not show a profit-oriented behaviour. A constellation ought to evolve (known from the "theory of clubs") where the market agents of some branch agree on a *neutral* speaker who advocates their common interests in the political sphere, but who does not act as a competitor within the group. It is still a contentious issue whether this solution is reached in an evolutionary process by way of market forces or by means of active governmental intervention.[74] The English example shows that well-meant economic policy regulations like Peel's Act of 1844 can prevent the emergence of an efficient allocation of public and private areas of responsibilities for a long time.

---

[71] For a discussion of Hayek's (1978) proposal of a competitive currency system see Hellwig (1985), Fischer (1986) and Issing (1999b).

[72] Cf. Andréadès 1909: 287-8, Kindleberger 1984: 89-90, Goodhart 1988: 13-8, 28, 48, Laidler 1991: 37-8, De Grauwe 1996: 7.

[73] Cf. Clapham 1944b: 372-3, 426-7, Cairncross 1988.

[74] Goodhart (1988: 45, 69-76) holds the first, Ziegler (1993) – with an eye also on the history of the Prussian Bank – the second opinion.

Summary of Part II

The "choice" of a medium of payment is not a mere technical matter, but rather a decision which shaped large chapters of economic (and political) history. A money medium has to meet high standards and its provision is intertwined with diverse interests within society. Given the indispensable services of money, it could be expected that evolutionary market forces would give rise to institutions taking over the task of supplying money. However, money is not like an everyday good: it can be compared to a network, the utility of which emerges from its dissemination. If the access to and the use of network or collective goods cannot be controlled by its producers, a private-market supply usually is precluded. But in the early stage of the modern monetary economy the function of money devolved upon precious metals, which could be mined at several locations, and upon promissory notes of well respected wealth owners and banks. These notes were not immediately redeemed, but circulated in the market, thus allowing the issuer a costless acquisition of goods and assets. Providing the market with money was a profitable business because, particularly with regard to bank notes, private costs of money production were lower than the money's value in terms of goods.

Therefore, on the one hand, there was no systematic shortage of money media; rather the economic policy issue was a regulation aiming at a restriction and stabilization of money supply. While, on the other hand, the monetary "system" and thus market exchange and production came to the verge of collapse if, for whatever reason, the market's confidence in the circulating money medium was shaken. Large-scale attempts to "cash in" previously issued notes left the financial system without a powerful "lender of last resort" who was able to provide the reserves which then were needed to calm down unrest and panic.

Persistent controversies, in the history of economic thought as well as in the sphere of practical banking, about the guaranteed exchange of money for some final "backing asset" point to a basic problem of confidence associated with any money: from the point of view of individual market agents striving for their private interests, the acceptance of money as a means of payment depends on the expectation that the possession of that money involves the option of executing a claim to goods and assets at any time; on a macro level, money performs as a symbolic device for the allocation of resources and the distribution of income. At first, the promissory note of a well respected wealth owner, i.e. a claim to a part of his wealth, was accepted by market agents as a means of payment because the promise of its redemption appeared to be credible. The effective use of this security however shows a crisis of that currency, the negation of money – for money is defined by being kept in circulation or held as an asset, and not by its redemption. Hence, the money function of any medium rests on a convention, on a collective expectation, and the "reputation equilibrium" of money depends on the mutual confidence on the part of market agents that such an equilibrium may exist.

The precarious instability of that equilibrium is reflected in the famous liquidity problem of commercial banks, which, as the key creators of money, propelled the economic development in Europe from the 12th century onwards by the extension of credit, although it took a while until public borrowers were supplanted by private entrepreneurs. The availability of finance as a barrier of economic activity was played down by classical economists for various reasons: they established the "modern" tradition of interpreting the economic process as a "real" exchange of goods and services; the classical macro model where capitalists had a saving ratio of unity seemed to suggest that firms would finance all investment through retained profits; and finally the banking system already appeared to be well developed. Classical economists failed to understand the mercantilist quest for trade surpluses: they analyzed international economic relations in terms of real barter and thus ignored the fact that, in the case of trade deficits, payment flows cause reserve losses of domestic banks which could hardly be compensated by balance-of-payment adjustments propagated by David Hume.

The question of the role of the state in the process of the establishment, evolution and maintenance of a monetary order provides no clear-cut answer. Governmental agencies at first appeared on the scene as beneficiaries of the emerging financial sector, demanding easy access to ample credit at low rates of interest. They actually supported the trend for a monopolistic note issue, which was however inherent to the market process of searching for an appropriate money medium, because of the positive returns to scale in the use of any money. In England, from the late 17th century onwards, the importance of banking for the macroeconomic development, the menacing instability of the financial system, and public credit demand motivated political interventions in the monetary system. Government performed a double role of a regulatory agency and a credit client vis-à-vis the large private Bank of England which, although founded on a political initiative and dependent on the periodical renewal of its charter, primarily pursued a commercial profit motive and for a long time was slow to recognize the macroeconomic repercussions of its business activities.

The passionate debate on the allegedly indispensable gold backing of the pound sterling in the 19th century was an anachronism, perhaps explainable by the "lag" of monetary theory understanding, because at that time, to all intents and purposes, the Bank of England was able, even in critical stages of the nation's financial system, to defend the stability of a paper currency. This achievement was not diminished by the fact that businessmen and wealth owners, opinion leaders in the City of London, in times of crises ostentatiously supported the Bank: which indicates that market agents are undoubtedly able to learn that it might pay to individually contribute to the preservation of a public good.

The institutional consequence of the Currency-Banking debate, the division of the Bank of England into two departments, was a landmark in the evolution of monetary economies because it aimed at a separation of money supply from the extension of credit, which is equally important for maintaining macroeconomic stability and microeconomic efficiency. Contrary to the intended monetary reform however, the central bank did not arise from the Issue Department, which worked under a strict rule controlling the reserve ratio of the pound sterling, but from the market-oriented Banking Department. This emphasizes the pattern of the emergence of central banking from the private banking business. It was not the rule-based management of the quantity of money, but rather a discretionary interest rate policy which over the years was able to stabilize the macro economy and to preserve the value of the pound. For a long time the Bank's interest rate policy was pursued for the sake of its profitability, the impact on the macro economy being an unintended by-product; the commercial banking sector did not acknowledge the Bank's supervisory and stabilizing role in the financial market before the Bank had given up its competitive behaviour.

PART III
THE EVOLUTION OF KEY CURRENCY SYSTEMS: A GAME-THEORETIC PERSPECTIVE

5.   The Hegemony of Pound Sterling in the Gold Standard

5.1   The Gold Standard as an International Monetary System

> The gold standard is the currency system of a free market economy.
>
> *Friedrich A. Lutz*[1]

> In the good old times of the gold standard, the problem of the stability of the value of money, defined in modern terms, was no issue. [...] Changes of prices were attributed to the sphere of goods, not of money. The currency was regarded as stable if the exchange rates were stable, and this was provided by the automatic mechanism of gold flows. [...] The gold standard did not guarantee absolute price stability. There were times when prices were falling, and there were times when they were rising. [...] This up and down of the price level, like booms and depressions in the business cycle, was accepted, more or less, as God-given. [...] Nobody hit upon the idea that money should be regarded as of a higher value in times of falling prices, and had a lower value when prices were on the rise.
>
> *Karl Blessing (former president of the Bundesbank)*[2]

If each country of a world economic system keeps a fixed "internal" exchange rate between its national currency and some units of a reserve asset (e.g. gold), an international parity grid of fixed exchange rates between these paper currencies is established, without any further institutional or political agreement, which works by simple market forces. If one pound contains x, and one franc z units of gold, the equilibrium exchange rate of the franc, expressed in pound sterling, can be computed as

---

[1]   Lutz 1935: 22.
[2]   Blessing 1962: 159-60.

$$e = \frac{x/z \; franc}{1 \; pound} \qquad [5.1]$$

If the franc should be devalued in terms of gold, i.e. if z was lowered, its exchange rate e was bound to rise vis-à-vis sterling.

As long as market agents can freely redeem each central bank's notes and freedom of international capital movements prevails, the equilibrium condition [5.1] holds by way of arbitrage. If the price of sterling notes (or bills) should rise on the foreign exchange, traders would sell franc to the Banque de France, ship gold to Britain, and buy sterling from the Bank of England (the first mentioned bank itself is charged with these transactions if it stood ready to "make" the foreign exchange market, i.e. fix the exchange rate by selling any excess demand for sterling or franc). The loss of reserves then forces the French banking system to curtail domestic credit supply.[3] As thus the French economy could not avoid a slowdown anyway, it was obviously preferable to bring about such a restriction through a rise of domestic interest rates, and *keep* the gold reserves unchanged: higher domestic interest rates would curb the growth of credit, money and income, and the interest rate differential would induce capital imports, which then stabilized the market exchange rate at the equilibrium level.

This consideration makes clear why, first, policy makers attached large and sometimes overriding importance to the state of the foreign exchange, and why, second, actual gold flows – contrary to Hume's model – were rather modest. The substitution of interest policies for gold movements is one deviation from the famous "Rules of the Game", which have been attributed to the gold standard *model*. But the predictions of that model would still hold if changes in the relative quantities of gold, as the driving forces of monetary and macroeconomic adjustment, would simply have been substituted by appropriate interest rate policies in all countries involved.

The gold standard, at most, provided a stable trend of prices in the long run, insofar as the conditions of production in the gold-mining industry did not differ from the conditions prevailing in other branches of the economy.[4] If monetary policy tried to control the path of prices in the medium term, a second deviation from the alleged symmetry of the gold standard's rules and results appears: central bankers who observed signs of a depreciating currency and concomitant reserve losses

---

[3] It has already been shown that – even in the best case – it would take some time until a possible monetary expansion abroad would turn the foreign exchanges again in favour of a gold-exporting country (see ch. 3.4).

[4] Cooper's assessment (1982: 7), "Price stability was not attained, either in the short run or in the long run, either during the period of the gold standard proper or over a longer period during which gold held dominant influence", throws too bad a light on the gold standard, particularly if contrasted with the empirical evidence reproduced in *figure 4.2.* Bordo (1993) also emphasizes the high degree of price stability in the era of the gold standard.

Box 10: The Rules of the International Gold Standard, 1879-1913[5]

All Countries

I. Fix an official gold price or "mint parity", and convert freely between domestic money and gold at that price.

II. Do not restrict the export of gold by private citizens, nor impose any other exchange restrictions on current or capital account transacting.

III. Back national bank notes and coinage with earmarked gold reserves, and condition long-run growth in deposit money on availability of general gold reserves.

IV. In short-run liquidity crises from an international gold drain, have the central bank lend freely to domestic banks at higher interest rates (Bagehot's Rule).

V. If rule I is temporarily suspended, restore convertibility at traditional mint parity as soon as practicable – if necessary by deflating the domestic economy.

VI. Allow the common price level (nominal anchor) to be endogenously determined by the worldwide demand for, and supply of, gold.

---

were definitely more eager to raise interest rates than bankers who enjoyed a strong performance of the home currency and a mounting gold stock to lower rates.[6] Thus the working of the system exhibited an asymmetric bias, a contractive tendency, as "weak" countries were forced to dampen macroeconomic activity, whereas "strong" countries were free to opt against an overheating of their economy by choosing to sterilize gold inflows.

As long as member countries of the gold standard were hit by unfavourable shocks deteriorating their trade performance *in a random-like fashion*, a "structural" leadership of any country was not expected to emerge. At best, an uneven distribution of gold reserves would confer more latitude to those countries possessing relatively large amounts of reserves. But in general, *all* central banks acted under a liquidity constraint, which was exogenously given by the – more or less – fixed amount of world gold reserves. None of them could behave in an independent way. In a fixed-exchange-rate system, $n - 1$ members have to adjust to the policy of the *n-th* country; thus in the gold standard, one is tempted to conclude, the role of that last member was played by the stock of gold.[7]

---

5 Reproduced from McKinnon 1993: 4.

6 "The dominant and overriding objective of monetary policy [...] was to maintain the convertibility of the national currency directly or indirectly into gold at the legal parity. [...] The major criterion or guide of policy was [...] the behavior of the reserve ratio of the central bank [...]. Decreases in the reserve ratio [...] characteristically led to increases in the discount rate [...]. On the other hand, when reserve ratios rose, central banks were under no similar compulsion to take measures of the opposite kind" (Bloomfield 1959: 23, cf. Lutz 1935).

7 Cf. McKinnon 1993.

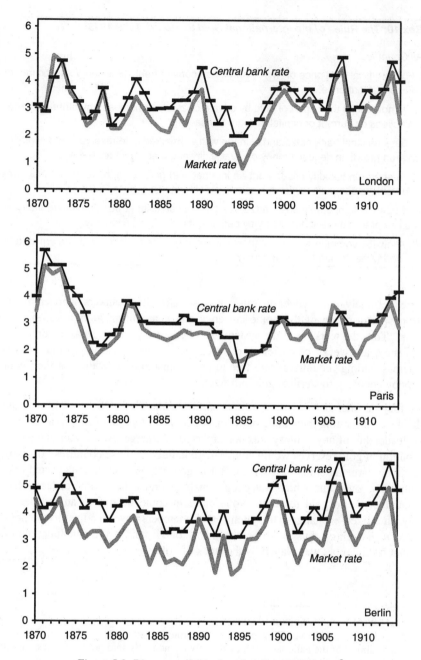

Figure 5.1: Discount rates in three key financial centres[8]

---

[8]   Data from Helfferich 1919: 614.

Central banks in France, England and Germany pursued a similar conduct of monetary policy vis-à-vis the domestic banking system: they all kept the discount bank rate above the market rate (*figure 5.1*). Thus the stock of bills of exchange held by central banks was relatively small as commercial banks made use of the central bank mainly as a lender of last resort.[9] But reserve keeping in the period 1880-1914 was markedly different: the Bank of England only held a gold reserve, whereas central bank reserves in other countries, besides gold, also consisted of financial assets denominated in pound sterling. Obviously, as a *reserve* asset is of a superior quality than the asset which is to be covered, this behaviour reflects a market ranking of the various national currencies. The fact that foreign central banks kept sterling assets indicates that they made every endeavour to guarantee the convertibility of their domestic currency in terms of pound sterling, whereas the Bank of England used interest policies in order to defend the *average* strength of the pound vis-à-vis all other currencies, so that no gold reserves were lost. Therefore, the gold standard in a way had been a sterling standard, a feature of the system which is hardly to be inferred from its symmetrical "rules".[10]

5.2   London as the World's Banker

> During the latter half of the nineteenth century, the influence of London on credit conditions throughout the world was so predominant that the Bank of England could almost have claimed to be the conductor of the international orchestra.
> *John Maynard Keynes*[11]

> Apparently the Bank was no more than the second violinist, not to say the triangle player, in the world's orchestra.
> *Donald McCloskey / Richard Zecher*[12]

By looking at economic fundamentals, one might guess that England was an average, or even "weak", member of the international gold standard, perhaps avoiding repeated balance-of-payment crises only by chance, i.e. by the poor knowledge of the relevant data in the public.[13] The trade balance, over the decades, had become negative, and the stock of gold reserves was relatively small compared to other countries (*figure 5.2*). With respect to the latter figures, the United States, France,

---

[9]   Cf. Andréadès 1909: 314, Lutz 1936.

[10]   Cf. Bloomfield 1963: 7, Kindleberger 1984: 68.

[11]   Keynes 1930: 306-7.

[12]   McCloskey/Zecher 1976: 65.

[13]   Because of the bad state of recorded statistics, American economists later envied the "lucky British": "When sterling was the leading key currency, their statistics were so bad that they did not even *know* when they had a balance-of-payment problem" (Strange 1971: 223, cf. Lindert 1969: 36).

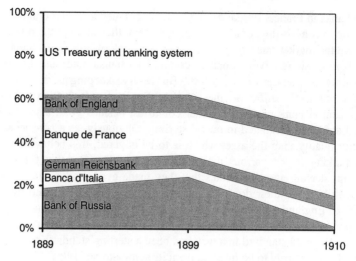

Figure 5.2: Distribution of gold reserves[14]

and Russia (!) should have been the dominant players, but not England. "How managed London to stay the centre of an international currency system which was based on gold, although the gold reserves of the Bank of England were far lower than the reserves of the US Treasury [...]? How could a country, exhibiting a persistent trade deficit, guarantee the stability of a worldwide exchange of goods, services and investments, of long and short-term credit, which surpassed its own economic capability to an ever growing extent?"[15]

Modern monetarist authors strictly denied the possibility that England might have performed a leading role, simply by referring to the fact that even the large volume of pound assets was but a small part of the world's quantity of money; therefore, the Bank of England's policy should have had only a minor impact on the world level of interest rates and prices.[16] This line of reasoning rests on the assumption that all currencies were alike. But on an international level, the same forces are at work which, in a closed economy, tend to bring forth a *ranking* of money assets, or even a monopolistic solution of only *one* currency. As a "big player" in the world economy with a strong trade performance in the 19th century; as a leading supplier of shipping and insurance services, England also gained in reputation on international financial markets.[17] Keeping working balances with

---

[14] Data from Fischer 1981.

[15] Fischer 1981: 165.

[16] Cf. McCloskey/Zecher 1976.

[17] "Financial distinction appears to have followed temporally after supremacy in trade and to have been causally connected with the decline in trade" (Kindleberger 1983: 79, cf. Kindleberger 1996, Schwarzer 1993).

British banks in London became a transaction-costs-saving behaviour for all agents trading on the world market, whether the English economy was directly involved in trade flows or not. If contract partners from all over the world accept a sterling-denominated transfer on their London giro account as a definite *payment*, sterling accounts carry a liquidity premium, which make them preferable – for businessmen at least – to money holdings denominated in their respective domestic currencies.

Over the decades, England thus built up a huge stock of foreign debt, mostly short-term, which exceeded the British gold reserve by far (whereas circulating sterling notes since the end of the 19th century actually were fully "backed" by gold). London served as a bank in the world economy, which was heavily exposed to a liquidity problem. It could only be managed by keeping up the foreigners' confidence in the pound. They *had* to believe that the Bank of England would always defend the pound's parity on the foreign exchange, which however came down to a sort of a collective illusion, as everyone knew that the Bank simply would not have been able to do so (because of the quantitative mismatch of foreign debt and gold reserves), if a massive withdrawal of funds should have happened. A key currency country may never give rise to an expected devaluation of its currency, because the withdrawal of foreign funds would bring about a severe disequilibrium of the balance of payments.

Despite this obvious risk for the value of sterling assets (in terms of foreign currencies), the convertibility and stability of pound sterling was never challenged until 1914.[18] The perseverance of that precarious equilibrium might be explained by taking a closer look at the structure of the British balance of payments (*table 5.1*). The balance of current account was positive, as the trade deficit was more than compensated by the proceeds from, mainly, shipping and insurance services, and the flow of interest payments accruing from the huge stock of foreign investment, which had been made during the preceding decades. England had a marked creditor status in her long-term financial relations; and perhaps was a debtor with respect to short-term capital deposits. Like any commercial bank, England turned short-term deposits into long-term lending; and consumed her "bank profit", resulting from the interest rate margin, in form of an excess of imported goods. "London banks became Europe's 'paymasters', not because of high saving on the British islands, but rather because of a large inflow of funds at low interest rates, which then were lent abroad at high rates."[19] The capital balance showed new lending, which was finally even smaller than the flow of profits from the stock of foreign investment, and a small rise of the stock of foreign deposits.

---

[18] Cf. Andréadès 1909: 385, Hawtrey 1923: 159-61, Bloomfield 1959: 21, Lindert 1969: 37-8.

[19] Stadermann 1994: 92, cf. Bloomfield 1963: 71-7, Lindert 1969: 58-68, Feis 1974: 17. For an early analysis of the English balance of payments, distinguished by its farsightedness, see Goschen (1861).

Table 5.1: England's Balance of Payments 1900-13[20]

Outflow	Influx
Trade deficit	Invisibles
Long-term credits	Property income
	Short-term deposits

The crucial point was that the Bank of England could stabilize the pound on the foreign exchange without any substantial welfare costs: because of the positive balance in the current account, any tendency of weakness stemming from the capital balance could easily be countered by marginal increases of the discount rate, which induced domestic banks to cut down foreign lending and foreigners to enlarge their holdings of sterling assets in London. Given the large volume of the sterling financial market, even an average elasticity of capital movements with regard to interest rate changes was sufficient to redirect the flows on the foreign exchange.[21]

Thus, the Bank could rely on its interest rate instrument in order to raise the external value of the pound, without being forced to dampen activities on the goods market. "There generally tended, over the cycle as a whole, to be no major conflict between external stability and internal stability."[22] Because there was virtually no trade-off between different goals of monetary policy, rational market agents expected that the Bank would always choose to defend the exchange rate of the pound. That is why the confidence of international investors in the pound remained unshaken for decades. Sterling balances in London were rated "as good as gold"; or even better: because they yielded an interest income. The credibility of the stability of the pound's exchange rate was (nearly) perfect, so that "England's commitment to convertibility [...] was aided by stabilizing private capital flows".[23]

Interpreting the international gold standard in analogy of a two-tier banking system does not show the "anomalies" of that international order[24], but rather its essence. One of the most important differences, compared to Hume's model of "specie flow", is that a key currency country does not necessarily lose gold reserves in

---

[20] Stylized record, data from Lindert 1969: 39, 64n, 69.
[21] Cf. Hawtrey 1923: 115-123, Minsky 1979.
[22] Bloomfield 1959: 42.
[23] Bordo 1993: 182.
[24] Cf. McCloskey/Zecher 1976.

case of a trade deficit, which then enforces a monetary restriction; most probably, only the country's creditors will change because foreign exporting firms will sell their sterling proceeds to the domestic banking system, which will be ready to hold these claims on the key currency country as an interest-earning reserve. A trade deficit thus neither produces a weakness on the foreign exchange nor a monetary restriction; it appears as a "deficit without tears".[25]

The stability of the gold standard as an international monetary system was not merely the result of automatic adjustment forces, but rather seems to have been supported, or even established, by England's role as a financial centre, and by the key currency status of the pound. International stability as a public good is not necessarily in short supply, if – as it had been the case with regard to England – the leading country's national interests are also served. It should not be overlooked however, that the economic and political gains accruing from its role as the world's banker obliged the country to always put financial solidity first on its agenda.[26]

The problem with the alleged hegemonic role of England in the international gold standard is twofold. First, that role is hard to find in the empirical data. The spread between short-term interests was rather low, at least, if compared to the later experience within the EMS (*figure 5.3*). The French discount rate generally was even lower than the British, so that a liquidity premium favouring the pound did not show directly; the Banque de France kept a higher ratio of reserves though. The finding of a more or less parallel movement of interest rates counters the above-mentioned monetarist argument, that the sheer size of the British quantity of money precluded the supposed control of the world money market; if the central banks in all countries involved pursued a similar policy stance, this course might even be prescribed by a small country. However, econometric work failed to confirm a "determination" of foreign interest rates by policy decisions on the part of the Bank of England (in the sense that foreign discount rates followed with a short lag the movements of the British rate); rather, *mutual* feedbacks between interest rates in the major countries were to be observed, suggesting that the gold standard was a more multipolar system.[27]

Second, the precondition for achieving stability of the *British* monetary system had been enforced by conferring a quasi-monopoly status upon the Bank of England – but on an *international* level a similar institutional solution was hardly con-

---

[25] Lindert 1969: 74.

[26] "The most important element in the success of any national gold standard is the public's confidence that the government's fiscal soundness and political imperatives will enable it to pursue indefinitely a monetary policy consistent with long-term price stability and continuous convertibility" (Hamilton 1988: 69-70, cf. Bloomfield 1963: 76-7, Eichengreen 1985, Eichengreen 1989).

[27] Cf. Bloomfield 1959: 29-40, Eichengreen 1987, Giovannini 1989, Tullio/Wolters 1996, Tullio/Wolters 2000.

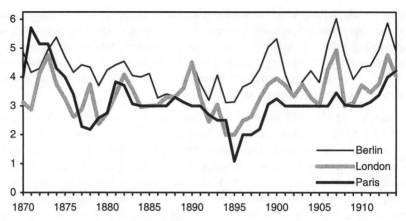

Figure 5.3: Central bank discount rates in three key financial centres[28]

ceivable. Certainly, England could not, and did not, force foreign central banks to hold sterling assets, simply by means of her political power. Why should all member countries agree on a leadership status for the British central bank? It is a widely shared opinion that England enjoyed such a leadership; but the analytical task is to explain why other countries might have voluntarily consented to a international monetary order, in which they took up a subordinate position. Kindleberger often expressed the view that key currency systems drew their stability from the management provided by a "hegemon", which induced other countries to accept the "rules" of the system.[29] But the interests of all participants in that "game" are to be scrutinized more thoroughly.

5.3   Macroeconomic Interdependence in a Game-Theoretic Model

> It is not clear from existing models why one country would prefer to lead while the other follows.
>
> *Barry Eichengreen*[30]

The basic premise of the following analysis is that the gold standard represented an international monetary system, which could only last if targets and strategies of the member countries were compatible. In a base-line model, at first, identical economies and policy strategies are assumed. From the macroeconomic interde-

---

[28] Data from Helfferich 1919: 614.

[29] Cf. Kindleberger 1986: 289-300, Kindleberger 1996. A critical comment is given by Skidelski/Nikolov (2000).

[30] Eichengreen 1987: 7.

pendence of these "players" in the world economy a set of equilibrium solutions can be derived. The basic economic logic of the issue of symmetry versus leadership can be studied by a simple two-country model, where the first (domestic) country is intended to become the dominant player; the group of all other member countries of the currency system, which in an way finally *choose* to subordinate their actions to the policy of the leader, is represented by the second (foreign) country.[31]

The working and interaction of these economies – two countries of equal size and efficiency – can be expressed by a set of equations, where all variables, except for interest rates, are expressed in logs; an asterisk denotes a foreign variable. Equation [5.2] shows aggregate supply, i.e. the price level p determined by autonomous wages w and rising marginal costs. Equation [5.3] defines aggregate income y depending on autonomous demand g, the rate of interest r and the real exchange rate (the fixed log nominal exchange rate is normalized to zero). The direct impact of foreign demand on home income is neglected; as α is supposed to be positive in both countries, this effect is captured indirectly via the price channel. Money demand, depending on nominal income and the rate of interest, is given by [5.4]. A mirror-image set of equations can be set up for the foreign country. Greek letters represent constant positive parameters; in order to avoid trivial causes for asymmetries they are identical in both countries.

$$p = w + \alpha y \qquad\qquad [5.2]$$

$$y = g - \beta r - \varepsilon\left(p - p^*\right) \qquad\qquad [5.3]$$

$$m = p + y - \sigma r \qquad\qquad [5.4]$$

Following the tradition of *IS-LM* models, money is assumed to consist of bank notes only. The commercial banking sector is omitted, private credit transactions are mainly carried through on the capital market. Non-banks may also satisfy their demand for cash by selling bills to the central bank, which – as the only active policy agent – abstains from open market operations on the capital market; its policy instrument is the discount rate i. Moreover, the central bank is obliged to issue notes if gold is offered for sale. Hence, high-powered money m is backed by a share $q < 1$ of the given world stock of gold (which as a constant is suppressed

---

[31] The methodology of the following study and the architecture of the model are basically the same as in Eichengreen (1987), although his results are being rejected. A short and preliminary version of chs. 5 and 7 is contained in Spahn (1998). Models of the gold standard and other key currency systems have been presented by Barro (1979), Giovannini (1989) and Jarchow (1997). Hamada (1979) and Cooper (1985) give surveys on the topic of strategic interaction and international economic policy coordination. See also the policy games modelled by Eichengreen (1984), Canzoneri/Gray (1985) and Barsky et al. (1988).

from the equations) and otherwise is being created by discounting bills. The domestic money supply function[32] can thus be approximated by

$$m = q - \mu i \qquad [5.5]$$

The foreign money supply accordingly is given by

$$m^* = (1-q) - \mu i^* \qquad [5.6]$$

Finally, due to unrestricted international capital movements, and neglecting any liquidity or risk premia, which as a constant parameter would not affect the results of the model, interest rate parity implies $r^* = r$. The omission of expected exchange rate changes can be justified by virtue of the traditional "Restoration Principle" according to which any short-term deviation from the once established exchange rate had to be reversed by means of economic policy actions. Market agents therefore expected a return to the previous level of the exchange rate and their activities supported the adjustment process.[33]

The solution of the macro system, where constant supply and demand parameters (w and g) have been set to zero in both countries, shows that monetary policies, i.e. variations of the discount rates, by proportionally changing market interest rates have a parallel influence on output and prices, but act adversely on the distribution of gold reserves:

$$\underline{r} = \frac{1}{2\Omega}\left[\mu\left(i+i^*\right)-1\right] \qquad [5.7]$$

$$\underline{q} = \frac{1}{2}\left[1+\mu\left(i-i^*\right)\right] \qquad [5.8]$$

$$\underline{p} = \underline{p}^* = \alpha\underline{y} = \alpha\underline{y}^* = \frac{\alpha\beta}{2\Omega}\left[1-\mu\left(i+i^*\right)\right] \qquad [5.9]$$

---

[32] Eichengreen (1987) seems to favour an alternative institutional set-up: the central bank and the commercial banks are integrated, money consists of bank deposits, which the public obtains by selling bills to, or demanding short-term credit from, the banking system. Both operations are controlled by the (official) bank or discount rate, which – as in the above model – is distinct from the long-term rate on the capital market (thus the term structure of interest rates is supposed to be variable in both countries). Equation [5.5] then is the money supply of the consolidated banking system. Eichengreen's approach has been modified in the text above (which has no bearing on the model's results), because it seems more appropriate to regard central banks as economic policy agents, which are separated from the private (banking) sector.

[33] Thus speculation was stabilizing (cf. McKinnon 1993). The conclusions drawn in this chapter do not change however, if expected exchange rate changes, for example leading to $r^* = r + \delta(p^* - p)$, are taken into account.

where $$\Omega = (1+\alpha)\beta + \sigma \qquad [5.10]$$

The two central banks are the main players of the policy game. They are assumed to act according to policy preferences, minimizing loss functions which represent the goal of maintaining external and internal equilibrium. In the gold standard, the former was considered to be of greater importance. "The view [...] of central bank policy as a means of facilitating the achievement and maintenance of reasonable stability in the level of economic activity and of prices was scarcely thought about before 1914, and certainly not accepted, as a formal objective of policy."[34] The external target is defined by some level $q_T > 0.5$ in both countries; this implies that both central banks cannot attract the desired amount of reserves at the same time. This assumption is necessary to constitute a binding liquidity constraint for both countries. Moreover, by making this assumption, Eichengreen aims to catch the restrictive bias, which sometimes is attributed to the gold standard.[35] On the other hand, the internal target (which has a relative weight b and b^*, respectively) is given by full employment $y_T = y_T^*$, normalized to zero. This target is equivalent to price stability, if supply shocks are absent.

$$L = (q_T - q)^2 + b\,y^2 \qquad [5.11]$$

$$L^* = \left[q_T - (1-q)\right]^2 + b^* \left(y^*\right)^2 \qquad [5.12]$$

Inserting the solutions from [5.8] and [5.9] into [5.11] and [5.12], and differentiating with respect to the policy instruments i and i^*, respectively, yield the reaction functions, which give the optimal answer of each player to any behaviour of its opponent. They exhibit a perfectly symmetric shape. Their positions and slopes depend, among other factors, on the policy preference parameters, which, at first, have been assumed as equal ($b = b^*$). If both players attach a low weight to internal equilibrium, these functions have a positive slope (*figure 5.4*).

$$i = \frac{\Omega^2 (2q_T - 1) + \beta^2 b}{\mu \left(\Omega^2 + \beta^2 b\right)} + \frac{\Omega^2 - \beta^2 b}{\Omega^2 + \beta^2 b}\, i^* \qquad [5.13]$$

$$i^* = \frac{\Omega^2 (2q_T - 1) + \beta^2 b^*}{\mu \left(\Omega^2 + \beta^2 b^*\right)} + \frac{\Omega^2 - \beta^2 b^*}{\Omega^2 + \beta^2 b^*}\, i \qquad [5.14]$$

---

[34] Bloomfield 1959: 24.

[35] The loss functions [5.11] and [5.12] attach the same weight to missing the reserve target in both directions, which might appear unconvincing. A reformulation which attaches a smaller weight to an overshooting leads to an increase of the level of interest rates; but this modification has no bearing on the problem of leadership. Choosing different reserve targets q_T for each country also does not alter the main conclusions of the model, as this resembles the case (which will be analyzed below) of attaching a different weight to the goal of external equilibrium.

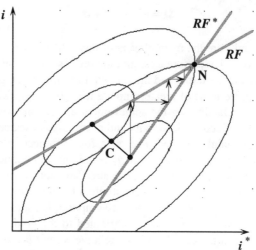

Figure 5.4: Cooperative and Nash solutions

Moving from any starting point in a south-western direction, i.e. if monetary policies embarks on an expansive course, increases output and prices in both countries. On the other hand, the home country gains on its gold stock, if the combination of discount rates is changed in the north-western direction. The ellipses reveal
the central banks' loss levels. Their centres show the optimal ratio of interest rates,
the zero-loss level, for each country.

Box 11: The Economic Logic of Reaction Functions and Loss Curves

The macroeconomic consequences of interest policies for the home country are de-
picted in *figure 5.5*. If domestic and foreign monetary policies march in opposite directions, the line $\dot{y} = 0$ (with a slope of minus unity), derived from [5.9], shows that the demand effects of domestic and foreign interest rate changes neutralize each other. A
parallel tightening or relaxing of monetary policies in both countries, on the other hand,
leaves the distribution of reserves constant; the line $\dot{q} = 0$ (with a slope of unity) is
based on equation [5.8]. Point A represents the general equilibrium with a zero-loss
level as both economic policy targets are attained.

Now let the foreign interest rate be increased from A to B and $b = 1$, i.e. the relative
importance of maintaining internal and external equilibrium be equal. If the macroeconomic impact of interest rate changes on both macro variables, y and q, were identical
in absolute terms, the equidistant position of B from both equilibrium lines would indicate that both targets were missed by the same amount. In that case, a circle drawn
around A, with the radius AB, would show all macroeconomic constellations, where
the welfare loss is equal to the state in B. Deviations from each target, resulting from
hypothetical movements of both interest rates, are such that gains in utility, with regard
to one target, are cancelled out by additional losses, with regard to the other.

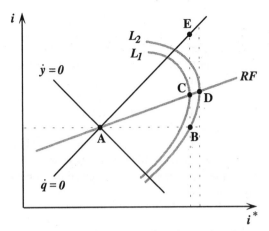

Figure 5.5: Welfare analysis of deviations from internal and external equilibrium

Actually, interest rate changes have a stronger impact on capital movements; it follows from [5.8] and [5.9] that $|dq/di| > |dy/di|$. Therefore, B represents a larger distance from the *external* equilibrium. By increasing the domestic interest rate the welfare loss could be reduced; in point C the lower loss level L_1 is reached. Applying Gossen's Second Law, in equilibrium it is impossible to lower the overall loss level by changing the extent to which both goals are attained. The asymmetric impact of interest rate changes on income and reserves deforms the initial loss circle into an ellipse, even if both targets are equally ranked. In the case of a further increase of i^* the optimal response would be point D. The line ACD represents the domestic reaction function.

If more emphasis is given to the external equilibrium ($b < 1$), starting from B, the domestic rate of interest has to be increased beyond C, in the extreme case (if $b = 0$) up to point E. The reaction function rotates, heading for the line AE; and the loss curve nestles into RF, until it finally (if $b = 0$) merges with that line. The economic implication is straightforward: if a player pursues only one goal, he can always find a domestic rate of interest, as a response to any challenge from abroad, which enables him to maintain a zero-loss level.

If both central banks do not pursue a strategic behaviour, the process of market interaction, i.e. the mutual response on each agent's policy decision, from any starting point will end up in the *Nash* equilibrium N (*figure 5.4*), which because of high interest rates has an unfavourable bearing on output and employment. Obviously both countries gain if a Nash outcome can be avoided. The *cooperative* solution C ensues, if both countries agree on the procedure of minimizing the (unweighed) sum of their individual loss functions [5.11] and [5.12] (neglecting weights implies a "fair" burden sharing of welfare losses). C is located on the Pareto-optimal contract curve, connecting the zero-loss levels of each player. Prohibitive transaction costs or mutual distrust may however preclude such an agreement being reached.

Moreover, the cooperative solution may be unstable because each player can reduce his individual loss by deviating from C. This might lead again to the Nash
solution. C might also be inferior to a *Stackelberg* solution where one player, the
"leader", chooses his optimal position on the reaction function of the second player, the "follower", who in turn confirms in a passive way the outcome of the
game. Formally, the domestic country minimizes [5.11] after inserting q and y
from [5.8-9] and then i^* from [5.14]. Obviously, the domestic country's leadership
solution S on RF^* is better than N, but an inspection of *figure 5.6* reveals that the
home country would gain even more if S^*, the leadership solution of the foreign
country, would prevail: the relatively higher domestic interest rate increases the
stock of reserves while the unchanged *average* stance of monetary policy in both
countries leaves output constant.

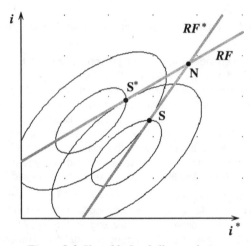

Figure 5.6: Unstable Stackelberg solutions

The general, somewhat ironic feature of the game is that both players would like
the other to be the leader, as the loss of each country is lower in a Stackelberg-follower position. The formal condition for that result to hold can be inferred from
the computed loss levels: $L(S) > L(S^*)$ and $L^*(S^*) > L^*(S)$, if $b^* = b < \Omega^2/\beta^2$.
The economic reason thus is to be found in the presumed low level of the internal
policy goal's weight, which brings about a positive slope of each country's reaction function. Thus both Stackelberg solutions are unstable. The unsuccessful attempt of both players to urge each other into the leading position ends up in the
Nash high-interest solution. In order to reach a stable leader-follower structure
some new features have to be added to an otherwise symmetric model.

5.4 Money Demand Effects of Sterling as a Reserve Currency

> If the interest of money be raised, it is proved by experience
> that money *does* come to Lombard Street, and theory shows
> that it *ought* to come.
>
> *Walter Bagehot*[36]

Eichengreen keeps to the assumption of identical policy preferences, but exploits
the well-known experience that financial assets denominated in sterling served as
a secondary currency reserve in the gold standard. The foreign banking system
used to back its home currency, besides gold, with these assets, i.e. accounts with
London banks and British bonds. Furthermore it could be observed until 1914,
that in periods of general monetary tightening England's capital import increased
even if interest rate differences remained unchanged. Private and institutional investors modified their portfolios, in times of monetary strain, in favour of currencies which exhibited a higher degree of liquidity. London drew funds from all
over the world, Paris and Berlin thus lost gold, but gained from peripheral countries, which had to bear the lion's share of monetary adjustment. "From the periph-
ery's viewpoint, the operation of the gold standard was anything but smooth."[37]

The foreign demand for sterling reserves can be expressed as

$$f^* = f_0^* + \phi r \qquad [5.15]$$

By dropping the constant f_0^* the foreign money supply [5.6] alters to

$$m^* = (1 - q) + \phi r - \mu i^* \qquad [5.16]$$

One part of f^* consists of interest bearing assets and is invested at the London
capital market (which by virtue of Walras' Law is suppressed from the model).
The share λ of f^* which is held as money forms a part of the overall sterling
money demand; if m were given, an increase in sterling demand from abroad reduces the amount of money which is available for British residents. Equation [5.4]
thus is modified:

$$m = p + y - \sigma r + \lambda \phi r \qquad [5.17]$$

The reserve and money demand modifications of the basic model imply that the
former symmetry of interest policy effects on the distribution of gold reserves is
lost. From the modified solution [5.8] it can be derived that changes of the British

---

[36] Bagehot 1873: 22.
[37] Eichengreen 1985: 18, cf. Eichengreen 1987, Bloomfield 1959: 42, Hawtrey 1923: 121-
2, Lindert 1969: 48-57, 78.

discount rate now have a larger influence on gold flows compared to changes of
the foreign rate. This is exactly what characterizes the specific power of the interest rate policy of a key currency central bank.

$$\frac{dq}{di} = \frac{(\Omega + \phi)\mu}{2\Omega + (1-\lambda)\phi} > \left|\frac{dq}{di^*}\right| = \frac{(\Omega - \lambda\phi)\mu}{2\Omega + (1-\lambda)\phi} \qquad [5.18]$$

But the additional term in the demand for sterling balances [5.17] also misleads
Eichengreen to believe that there is a particular pressure on output and prices in
England if, due to a parallel increase of discount rates in both countries, the rise in
the long-term rate of interest produces a further demand for sterling assets.[38] Actually however, the reserve and money demand effects have only gradual *and
symmetrical* repercussions on output and prices in both countries, by adding a
term $(1-\lambda)\phi$ in the denominator of the solutions [5.7] and [5.9].

Table 5.2: Balance sheets of central banks in the gold standard

England		Foreign country	
Gold ↑	Notes	Gold ↓	Notes
Bills and bonds	- *abroad* ↑⇓	Sterling reserves	
	- *in Britain* ⇑	- *Notes* ↑⇓	
		- *Bonds* ⇑	
		Bills and bonds	

Eichengreen seems to ignore a market channel whereby an additional demand for
sterling assets induces a concomitant increase of sterling money supply. This can
be inferred from an inspection of the balance sheets of the consolidated banking
systems in both countries (*table 5.2*): if the foreign bank system wishes to increase
its sterling reserves, it can do so only by shipping gold to England. In the foreign
country, the quantity of money remains constant; only the structure of the central
bank's assets will change (gold ↓, sterling notes ↑). On the other hand, the Bank of
England increases its gold reserves by issuing additional notes, which then are
held abroad (gold ↑, notes abroad ↑). If foreign agents prefer to hold interest-bearing reserve assets $(\lambda = 0)$, the acquired sterling notes are exchanged for sterling
bonds (⇓⇑), whereas the quantity of notes held by British non-bank sellers of these
bonds rises (⇑). In no case any shortage of sterling notes does emerge, because the

[38] "If in response to a discount rate increase abroad, the domestic central bank responds in
kind, the increase in interest rates world-wide will provide an incentive for the foreign
country to augment its stock of interest-bearing foreign exchange reserves. The supply
of money available to domestic residents will be correspondingly reduced [sic!], requir-
ing domestic money demand to decline to the level of supply through the reduction of
prices, output and employment" (Eichengreen 1987: 23).

foreign demand for sterling assets leads to a parallel creation of money in England.

Moreover, if the motive of earning interest payments is neglected, it makes no sense for the *foreign banking system* to substitute gold for sterling assets in times of financial crisis, because at that times the former should rank higher than the latter. It is more realistic to assume that *non-bank agents* abroad might decide to enlarge the share of sterling assets in their portfolio of financial wealth. For example, export sales proceeds then are no longer converted into home currencies, but are kept as investments at the London capital market. But an additional demand for interest-bearing sterling assets will lower the capital market rate, spurring monetary expansion in both countries; only an extra demand for sterling cash causes a monetary squeeze, again in both countries.

The asymmetric reaction of capital flows to interest rate changes also modifies the shape of the reaction functions. During a period of rising world interest rates, the Bank of England is not forced to counter interest rate increases abroad by similar adjustments at home as the direction of gold movements is biased towards Britain. This effect may flatten the slope of the home country's reaction function. According to Eichengreen, this function may even reach a zero slope so that a stable Stackelberg equilibrium solution with Britain as the leading country emerges. The Bank of England chooses its optimum point S on RF^*, which will be accepted by the other player: the foreign central bank's loss in S is lower compared to its own leadership point S^*, which due to the zero slope of RF coincides with the Nash solution N (*figure 5.7*).

Unfortunately, Eichengreen reached this conclusion by means of a back-of-the-envelope analysis only. The same forces which may flatten RF will make RF^* steeper so that a Nash solution will emerge. Moreover, an algebraic examination

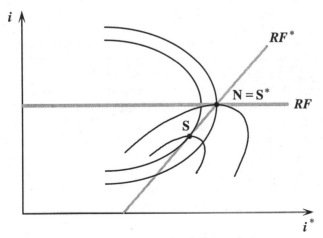

Figure 5.7: Eichengreen's Stackelberg solution

of the loss levels show that in case of identical policy preferences ($b = b^*$) the foreign country would accept S because of $L^*(S) < L^*(S^*)$, but the home country would not, as $L(S) < L(S^*)$ does *not* hold. Again, as in the basic model, each player intends to become the Stackelberg *follower*. Thus an agreement is precluded. The indisputable demand for sterling accounts and bonds as reserve assets does not suffice to establish a stable hierarchy of countries in the gold standard model.

5.5   Different Policy Preferences and Shocks

> In deciding whether to change Bank Rate, the Bank of England [...] looked almost exclusively at the size of its reserve. [...] On the other hand, the Bank was little sensitive to the state of trade in Britain.
>
> *Richard S. Sayers*[39]

A second – and more successful – attempt for establishing a stable hierarchical order in a model of the international gold standard builds on the assumption of different policy preferences with respect to the maintenance of internal and external equilibrium. There is a widely shared consensus that defending the value of the pound on the foreign exchange was the overriding objective of British monetary policy. Accordingly, it is now assumed that the relative interest in maintaining internal equilibrium is lower in Britain than in the foreign country ($b < b^*$). In order to simplify the analysis, the foreign sterling demand effect now is disregarded as it has no essential influence on the players' strategies and the game's solutions.

The *process* of lowering b, i.e. increasing the weight of the reserve target in England, implies that the British reaction function becomes steeper, because the home discount rate has to be increased relative to each given level of the foreign rate in order to attract more capital imports. At the same time the shape of the loss ellipse flattens and lowers its vertical distance around *RF*, because the loss function approaches the one-target case where the loss ellipse coincides with the reaction function. The British Stackelberg-leader point S thus moves along RF^* in a north-eastern direction (as indicated by the arrow in *figure 5.8*), thus substituting reserve gains for output losses. But the foreign central bank per assumption ($b < b^*$) cannot tolerate these losses for long. There is a switch point where it is no longer advantageous for the foreign player to favour the S-solution (as in *figure 5.6*); a superior strategy then is to head for S^*. Here, both discount rates are reduced: the British rate remains somewhat higher, compared to the foreign country, say, France (this corresponds to the empirical finding, *figure 5.3*).

---

[39] Sayers 1957: 61.

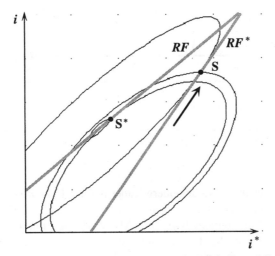

Figure 5.8: The key currency country as the Stackelberg follower

The Stackelberg-leader position of the foreign country in turn is also accepted by the Bank of England, because the switch from S to S* implies a substantial reduction of its welfare loss. Interestingly enough, this reduction occurs – because of monetary ease at home and abroad – particularly with respect to the output target, which had been ranked lower at the outset! This clearly shows that a "hard-nosed" policy with respect to a dominance of the balance-of-payment target in no way requires a renunciation of home employment. Rather, this policy forces other players to acknowledge that the home country has more staying power in the sphere of finance. It is just because more weight is given to the employment target, that these players in turn appear as "weak-currency" countries on the international financial market.

The idea, that England as the dominant agent in the international gold standard also acted as a Stackelberg leader in terms of game theory, is often taken for granted.[40] But economic theory reveals that this would only have been possible if England had given *more* emphasis to the goal of internal equilibrium than other member countries (*table 5.3*). It is not paradoxical that a powerful central bank in a key currency system acts as a Stackelberg follower. The very behaviour that indicates dominance in the general setting of game theory expresses weakness in currency policy matters. The threat of a hard-nosed central bank to pursue restrictive interest rate policies in favour of strengthening the currency, forces foreign countries to orient their monetary policies by the signals sent out by that central bank. By acting according to that bank's reaction function, a weak-currency country has to take into account, and to anticipate, the monetary policy stance of the

---

[40] Cf. Eichengreen 1987, Bordo 1993.

Table 5.3: Policy preferences and Stackelberg solutions

Preferences	$b < b^*$	$b > b^*$
Stable solution	S^*	S
Formal conditions	$L(S^*) < L(S)$ $L^*(S^*) < L^*(S)$	$L(S) < L(S^*)$ $L^*(S) < L^*(S^*)$
Implikation for U.K.	Stackelberg follower	Stackelberg leader

powerful central bank. The Stackelberg leader is forced to *optimize* his policy decisions, because he pursues conflicting targets which exposes him to the risk of the emergence of unfavourable trade-offs. The strong position of his opponent, on the other hand, rests on the fact that his more one-sided preference order is less dependent on external interferences, which allows him to employ a more mechanistic rule of behaviour.

The essential prerogative of the Stackelberg leader is to have the "first move". But this metaphor should not be understood as a description of the players' behaviour in "historical time". It merely says that an agent adjusts to an expected policy of its opponent, which is supposed to be *given*, i.e. which will not change in response to the decisions of any other agent involved in the game. Of course, interest rates set by the key currency country and other members of the currency system are subject to changes, if any of the economies is hit by some shock. The sequence of moves and adjustments, which are then to be observed, depends on the origin and location of the shock. Therefore, an econometric analysis of interest rate moves and responses, unwinding in historical time, hardly allows safe conclusions on the leader-follower structure of the currency system.

If the condition $b < b^*$ was the essential feature of the international gold standard, the analysis can be further simplified by letting $b = 0$. But $b^* > 0$ has to be maintained because otherwise the reaction functions exhibit a parallel slope and no equilibrium could be achieved. Because of her low stock of gold, and the obligation to preserve her reputation as the world's banker, England attributed absolute priority to the equilibrium of the balance of payments, whereas other countries in view of a higher reserves, and being less exposed to the risk of losing financial reputation, could afford also to pursue output targets.[41]

---

[41] The fact that British monetary policy seemed to neglect the sphere of trade and commerce has even been criticized as a result of an institutional *defect*: "The Bank of England, because of its organizational structure and the social composition of its management, is almost a classical example for the hypothesis, that, at least up to the First World War, England failed to build a way of economic policy making, which rested on a consensus between agrarian, industrial and commercial interests" (Ziegler 1990: 142, cf. Bloomfield 1959: 32).

The assumption $b = 0$ implies formally that England's loss ellipse coincides with her reaction function, and that – as long as the foreign country chooses S^* on *RF* – England's loss level is zero, irrespective of any shock which may occur at home or abroad. If the Bank of England is only interested in the desired level of gold reserves it optimizes the *difference* of the two discount rates, neglecting their *levels*. The reserve target then is achieved on any point of the British reaction function. This has a remarkable implication for the scope of monetary policy abroad: the foreign central bank has to accept that its reserve target cannot be reached, but it can choose the level of discount rates so that the desired output level can be achieved; this holds true regardless of any disturbances which may occur.

Simple supply and demand shocks can be incorporated into the model by letting $w > 0$ or $g > 0$ in [5.2] or [5.3]; foreign supply and demand equation are modified by analogy. Both reaction functions' intercepts vary with all shocks, at home or abroad, irrespective of the value of the policy preference parameters b and b^*. Even in the simple case, where the Bank of England pursues only a reserve target, the net effect of all interest rate adjustments cannot unambiguously be determined (*table 5.4*).

Table 5.4: Interest rate responses to shocks in the S^* solution (with $b = 0$)

	dg	dw	dg^*	dw^*
di	?	(+)	+	–
di^*	+	+	+	–

• An autonomous increase of domestic goods demand brings about, via a money demand effect, a higher rate of interest on the capital market; this is cushioned by the income loss due to lower net exports, as a consequence of higher domestic prices. The net effect might be an inflow of reserves which allows a lowering of the discount rate. *RF* thus will shift downwards. The foreign country has to increase its discount rate in order to dampen the excess demand on the goods market.[42] RF^* shifts to the right. Accordingly, both players will adjust their discount rates, and the new equilibrium S^* will be found in an interactive way (*figure 5.9*): England, as the shock's country of origin might lower her discount rate first, followed by a Stackelberg-leader move of the foreign country, which then causes England to adjust again. Or, in a clockwise movement, the foreign player might

---

[42] This aspect is neglected in England because of the $b = 0$ assumption. If $b > 0$, a conflict would arise anyhow, because a monetary restriction, necessary to contain goods market dynamics, would induce further capital imports via the interest rate channel. If sterilization is precluded, the increase of interest rates is "self defeating" as it induces an involuntary monetization of gold inflows.

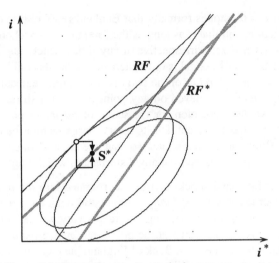

Figure 5.9: Demand expansion in the key currency country

increase his rate first. Even a "rational expectation solution" is conceivable where both agents simultaneously switch over to the new equilibrium at one stroke.

• A wage increase in the key currency country acts directly on prices and thus money demand, which allows a lower discount rate. But this effect is dominated by the lower income, due to the revaluation of the real exchange rate, which in turn will also check the price increase. The overall net effect on interest-rate-induced gold flows may well be negative so that the Bank of England will raise its discount rate. The foreign central bank will respond in a similar manner, but in order to compensate the export-induced overheating of the economy.

• A demand shock in the foreign country makes the foreign central bank feel bounded to raise the discount rate in order to maintain internal stability. It thus brings forth a redirection of gold flows, which then forces the home country to raise the bank rate even more so that the reserve target can be met.

• A rise in foreign wages leads, somewhat surprisingly, to lower interest rates throughout, because no player bothers about the price level as such. The foreign country eases monetary policy in order to neutralize the negative cost push effect on output and employment, whereas the home country reacts to the initial rise in the market rate of interest, due to gains in export demand, and lowers the discount rate in order to ward off the emergence of excess gold reserves.

5.6 The End of the Game: From the Gold to the Wage Standard

> If the English pound is not to be the standard which every-
> one knows and can trust [...], the business not only of the
> British Empire, but of Europe as well, might have to be
> transacted in dollars instead of pounds sterling. I think that
> would be a great misfortune.
>
> *Winston Churchill in 1925*[43]

> The [...] complaint against the gold standard is [...] that it at-
> tempts to confine the natural tendency of wages to rise be-
> yond the limits set by the volume of money, but it can only
> do so by the weapon of deliberately creating unemployment.
> This weapon the world, after a good try, has decided to dis-
> card.
>
> *John Maynard Keynes*[44]

> In order to buy labor peace during the war, many govern-
> ments greatly expanded the rights of workers to participate
> in the political process and to unionize. [...] This democrati-
> zation, coupled with a better understanding of the links be-
> tween central bank actions and domestic economic activity,
> eliminated the presumption that external stability would al-
> ways take precedence over internal stability as a goal for
> monetary policy.
>
> *Ben S. Bernanke*[45]

It is widely held that the international gold standard was remarkably durable in the face of substantial disturbances; but, in a way, the First World War was the first global shock, and it marked the beginning of the system's decline.[46] England had lost much of her international competitiveness due to different paths of inflation at home and abroad, and by re-entering the gold standard at the old parity of the pound. The ensuing real overvaluation of sterling was the price to be paid for ad-hering to the venerable "Restoration Principle".

Undoubtedly, the huge trade deficit indicates a relative decline of the British in-dustry, which has been apparent since the late 19th century. It is a tempting hypo-thesis to argue that a key currency country typically runs the risk of sowing the seeds of its own decline by resting on its laurels, which it had earned on account of its reputable currency. As long as foreigners are prepared to finance lasting trade deficits, the economic and social costs entailed in a policy of technological restructuring always appear too high. "Thus the very centrality of Britain's finan-

---

[43] Quoted from Kindleberger 1984: 341.

[44] Keynes 1943a: 31-2.

[45] Bernanke 1993: 261.

[46] For diverging opinions on the stability of the international gold standard see Bordo (1993) and Pierenkämper (1999).

cial position created a weakening of adjustment 'discipline', a bias towards deficits [...]. It is difficult to see why Britain should have wished to escape from the special financial position. Key-currency status allowed her (and France and Germany to lesser extents) to postpone otherwise necessary contractionary adjustments."[47]

The decision to restore the parity of the pound was clearly meant to be a reputation-preserving signal to the world financial market. In terms of the modern theory of central banking, the gold standard might be conceived as a commitment with an escape clause. "The rule is contingent in the sense that the public understands that the suspension will last only for the duration of the wartime emergency plus some period of adjustment. It assumes that afterwards the government will follow the deflationary policies necessary to resume payments at the original parity."[48] The problem was that central bankers underrated the macroeconomic adjustment costs. The Bank's director Addis even expected first of all benefits for the working class.[49] Political quarters aimed at the defence of England's position as the key currency country, but the policy they chose produced the opposite effect: from a goods market perspective the high price of sterling made gold England's cheapest export commodity; and the low price of the dollar was seen as a one-off chance to buy dollar assets. Churchill, who "was deafened by the clamorous voices of conventional finance", in the end could neither prevent the descent of the pound nor the emergence of a deep-seated stagnation of the British economy.[50]

England's problem can be analyzed in the same way as a domestic wage shock ($dw > 0$). If the extreme assumption $b = 0$ is dropped and generalized again to $b < b^*$, the decrease in competitiveness (due to an overvalued real exchange rate) in the transition to the new S^*-solution demonstrates the severe increase of English welfare losses (*figure 5.10 a*). Both central banks increase their discount rates: the foreign bank, because the additional export demand threatens internal macroeconomic stability; the British, because the deterioration of the trade balance, via the income effect of money demand, leads to an external drain of gold.

If the British supply-side problem increases ever more, England might feel herself compelled to fundamentally change her monetary policy strategy (*figure 5.10 b*): the widening of the British loss ellipse shows that a transition to a Stackelberg-leader behaviour might be advantageous (S becomes equivalent to, and would do-

---

[47] Lindert 1969: 74-5, cf. Emminger 1934, Eichengreen 1989. The conclusion that England failed because of a "wrong" industrial policy however, can be countered by the consideration that the U.S. resource-intensive way of production on a large scale for the U.K. was simply not an available and appropriate strategy (cf. Crafts 1998).

[48] Bordo 1993: 161, cf. Giovannini 1993.

[49] "I think it would not be too high a price to pay for the substantial benefit of the trade of this country and its working classes, and also, although I put it last, for the recovery by the City of London of its former position as the world's financial center" (quoted from Moggridge 1972: 41-2).

[50] Keynes 1925: 212, cf. Stadermann 1994: 162-5. A view on *figure 4.2* reveals the severe, and useless, deflation which England had to endure after the First World War.

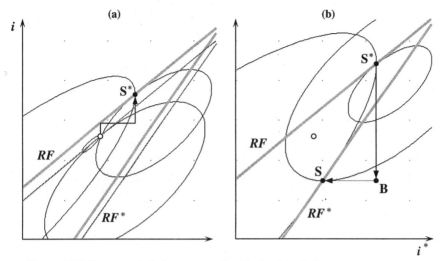

Figure 5.10: Regime switch due to a supply-side shock in the key currency country

minate S^*, if the revaluation of the real exchange rate be continued). But it is also evident that England's opponent would not appreciate a transition from S^* to S as this would aggravate his problem of maintaining internal stability. Therefore, S can be no solution of the game. If the home country tried to initiate a regime shift by lowering its discount rate to B, the foreign player does not necessarily have to give in and reduce his rate likewise. He might decide to stay in B for a while, knowing – by assessing the relative deterioration of welfare levels – that this puts heavy pressure on the first country to return to S^*. The attempt of both players to stick to their favourite Stackelberg choices ends up in the *Bowley* solution where both agents are worse off, compared to each of the Stackelberg solutions.

Already in the mid-1920s England had fallen into dependence on another foreign country: the Banque de France, which possessed an amount of sterling assets matching the whole gold stock of the Bank of England, was in a position to threaten the British balance of payment. In view of the British deficit, "Paris had the power to force upon London a Bank Rate increase, but Norman [governor of the Bank of England] suggested to Moreau [governor of the Banque de France] the alternative of a reduction in the Paris rate. The French, suspicious always of what Moreau referred to as 'the imperialism of the Bank of England', maintained that the responsibility for corrective measures rested with the deficit country".[51]

Later, the reluctance of the U.S. to lower its discount rate corresponds to the American practice of sterilizing the monetary effects of gold inflows so that the increase of goods prices was moderated. Thus British hopes, that – according to

---

[51] Eichengreen 1984: 80.

the rules of the gold standard – an inflationary adjustment of the U.S. economy would relieve the problem of the misalignment of the pound, were shattered. Keynes complained about the U.S. monetary policy: "In practice the Federal Reserve Board often ignores the proportion of its gold reserve to its liabilities and is influenced, in determining its discount policy, by the object of maintaining stability in prices, trade, and employment. Out of convention and conservatism it accepts gold. Out of prudence and understanding it buries it. [...] For the past two years the United States has *pretended* to maintain a gold standard. *In fact* it has established a dollar standard."[52] But Keynes' underlying reproach that the U.S. had violated the "Rules of the Game" is hardly convincing. First, the Bank of England also did not stuck to a rigid ratio of gold and money supply. Second, the Fed pursued that type of policy Keynes himself had emphatically recommended as the only appropriate target in his "Tract": stabilization of the internal price level.

How did the U.S. "establish a dollar standard"? A spontaneous answer might be: by keeping the dollar in short supply so that other members of the world economy have to obey to the monetary standard, i.e. formally: adjust to a reaction function, which is set by the one dominant agent who demonstrates that he can afford to sustain high interest rates. But this answer is misleading; attracting capital imports by means of a monetary restriction does not generally indicate the strength and reputation of a currency. The crucial factor is the expectation of market agents that the *liquidity and stability of a currency* (in terms of goods, assets and competing currencies) is "guaranteed" so that it serves as a perfect (international) means of payment, and assets denominated in units of that currency bear no exchange rate risks. And there were definitely no signs indicating a possible devaluation of the dollar in terms of gold.

The British position as the leader of the international gold standard could not be perpetuated, not because the U.S. struggled for a dominance in the field of international finance, but rather because they intended to dampen wage and price increases at home. Otherwise, if more emphasis had been given to the state of the U.S. capital balance, the Fed should have *lowered* interest rates (and tolerated inflation).[53] On the other hand, the attempt to restore British competitiveness by imposing a downward pressure on wages proved unsuccessful due to an increased rigidity of wages. The Bank of England felt that it was impossible to further increase British interest rates, without "provoking a riot", given the bad state of industry and high unemployment.[54] Therefore, speculation was spreading, gathering momentum as the British deficit continued, that England might be forced to go off gold, i.e. to devalue the pound. Thus, the pound lost its liquidity premium (which generally is attributed to the world's key currency) to the dollar.

---

[52] Keynes 1923: 197-8, cf. Crabbe 1989.

[53] In case of $b^* = 0$ the multiplier di^*/dw, contrary to the regime represented in *table 5.4*, is unambiguously negative.

[54] Cf. Eichengreen 1984: 80.

A new feature of monetary policy making in nearly all countries was that the weight of goods market equilibrium as a policy target increased substantially. The growing knowledge of the macroeconomic impact of monetary policy undermined the understanding of the business cycle as an inevitable fate. Government felt more and more responsible for employment and prices. Moreover, the emergence of a democratic welfare state and the strengthening of unions brought about increased wage rigidities and, more generally, made the state of the labour market a political issue. Apparently wage setting could no longer be subordinated to the requirements of the foreign exchange, and the nominal standard of a nation's money henceforth was governed by the price of labour, and not by the price of gold.[55]

The idea of an institutional erosion of the gold standard may appear convincing; but patterns and norms of wage formation ought to be treated as endogenous elements of economic development. It was simply the choice of a wrong nominal exchange rate when re-entering the gold standard which destroyed the binding force of the gold parity as a credible constraint on wage formation. In general, market agents ought to be able to *meet* a commitment if it is to preserve its normative reputation. If a reasonable degree of wage restraint is not honoured by perceptible employment gains, a regime switch of market behaviour is obvious. Instead of increasing their efforts forever, people will demand new "Rules of the Game". Removing the constraints given by the old rules sometimes is an efficient *and* cheap way out. When the pound was devalued in September 1931, a widespread surprise was felt that the sacrilege of giving up the "mystic" fixed parity went unpunished; a member of the British aristocracy was baffled: "Nobody told us we could do this".[56]

---

[55] "The nominal wage and not the quantity of money establishes the national character of a currency. [...] The basic reason for the gradual erosion of the gold standard thus is to be found in the strengthening of unions, as an autonomous fixing of nominal wages contradicts the conditions of a proper working of the gold standard. Free collective bargaining, the sacred cow of national economic policy, therefore precludes the existence of a currency, the international character of which corresponds to the working of free world trade. From this point of view, the erosion of the gold standard implies the enthronement of a wage standard and the transition to a world economic regime where the genuine money of wealth owners no longer plays the dominating role" (Riese 1986: 285-6, cf. Keynes 1923, Eichengreen 1992).

[56] Quotation from Artis/Lewis 1993: 50.

6. The Loss of Credibility and Stability in the Bretton Woods System

6.1 American Monetary Policy Without a Nominal Anchor?

> The plan aims at the substitution of expansionist, in place of contractionist, pressure on world trade.
>
> *British statement on the Bretton Woods plans*[1]

> National macroeconomic autonomy is central to what the negotiators wanted.
>
> *Ronald McKinnon*[2]

The Bretton Woods currency order exhibited a double nature:

• On the one hand, a two-tier system, continuing the external constraints on monetary policy making, was established where fixed exchange rates of national currencies were set up vis-à-vis the dollar, which in turn was defined as containing some fixed amount of gold. This framework was chosen in order to evade difficulties stemming from the actual uneven distribution, and a possible overall scarcity of gold reserves, in the future.

• On the other hand, the desire to end the subordination of internal policy goals to balance-of-payments restrictions runs all the way through the negotiations and agreements of the treaty. Keynes could not get his plan accepted which was to establish an artificial world currency – the "bancor" – and to some extent abolish the budget constraint of deficit countries. Full convertibility of national currencies was not restored until 1959; and governments felt encouraged to employ restrictions on capital movements[3] and sought to sterilize the monetary effects of exchange rate interventions. Moreover, in the case of "fundamental disequilibria", each member country was allowed unilaterally to alter its exchange rate. There was no rule or norm enforcing a return to the former parity. With the traditional

---

[1]   Quoted from Giovannini 1993: 118, cf. Keynes 1942: 176, Kregel 1994/95.

[2]   McKinnon 1993: 13.

[3]   In 1943, Keynes expressed a widely shared opinion: "We think it entirely impracticable that individual nationals of a country should be free to move assets abroad or to invest abroad quite irrespective of whether their country had a favourable balance which made such transactions possible. [...] Foreign investment of individuals that does not correspond to a favourable balance is clearly something which can only cause trouble and can do no good, in the same way as flights of capital for reasons of political fear or fluctuating ideas of where the 'better 'ole' is. All that we want to get rid of. [...] We can not hope to control rates of interest at home if movements of capital moneys out of the country are unrestricted" (1943a: 212, 276, cf. Moggridge 1986, Giovannini 1993).

Box 12: The Bretton Woods Agreement in 1945 – The Spirit of the Treaty[4]

All Countries

I. Fix a foreign par value for the domestic currency by using gold, or a currency tied to gold, as the numéraire; otherwise demonetize gold in all private transacting.

II. In the short run, keep exchange rate within one percent of its par value; but leave its long-run par value unilaterally adjustable if the International Monetary Fund (IMF) concurs.

III. Free currency convertibility for current-account payments; use capital controls to dampen currency speculation.

IV. Use national monies symmetrically in foreign transacting, including dealings with the IMF.

V. Buffer short-run payments imbalances by drawing on official exchange reserves and IMF credits; sterilize the domestic monetary impact of exchange-market interventions.

VI. National macroeconomic autonomy: each member government to pursue its own price level and employment objectives unconstrained by a common nominal anchor or price rule.

Restoration Rule abolished, speculation no longer acted as a stabilizing force. Finally, the U.S. gold reserve was, in a way, protected by the proviso that private agents were not allowed to demand gold at the fixed dollar price from the Federal Reserve, but only foreign official institutions, which could be deterred from doing so by means of political pressure. "The reason why the major industrial countries failed to use their disciplinary device had more to do with politics than with economics."[5]

Perhaps gold was left as a "final reserve" or "backing" of the international currency system, because of a lack of confidence in the stability of a pure fiat money standard. Moreover, the fixed dollar price of gold exposed also the U.S. to an exogenous constraint; thus to some extent weakening the privileged position of the dollar which was perceived, but not striven for, from the outset. Finally, with a gold-backed dollar, in principle the U.S. also had the possibility to devalue, if all other currencies maintained their former (implicit) gold price. But the dollar became *the* reserve asset, which surprisingly, in view of the preceding history of the emergence of key currencies, was not generally expected (the statutes allowed all currencies for intervention purposes).[6] Therefore all Bretton Woods member

---

[4] Reproduced from McKinnon 1993: 13.
[5] De Grauwe 1996: 36, cf. 16-22, 32-39.
[6] "The system that operated [...] turned out to be quite different from what the architects had in mind. [...] Instead of a system of equal currencies, it evolved into a variant of the gold exchange standard – the gold-dollar system. [...] Concurrently with the decline of sterling was the rise in the dollar as a key currency" (Bordo 1993: 168).

countries kept gold *and* dollar reserve assets. Thus an independent gold policy of the U.S. would have produced an instability in financial markets, similar to those prevalent in a bimetallism standard, and a loss of confidence in the dollar's gold backing. An unilateral devaluation of the dollar in terms of gold thus would have caused foreign countries also to devalue their national currencies.[7]

The structural dollar demand, in connection with the impossibility to devalue, amounted to the emerging risk of a dollar overvaluation, which implied a mirror-image effect on the competitiveness and growth perspectives of foreign countries. "A reserve currency regime with fixed exchange rates permits other currencies to be undervalued and thus permits other countries to enjoy export-led growth."[8] At the same time, the American key currency privilege of relying on the readiness of foreigners to finance external deficits, should they ever occur, could easily lure U.S. economic policy to choose the cheap strategy of "printing dollars" instead of embarking on a solid path of painful supply-side adjustments. This threat was a real one; all the more so as it was the obligation of the *foreign* central banks to stabilize their national currencies vis-à-vis the dollar, by eventually buying any excess supply of dollars, so that the Fed was exempt from the task of defending the value of the dollar on the foreign exchange – indeed, what a difference compared to the rules of the international gold standard!

This set-up of the Bretton Woods system does not necessarily hint at a hidden strategic element[9] in the treaty, but simply to the constructional flaw of establishing the postwar currency order as a half-way house between an asset-backed system and a paper money standard. As long as the currency system is built on a more or less exogenously given quantity of a reserve asset, even the most powerful central bank is but one of the $n-1$ players who has to use his interest policies to prevent an external drain. But if there is no such basic reserve asset, the necessary nominal anchor has to be provided by one of the n countries. In that case, the leading central bank, in general, should not carry through large-scale, uni-directional interventions on the foreign exchange, because this might destabilize the world's price level, as a massive increase or decrease of the gold stock would have done centuries ago.

It appears too obvious that the leading central bank should then try to stabilize the price (level) of a basket of home produced goods instead of the price of gold, which enables other countries to "import" price stability by means of a fixed nom-

---

[7] Cf. Grubel 1969: 196-7, Cooper 1975, Eichengreen 1989.

[8] Cooper 1975: 73.

[9] Stadermann (1994: 247) reverses the predominant picture of Keynes as the "loser" of the Bretton Woods negotiations. Given the probability of an emerging overvaluation of the dollar, and the American incentive to run expansive policies, the growing trade surpluses of other countries would turn creditor-debtor relations against the U.S. Thus the Bretton Woods agreement is interpreted as a "cunning device" enabling Britain "to regain her former position in the world economy. The plan failed [...] because Japan and Germany learnt to exploit the opportunities of the system better than Britain."

Box 13: The Fixed-Rate Dollar Standard, 1950-70[10]

Industrial Countries Other than the United States

I. Fix a par value for the national currency with the U.S. dollar as the numéraire, and keep exchange rate within 1 percent of this par value indefinitely.

II. Free currency convertibility for current-account payments; use capital controls to insulate domestic financial markets, but begin liberalization.

III. Use the dollar as the intervention currency, and keep active official exchange reserves in the U.S. Treasury Bonds.

IV. Subordinate long-run growth in the domestic money supply to the fixed exchange rate and to the prevailing rate of price inflation (in tradable goods) in the United States.

V. Offset substantial short-run losses in exchange reserves by having the central bank purchase domestic assets to partially restore the liquidity of domestic banks and the money supply (Bagehot's Rule).

VI. Limit current account imbalances by adjusting national fiscal policy (government net saving) to offset imbalances between private saving and investment.

The United States

VII. Remain passive in the foreign exchanges: practice free trade with neither a balance-of-payments nor an exchange-rate target. Do not hold significant official reserves of foreign exchange, and (passively) sterilize the domestic monetary consequences of other countries' foreign exchange interventions.

VIII. Keep U.S. capital markets open to foreign governments and private residents as borrowers or depositors.

IX. Maintain position as a net international creditor (in dollar denominated assets) and limit fiscal deficits.

X. Anchor the dollar (world) price level for tradable goods by an independently chosen American monetary policy based on domestic credit expansion.

---

inal exchange rate in terms of the key currency. "Once the regime had evolved into a *de facto* dollar standard, the obligation of the United States was to maintain price stability."[11] To put it in a nutshell: the Fed should have defended the value of the dollar on the U.S. goods market, and not on the foreign exchange. An obligation to sell gold on demand at a fixed dollar price should *not* have been part of such an international currency order, "a necessary omission for the dollar standard to continue indefinitely".[12]

Admittedly, the substitution of a fixed gold price by a stable price level of domestic goods entails some serious pitfalls (which will be studied in the subsequent

---

[10] Reproduced from McKinnon 1993: 16.
[11] Bordo 1993: 178.
[12] McKinnon 1993: 16, cf. McKinnon 1969.

EMS chapter). But the twofold immediate flaw of the Bretton Woods system was that, first, no particular emphasis was attributed to the importance of the goal of price stability in the U.S. and, second, the dollar's gold backing, though limited, created an unnecessary liquidity problem for the Fed, which might give rise to speculative instabilities on the international financial market.

6.2   The Bretton Woods Model

> The architects never spelled out exactly how the system was supposed to work.
>
> *Michael D. Bordo*[13]

> There is no plausible definition of a deficit in the balance of payments of the *N*th country which is also a reserve center. [...] However the United States would have an increased obligation to maintain stable internal policies.
>
> *Ronald McKinnon*[14]

The simple two-country model introduced above is used to analyse the working, and the downfall, of the Bretton Woods system. Again, the domestic country is supposed to be the dominant agent (the U.S.), and the foreign player represents the aggregate of other member countries. Supply and demand equations [5.2] and [5.3], and their foreign counterparts, continue to apply; supply and demand shocks are ignored ($w = w^* = g = g^* = 0$). The dollar money supply [6.1] depends on the American gold reserve (which for simplicity equals the total world stock, i.e. $q = 1$), and on the short-term interest rate as the active policy instrument. Foreign money supply [6.2] is "backed" by dollar assets f^*, and also influenced by the central bank's interest rate. The part λ of f^* which is being held in dollar notes adds to the overall dollar demand [6.3]. Foreign money demand [6.4] is unaffected by the key currency structure of the model.

$$m = q - \mu i \qquad\qquad [6.1]$$

$$m^* = f^* - \mu i^* \qquad\qquad [6.2]$$

$$m = p + y - \sigma r + \lambda f^* \qquad\qquad [6.3]$$

$$m^* = p^* + y^* - \sigma r \qquad\qquad [6.4]$$

Contrary to the traditional rule of the gold standard, gold no longer serves as a medium for foreign exchange interventions; therefore its distribution does not

---

[13] Bordo 1993: 165.
[14] McKinnon 1969: 156.

Table 6.1: Balance sheets of central banks in the Bretton Woods system

U.S.		Foreign country	
Gold Bills and bonds	Notes - *in the U.S.* ↓⇑ - *abroad* ↑⇓	Dollar reserves - *Notes* ↑⇓ - *Bonds* ⇑ Bills and bonds	Notes ↑

change according to market forces or interest policies. The endogenous monetary variable thus is given by f^*. Therefore, it is no longer possible – as in Eichengreen's model of the gold standard – for the foreign central bank to orient its demand of f^*, as a behavioural choice, by its market yield; conversely, the bank is forced to use interest rate policies in order to attract a sufficient amount of dollar assets. Finally, the *world* supply of dollars depends only on the domestic component of money creation by the Fed.

The structure of foreign reserve keeping has a marked influence on the macroeconomic working of the system. Assume a rising interest rate on the German capital market, perhaps induced by the Bundesbank. Dollar bonds will be sold on the U.S. capital market, and the proceeds are used to buy marks, which then finance the acquisition of German bonds. This transaction withdraws dollars from the American economy, and, in order to maintain the dollar exchange rate, they are bought by the Bundesbank, which thus increases the German money supply (arrows ↓↑ in *table 6.1*). Hence, the initial German interest rate increase to some extent is transmitted to the U.S., but the Bundesbank itself involuntarily cushions the monetary squeeze on the German money market by the obligation to absorb any excess dollar supply. Similar considerations apply in the case of a loss of American competitiveness which, due to a trade deficit, causes an outflow of dollars. The concomitant increase of foreign money supply mitigates an overvaluation of the dollar, but there would be no compulsion to reduce the U.S. deficit.[15]

German monetary policy loses even more of its limited power if it decides to keep all reserve dollar assets in U.S. bonds. In that case, dollar notes acquired on the foreign exchange would be immediately recycled to the American capital market, thus relieving the liquidity shortage (arrows ⇓⇑). Accordingly, the German influence on the American interest rate disappears completely, U.S. capital exports – and mark creation by the Bundesbank – continue until the initial interest rate increase is reversed.[16]

---

[15] Cf. Rueff/Hirsch 1965.

[16] "The accumulation or decumulation of dollar exchange reserves by foreign central banks would not affect the American monetary base. Only foreign holdings of 'nonmonetary' U.S. Treasury bonds would change. Therefore, exchange interventions by foreign central banks were 'passively' or automatically sterilized from changing the American money supply [...]. Foreign money supplies were affected by exchange intervention by

The solution of the macro system confirms the limited market power of foreign monetary policy: it has a clear impact on the allocation of dollar assets [6.6], but acts on the capital market rate [6.5], output and prices [6.7] only insofar as it keeps a fraction $\lambda > 0$ of non-interest bearing dollar reserves. In contrast to the gold standard (equations [5.7-9]) the world level of interest rates, demand, employment and prices is mainly determined by the key currency country. The Fed thus, on the one hand, enjoyed the privilege that its balance-of-payment restriction was abolished by the reserve keeping behaviour abroad, but on the other hand was charged with a responsibility for world growth and inflation: "Unemployment in France should enter American decision-making."[17]

$$\underline{r} = \frac{1}{(1+\lambda)\Omega}\left[\mu\left(i+\lambda\,i^*\right)-q\right] \qquad\qquad [6.5]$$

$$\underline{f^*} = \frac{1}{1+\lambda}\left[q+\mu\left(i^*-i\right)\right] \qquad\qquad [6.6]$$

$$\underline{p} = \underline{p^*} = \alpha\,\underline{y} = \alpha\,\underline{y^*} = \frac{\alpha\,\beta}{(1+\lambda)\Omega}\left[q-\mu\left(i+\lambda\,i^*\right)\right] \qquad\qquad [6.7]$$

In actual fact however, in all countries domestic policy goals were to the fore which may also be partly explained by the politicization of monetary authorities. "In practice, central banks became junior branches of the treasuries."[18] Both targets – employment and prices – can be used interchangeably (they are linked by a constant parameter α) as long as supply shocks are absent. Nevertheless, let the U.S. target be some output level y_T, whereas the foreign country aims at a constant price level (which for simplicity is normalized to unity).[19] The U.S. target mainly serves as a rough proxy for ambitious social policy programs in the 1960s and military spending (particularly in the Vietnam war). The target of price stability abroad is not chosen to deny the importance of the employment goal in the European countries (actually Germany supported her employment by keeping an undervalued currency, i.e. by means of a relatively low rate of inflation compared to her trading partners), but to "prepare" the model for the final Bretton Woods conflict concerning the problem of inflation import from the U.S.

The conditions of external equilibrium were perceived as restrictions, rather than aims; the weight attached to them, x and x^*, respectively, in the loss functions is supposed to be small. The Fed may want to confine dollar assets held by foreign

---

foreign governments, but the American money supply was not" (McKinnon 1993: 19, cf. Balbach 1978, De Grauwe 1996: 36-7).

[17] McKinnon 1969: 157.

[18] Capie/Goodhart 1995: 151.

[19] This is even "tougher" than a zero-inflation target, because true deflation is required after discrete price-level increases. But this rule is chosen here only to keep the model as simple as possible.

agents to the amount of its own gold reserve so that its liquidity problem is eliminated. The foreign central bank feels a somewhat more urgent need to keep dollar assets in a sufficient amount f^* in order to meet the demands arising from imbalances on the foreign exchange.

$$L = (y_T - y)^2 + x(f^* - q)^2 \qquad [6.8]$$

$$L^* = (p^*)^2 + x^* (f_T^* - f^*)^2 \qquad [6.9]$$

Minimizing these loss functions yields two reaction functions, where – in accordance with the historical facts – it has been assumed that foreign central banks kept their dollar assets invested at the American capital market ($\lambda = 0$). As a consequence, monetary policy abroad loses its influence on all macro variables except for the distribution of dollar assets f^*.[20] The formal implication is that the relative weight x^* given to the external target vanishes from the foreign reaction function RF^*. Starting from a base level determined by the gap between the aggregate foreign reserve target and the U.S. gold stock, foreign monetary policy tracks the Fed's interest rate decisions. A close look at [6.6], [6.9] and [6.11] reveals that at any point on RF^* the foreign central bank attains its reserve target.

$$i = \frac{\beta (\beta q - \Omega y_T)}{\mu (\Omega^2 x + \beta^2)} + \frac{\Omega^2 x}{\Omega^2 x + \beta^2} i^* \qquad [6.10]$$

$$i^* = \frac{f_T^* - q}{\mu} + i \qquad [6.11]$$

If $x > 0$, the Fed also responds, although in a weaker manner, to interest rate increases abroad in order to limit the gap ($f_T^* - q$), which, as a general assumption, is taken to be positive (because otherwise the American liquidity problem would be of no importance). Furthermore, the Fed chooses the base level of American interest rates according to its output target y_T.

An analytical comparison of all possible solutions of the policy game confirms the impression gained from the graph (*figure 6.1 a*): both players definitely prefer a Stackelberg solution over the Nash outcome. But the emergence of a stable equilibrium depends on preferences and the scale of policy targets.

---

[20] Actually these assets were mostly held with the American banking system, which in the above model is amalgamated with the private non-bank sector. The gain of interest payments of course is a poor compensation for the loss of market power of the national central bank; but, contrary to the two-country model above, any single member country of the Bretton Woods system could not expect to gain substantial influence on world monetary conditions by keeping its foreign reserves in cash.

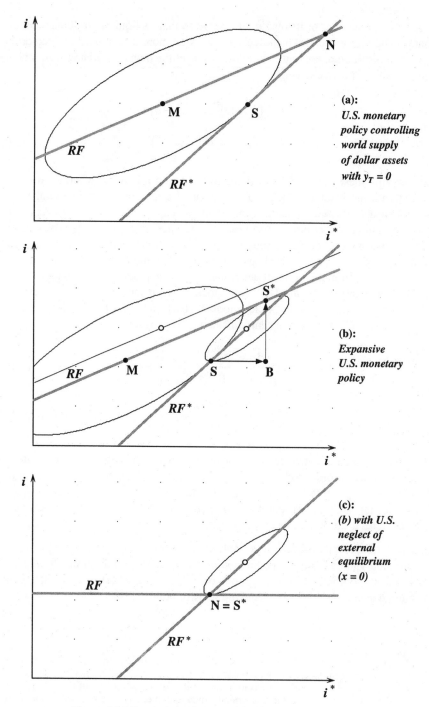

Figure 6.1: Alternative solutions of the Bretton Woods game

Table 6.2: Evaluation of the Stackelberg solution S

$y = y^*$	$p = p^*$	f^*	L	L^*
y_T	$\alpha\, y_T$	f_T^*	$x\left(f_T^* - q\right)^2$	$\left(\alpha\, y_T\right)^2$

• Let the Fed choose an interest rate which hits the U.S. output target (in the overall zero-loss point M). According to his reaction function, the foreign player responds so that point S is reached. As this is the best position the Fed can reach, it will stick to that Stackelberg-leader policy. The output goal, due to the Fed's absolute control over macro variables at home and abroad, can always be reached; but the gap $(f_T^* - q)$ produces a welfare loss. On the other hand, a Stackelberg-leader strategy does not pay for the foreign agent, as long as the U.S. output target is moderate and the foreign country thus does not "import" too much inflation (*table 6.2*; in *figure 6.1 a* the target has been chosen at the monetary equilibrium level $y_T = 0$).

• If y_T is increased ever more, the home reaction functions shifts downwards and the U.S. "bliss" point M moves to the south-west; so also does S. The foreign central bank might wish to defend price stability at home by changing to a solution with higher interest rates (*figure 6.1 b* shows the switch case where S equals S*). By assumption ($\lambda = 0$) foreign monetary policy has no influence on output and prices (therefore RF^* does not move), and thus needs the consent on the part of the Fed. But S* is unacceptable for the U.S., and for a while the system might be hung up in the Bowley solution B, where the foreign central bank has to absorb a growing amount of dollars and thus is unable to stop inflation at home.

• The transition to S* is precluded, on principle, if the Fed should decide to drop its external policy target ($x = 0$). In that case U.S. monetary policy no longer tries to keep the foreign claim to the American gold stock in check; the Fed's loss becomes zero. RF turns horizontal and, although the actual solution S remains unchanged as a matter of substance, i.e. with respect to the level and ratio of interest rates, it corresponds formally to a Nash game or a Stackelberg-leader position of the foreign country (*figure 6.1 c*). Similar to the constellation in the gold standard, this solution does not express strength, but a *strategic weakness* of the foreign player, who has to settle in a world macroeconomic situation dominated by U.S. monetary policy. If monetary expansion at home speeds up (with a higher y_T), RF shifts downwards, and the foreign loss ellipse becomes larger and larger.

The hypothesis of an American Stackelberg-leader policy – in "normal" times – with its implication of a relatively low U.S. rate of interest seems to be consistent with the empirical data (*figure 6.2*). But because of the faulty design of the Bretton Woods system the stable equilibrium did not endure for long.

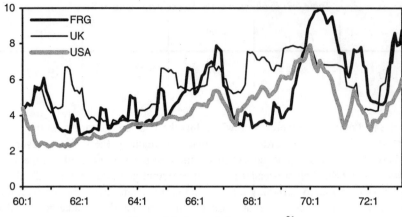

Figure 6.2: 3-month interest rates[21]

6.3   Triffin's Dilemma: The Liquidity Problem of the Federal Reserve

> The country whose currency is functioning as a key or re-
> serve currency in international monetary relations, and there-
> fore as the currency of denomination in international trans-
> actions, must act as if it is on a gold standard.
>
> *Hyman P. Minsky*[22]

In 1960 Triffin called attention to a long-run trade-off problem stemming from the dollar's gold backing.

• *A dollar shortage*: if U.S. monetary policy should try to limit the gap between foreign dollar holdings and the American gold stock by means of a restrictive policy, the expansion of the *world* quantity of money would be limited likewise, and world growth would be severely hampered.

• *A dollar glut*: if otherwise the Fed allowed a steady monetary growth, an ever increasing gap $(f^* - q)$ would undermine the confidence in the fixed gold parity of the dollar. Only foreign official institutions had the right to redeem dollar assets, but the French, grudging the U.S. the privilege of neglecting balance-of-payments deficits, threatened to do so in the 1960s. Private market agents would expect a dollar devaluation, also in terms of other currencies, if any attempt to cash in gold for dollar were rejected and/or the dollar be devalued in terms of gold. There were

---

[21] Data from OECD: Main Economic Indicators, Bundesbank: 50 Jahre Deutsche Mark (CD-ROM).

[22] Minsky 1979: 103.

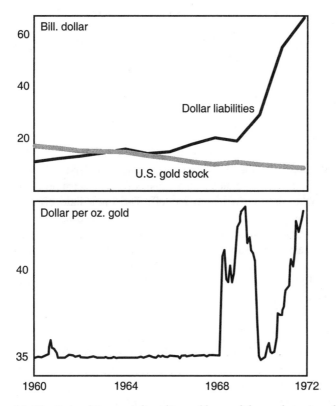

Figure 6.3: The Federal Reserve's liquidity problem and the market price of gold[23]

also discussions to revalue *all* currencies vis-à-vis the dollar *and* gold in order to relieve the growing shortage of gold as the basic reserve asset of the system.[24]

The critical gap between foreign holdings of dollar assets and the American gold stock became positive in the mid 1960s (*figure 6.3*). From 1961 until 1968 all central banks had intervened in the private world gold market, aiming to keep the market dollar price of gold constant at the fixed rate which had been determined in the Bretton Woods treaty. When that concerted action was ended, the market price of gold exploded, and it became evident that the dollar was irredeemable.

The formal logic of asset markets implies that the interest rate parity between domestic and foreign bonds be modified by the expected rate of dollar devaluation $\dot{e}^e$ (vis-à-vis gold and other currencies), which might be modelled as depending on the quantitative extent of the Fed's liquidity problem. Furthermore, an addi-

---

[23] Data from De Grauwe 1996: 46, Bordo 1993: 174, cf. Grubel 1969: 138-9.

[24] Cf. Triffin 1960, Kenen 1960, Balogh 1973: 73. Later in 1970, when no longer needed, *Special Drawing Rights* were created to perform as additional, artificial currency reserves.

tional element h is inserted into the U.S. money supply function [6.1], representing the long-term element of dollar creation on the basis of home assets, as distinct from "daily" operations of varying short-term interest rates.

$$r = r^* + \dot{e}^e = r^* + \delta\left(f^* - q\right) \qquad [6.12]$$

$$m = q + h - \mu i \qquad [6.13]$$

The consequences of the aggravation of the American liquidity problem, *independently* from a general monetary expansion, can be understood by studying the effects of $dh = -dq$ (which enables an analysis of a long-term problem in the setting of the above short-term macro model). The immediate effects of such a change of composition of the Fed's asset holding are, according to [6.12], in the U.S. an outflow of capital; additional creation of foreign money due to the acquisition of the excess dollar supply on the part of the foreign central bank; and the lowering of the foreign capital market rate, which in turn increases output and prices abroad. Expansion of goods demand spills over via the trade balance to the U.S., where – with the quantity of money being constant – the long rate of interest will rise (*table 6.3, first row*).

Due to expected dollar devaluation, foreign interest rate policy also acquires an influence on macro variables in both countries (*table 6.3, second row*), even if dollar assets are not held in cash ($\lambda = 0$). The "perverse" multiplier $dr^*/di^* < 0$, creating an *expansive* effect of restrictive monetary policy on output and prices, can easily be explained by the traditional force $df^*/di^* > 0$ which intensifies devaluation expectations and thus, again by virtue of [6.12], leads to capital imports.[25]

In terms of the policy game, the – albeit small – effect of foreign monetary policy on U.S. goods demand implies that the home reaction function RF shows some sensitivity with respect to interest rate changes abroad; therefore its slope is slight-

Table 6.3: Monetary policy effects in case of an expected dollar devaluation[26]

	df^*	dr^*	dp^*	dy	dr
$d(h/q)$	(+)	(−)	(+)	(+)	(+)
di^*	+	(−)	(+)	(+)	(+)
di	−	+	−	−	+

[25] The impact of U.S. interest policies on the model's variables (*table 6.3, third row*) remains qualitatively unchanged.

[26] Signs in brackets depend solely on $\delta > 0$. Because of the dimensional differences in [6.12] the parameter δ should take on very small values only.

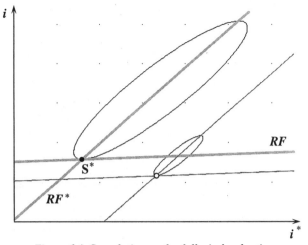

Figure 6.4: Speculation on the dollar's devaluation

ly positive (*figure 6.4*). As the assumption $x = 0$ still holds (the Fed does not bother about foreign claims to American gold), U.S. loss is zero in all points on *RF*. The foreign player will choose its Stackelberg-leader position S^*, which is accepted by both agents. Assume that the Fed does *not* pursue excessive output targets ($y_T = 0$). Nevertheless, if the composition of the Fed's assets changes in favour of h, the involuntary money creation abroad creates an ever growing loss for the foreign player: in order to ward off excessive speculative capital inflows, he is forced to lower his interest rate (RF^* shifts to the left), which fuels inflation from domestic credit creation; and the same effect would result from the decision to keep rates high, where money growth emerges from the purchase of the excess dollar supply on the foreign exchange. On the other hand, the increase of the U.S. rate of interest, brought about by the upward shift of *RF*, always suffices to neutralize the imported goods demand effect from foreign monetary expansion.

In spite of the formal logic of the above argument however, it can be doubted whether Triffin hit the crucial point. Actually, despite some rhetorics, there were practically no attempts to substitute gold for dollar assets. France was the exception: she began to convert dollar assets into gold – and proposed to double the gold price. Instead of a shrinking of the U.S. banking system's balances, which such a conversion would have brought about, dollar liabilities surged at the end of the 1960s (*figure 6.3*).[27] And when the dollar was declared irredeemable in 1971, it did not terminate the Bretton Woods system.

---

[27] The "first generation" model of exchange rate crises teaches that a dwindling stock of reserves is absorbed by speculators in one sweep (cf. Krugman 1979, Bordo 1993, De Grauwe 1996: 44-8).

6.4   The Deterioration of the External Balance and World Inflation

> The United States has had no external reason for trying to
> avoid inflation, because any consèquential deficit would be
> financed by accumulations of dollars in the rest of the world;
> and because a U.S. deficit implies a surplus in the rest of the
> world, the rest of the world as a whole has had no external
> reason for trying to avoid inflation either.
>
> *Harry G. Johnson*[28]

> A nation, most of all a great world power, does not want to
> be hampered in its domestic policies, or in its international
> security or political objectives, by external economic con-
> straints, and specifically by the need to guard against a
> breakdown of the monetary system.
>
> *Paul A. Volcker*[29]

The opinion that the limitedness of the American gold stock would inevitably
cause a confidence problem can be countered by looking back at the gold standard. The Bank of England had managed to maintain the credibility of the exchange rate of the pound, given an even larger imbalance between foreign indebtedness and domestic gold reserves. But in the British case the structure of the balance of payments supported the efficacy of the Bank's interest policy, as the surplus in the current account reduced the stabilization problem to the restriction of
net capital exports.

The U.S. were in a similar position until the mid 1960s (*table 6.4*). Despite substantial military spending abroad the overall deficit was produced by net private
foreign investment which – as in the British case – could easily be matched by
short-term capital movements. But in the 1970s things had changed markedly: a
mounting trade deficit was responsible for the deterioration of the basic balance. It
became evident that the stabilization of the dollar, in times of pressure, now entailed heavy welfare costs in terms of lost output and employment. After the 1970
recession, which had not stopped U.S. inflation, there was little hope that the Fed
would "invest" anew in the external stabilization of the dollar by a hike in interest
rates; instead, rates were further lowered (*figures 6.2, 6.5*).

Henceforth, the scenario of producing a recession at home for the mere purpose of
defending the external value of the dollar seemed to be an incredible option. "The
high current account deficit shows that there is no way, except by measures that
would seriously deflate the economy in order to reduce imports, the Federal Reserve can make dollars scarce. And, without the Federal Reserve being able to
make dollars scarce relative to foreigners' payment commitments by 'controlling'

---

[28] Johnson 1972: 334.
[29] Volcker 1978/79: 7.

Table 6.4: U.S. balance of payments (bill. dollar)[30]

	1960	1964	1971	1977
Trade in commodities and services	2.2	3.9	-5.8	-30.7
Capital income	2.3	3.9	4.6	11.9
Balance	*4.5*	*7.8*	*-1.2*	*-18.8*
Military and government expenditure	-3.9	-3.8	-4.8	-1.3
Balance	*0.6*	*4.0*	*-6.0*	*-20.1*
Long-term private investment	-3.9	-6.6	-9.8	-10.3
Deficit: Short-term and reserve movements	*3.3*	*2.6*	*15.8*	*30.4*

offshore investments, the continued use of the dollar as an international currency is in jeopardy."[31]

The Bretton Woods system did not collapse because of a credibility problem with respect to the partial gold backing of the dollar, but rather because the general course of American economic policy making appeared less and less to conform to the requirements which have to be met by a key currency country. Throughout the 1960s, the U.S. had hardly shown any hesitation in financing a war abroad, and employment and social policies at home by way of monetary expansion. The continuous worsening of the current account[32] was accompanied by a fiscal behaviour which was not in line with the other G7 countries, if notorious high-deficit Italy is excluded (*figure 6.5*).

The U.S. felt no external compulsion for a monetary restriction; but this is, in a way, a typical privilege of a key currency country. The crucial flaw in the working of the international monetary system was that the Fed, being the world's key central bank, failed to exert the necessary liquidity pressure on its "tier-two" banks abroad: foreign countries were flooded with dollars, and thus likewise felt no need

---

[30] Data from Minsky 1979: 112, cf. Frankel 1988.

[31] Minsky 1979: 113.

[32] Volcker's attempt to put the loss of American competitiveness down to an initial misalignment in the Bretton Woods treaty is hardly convincing, because the deterioration of the U.S. current account can be explained by altering inflation differentials in the 1960s: "With the benefit of hindsight, it would seem that an erosion of the United States competitive position was implicit in the postwar arrangements. First Europe and later – with even greater momentum – Japan brought its industrial capacity and efficiency close to United States standards. It took some twenty years, but eventually the United States payment position was irreparably undermined" (1978/79: 6).

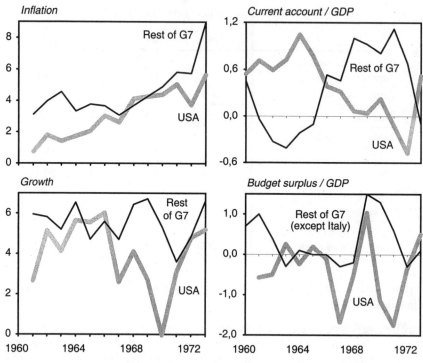

Figure 6.5: U.S. macro variables compared to G7 countries[33]

to contain nominal demand. But even if they preferred to do so on their own account, they were not able to protect their money, goods and labour markets from
the dollar glut. Inflation in G7 countries finally was even higher than in the U.S.,
as a combined result of the two scenarios illustrated above (*figures 6.1 c, 6.4*).
Finally foreign countries, first and foremost Germany, chose to uncouple from the
inflationary money machine by abolishing the fixed dollar exchange rate.

It is tempting to ask whether Bretton Woods collapsed because of a *constructional
flaw* of the system or because of *inappropriate actions* in economic policy.
Whereas the gold standard was not "constructed" by politicians, but emerged out
of the tradition and the practice of the (international) banking sector, the Bretton
Woods rules reflected explicit or implicit policy goals. But over the time, the factual working of the system (the "rules" of market forces) diverged from written in-
structions and theoretical views.

One commitment, which was laid down explicitly, the fixed dollar price of gold,
was unnecessary and proved to be destabilizing; whereas one other requirement,
some device for a credible long-run stability of money prices, received insuffi-

---

[33] Data from OECD: Main Economic Indicators, Economic Outlook.

cient attention. The half-hearted gold backing of the dollar should have been eliminated from the treaty.[34] There is little doubt that the rise in world inflation is to be
explained by a monetary expansion in the U.S. "whose monetary authorities essentially played the role accorded to gold miners in 19th century monetarty theory".[35] It is true that the link between dollars and gold might have been established,
just in order to enforce economic policies in the U.S. which strive for nominal stability of market values; but then the commitment should have been designed more
effectively, allowing also private market agents to exchange dollars for U.S. gold.
The high rate of world growth which is causally attributed to the Bretton Woods
system, the "golden age of economic development"[36], should be seen in context
with a progressive erosion of the nominal-standard economy which made itself
felt in the early 1970s.

Compared to the preceding gold standard, political considerations began more and
more to dominate attitudes towards currency matters. This applies to the reluctance of the U.S. to acknowledge the currency order as a restraint for the making
of world and domestic policies; but also seems to be true with regard to the
dwindling acceptance of the "hegemony" of a key currency country and its supposed "privileges". The financing of (temporary) U.S. balance-of-payments deficits by foreign financial investment, in principle, was a usual by-product of a national money functioning as a key currency, but was even associated with U.S.
imperialism in the 1960s. The indisputable failure of the U.S. to act according to
the behavioural requirements of a responsible guide of the world currency system
was condemned as if arising from almost a criminal intent.[37] Perhaps sterling was
the last currency which was used on a world scale without unnecessary political
reservations against its "nationality".

---

[34] "This collapse of dollar-based par values was hardly inevitable. If the U.S. Federal Reserve System had continued to anchor the common price level, and if the Americans had
not asserted their legal right to adjust the dollar exchange rate as promised by the Bretton Woods Articles, the fixed dollar exchange parities could have continued indefinitely
once the residual commitment to gold convertibility was terminated" (McKinnon 1993:
26).

[35] Laidler/Nobay 1976: 305.

[36] Davidson 1999: 97, cf. Bordo 1993.

[37] "It was not 'high living' that wrought the change in the dollar. Rather was the deliberate
exploitation of its role in the international system to defray current government expenditure abroad, to obtain resources and to accumulate high-income-bearing assets against
paper obligations of steadily depreciating value. It was the result of military and corpo-
rate megalomania" (Balogh 1973: 33, cf. Kindleberger 1967).

7. The European Paper Money Standard: A "DM Club"[1]

7.1 The Determination of the Key Currency by Market Forces

> Markets, not governmental intentions, make and sustain an international currency.
>
> *Paul A. Volcker*[2]

> For political reasons the dominance of one currency cannot be justified in the long term.
>
> *Toni Pierenkämper*[3]

The driving forces for the foundation of the European Monetary System (EMS) in 1979 were located mainly in the sphere of politics, and not in the financial market sector; only later the Bundesbank was initiated into the plans. The Germans hoped to achieve a better protection against unwanted spells of mark appreciation by forming a fixed-exchange-rate union containing also weak-currency countries; and the French wished to escape from German leadership in monetary policy affairs which they had painfully perceived, more and more, in the postwar era. France's aim was to gain some influence on German monetary policy making, without sacrificing parts of her own national autonomy.[4]

The attempt to built a European "democratic" currency system without any explicit "leadership" shows in the creation of an artificial currency, the European Currency Unit, intended to become the common reference point of national currencies. Each national currency was fixed in ECU units, but the ECU itself was constructed as a *basket* of all currencies; which implied that – in case of bilateral exchange rate changes – the "anchor" of the EMS over the years would devalue against better performing national currencies. Thus it is no surprise that the ECU remained in the status of a pure official money of account, and was hardly used in market contracts. Interestingly enough, the question of how to provide for a nominal anchor in the EMS was left unanswered in the institutional set-up of the system. This omission was all the more grave because, for the first time in the history of currency orders, an international monetary system was created where no single currency was linked to a metallic "reserve"; gold had been completely demonetized.

---

[1] The term "Deutsche Mark Club" was coined (presumably among others) by Dornbusch (1987).

[2] Volcker 1978/79: 5.

[3] Pierenkämper 1999: 45.

[4] Cf. Story 1988, Bernholz 1998.

Box 14: The European Monetary System in 1979 – The Spirit of the Treaty[5]

All Member Countries

I. Fix a par value for the exchange rate in terms of the European Currency Unit, a basket of EMS currencies weighted according to country size.

II. Keep par value stable in the short run by symmetrically limiting range of variation in each bilateral exchange rate to 2.25 percent on either side of its central rate.

III. When an exchange rate threatens to breech its bilateral limit, the strong-currency central bank must lend freely to the weak-currency central bank to support the rate.

IV. Adjust par values in the intermediate term if necessary to realign national price levels – but only by collective agreement within the EMS.

V. Work symmetrically toward convergence of national macroeconomic policies and unchanging long-run par values for exchange rates.

VI. Keep free convertibility for current-account payments.

VII. Hold reserves mainly as European Currency Units with the European Fund for Monetary Cooperation, and reduce dollar reserves. Avoid holding substantial reserves in other EMS currencies.

VIII. Repay central bank debts quickly from exchange reserves, or by borrowing from the European Fund for Monetary Cooperation within strict longer-term credit limits.

IX. No member country's money is to be a reserve currency, nor is its national monetary policy to be (asymmetrically) the nominal anchor for the group.

The character of any fixed-exchange-rate system is revealed by its intervention rules. If a bilateral exchange rate should deviate from its target level, the central banks of *both* countries involved were obliged to intervene in a *symmetrical* fashion: any currency's excess supply on the foreign exchange would be absorbed by purchases on the part of the "strong" currency bank and by sales of reserves on the part of the "weak" currency bank. Thus the concomitant monetary effects of interventions work from both sides to correct the imbalance. Obviously, the burden of adjustment ought not to fall on the deficit country alone. A loss of competitiveness in one country should also trigger a monetary expansion in the surplus economy.

Let the domestic country be Germany, and all other EMS member countries be integrated into the foreign player. Supply and demand equations [5.2] and [5.3], and their foreign counterparts, continue to apply. Money demand at home and abroad is given by [5.4] and [6.4], respectively. But with inflation differentials playing a prominent role in the EMS, in spite of the before-mentioned adjustment procedure market agents take into account the possibility of exchange rate realignments; thus the market rate of interest in the foreign country diverges from the German rate by

---

5   Reproduced from McKinnon 1993: 36, cf. De Grauwe 1994a: 98-103.

some expected rate of devaluation which depends on differences of national price levels.[6]

$$r^* = r + \delta\left(p^* - p\right) \qquad [7.1]$$

With respect to money supply, at first it is assumed that both central banks keep home (*h*) and foreign (*f*) interest bearing assets[7], as basic balancing items of domestic money creation, distinct from short-term operations of interest rate policies. The economic logic of the money supply equation is unaffected by the empirical trend that the traditional policy of discounting bills has been more and more displaced by repurchase agreements with the commercial banking system, where long-term bonds are bought and sold on a short-term basis.

$$m = h + f - \mu i \qquad [7.2]$$

$$m^* = h^* + f^* - \mu i^* \qquad [7.3]$$

Counting equations and variables reveals that not all monetary aggregates can be endogenous. This is the other side of the $n - 1$ problem: one country *has* to pursue an independent monetary policy. The EMS tried to circumvent the involuntary rise of a key currency by prescribing a symmetrical intervention rule (so that the autonomous money variable is "shared" by all system members)

$$df = -\eta\, df^* \qquad [7.4]$$

where the coefficient η should equal unity in the ideal case. If all domestic factors of money creation are kept constant, the change of foreign reserves abroad can be computed as

$$df^* = \frac{\delta(\beta+\sigma)+2\varepsilon-1}{(1+\eta)\Psi}\left(dw-dw^*\right) + \frac{\delta\alpha\sigma-(1+\alpha)}{(1+\eta)\Psi}\left(dg-dg^*\right) \qquad [7.5]$$

where $\qquad \Psi = 1 + \alpha\left(2\varepsilon + \delta\beta\right) \qquad [7.6]$

A wage shock abroad, or any supply-side deterioration of foreign competitiveness relative to the home country ($dw^* > dw$), will cause a reserve loss of the foreign central bank and, according to [7.4], an increase of foreign assets on the part of the domestic central bank. This sets off a monetary restriction abroad and an ex-

---

[6] This formulation appears to be particularly appropriate as a constant or even shrinking difference of national rates of *inflation* still implies a continuous divergence of *price levels* and, hence, competitiveness (cf. De Grauwe 1994a: 122-3).

[7] As in the Bretton Woods model, foreign reserves are invested at the bond market, so that no complications arise with regard to national money demand equations.

pansion at home.[8] Note that domestic prices then rise on account of the twofold effect of the direct impact of increased export demand and as a consequence of the induced monetary expansion (due to $\eta > 0$):

$$\frac{dp}{dw^*} = \frac{\varepsilon\alpha\sigma + \eta\alpha\left[(\delta\beta + \varepsilon)(\beta + \sigma) + \beta(\varepsilon - 1)\right]}{(1 + \eta)\Psi\Omega} \qquad [7.7]$$

But the immediate symmetrical liquidity effect is supplemented by an overall monetary restriction in both countries in the medium term: the foreign central bank is forced to replenish its stock of foreign assets, or is obliged to refund reserves if lent from the domestic central bank in the first place; and the latter – just because the EMS did not provide any rules for national policy making – may feel inclined to sterilize the monetary effect of exchange rate interventions from its money supply by choosing $dh = -df$ (which let the Bundesbank agree to the EMS treaty). The net result is after all that the deficit country alone has to bear the adjustment costs: the basic "law" of international monetary relations, which the EMS treaty aimed to abolish.

The general message is straightforward: if countries with different long-run price trends form a fixed-exchange-rate system, and if monetary policy in the most-stability-oriented country is able and willing to continue its course, an excess demand for that stable currency will build up. It will become the key currency via an excess demand as a means of payment, due to its relative scarcity in cross-border goods market transactions. Other central banks then are forced to follow the key country's interest rate in order to attract a sufficient amount of key currency reserves which are needed to balance the foreign exchange. Of course, a relatively low rate of inflation and a permanent pressure for revaluation will also induce agents to keep key currency financial assets.

These joint effects had strengthened the international role of the mark already since the 1950s – incidentally against the preferences of German politicians and (central) bankers. The president of the Bundesbank explicitly called the mark a *"reserve currency against the will"*: "First, the capacity of our financial markets is too small. Foreign monetary authorities cannot be provided with sufficient and fast-to-liquidate investment assets without straining the working of our markets or without forced interventions on money and capital markets which are not justifiable for internal reasons. Second, the economic and financial power of the FRG is too weak to bear the burden which can come along with international reserve movements. Finally, during the building up of a reserve currency, there is a tendency of overvaluation which however may become effective later when that phase is over or when reserves held in that currency are reduced. Therefore, the

---

[8] The second term on the r.h.s. of [7.5] indicates that the consequences of divergent demand shocks are more ambiguous as the direct effect of a demand expansion on reserve flows is countered by expected devaluation, due to rising prices.

Bundesbank has resisted the tendency of keeping the mark as a reserve asset, but had to accept it willy nilly to some extent".[9] In the late 1970s, during the flight from the dollar, the international role of the mark increased when investors diversified funds in various currencies, and "the mark was appreciating because of an insufficient creation of mark assets".[10]

Box 15: The European Monetary System as a Greater Deutsche Mark Area 1979-92[11]

All Member Countries

I. through V. Same as in EMS "Spirit of the Treaty" (Box 14).

VI. Avoid using the credit facilities of the European Fund for Monetary Cooperation.

Member Countries Except Germany

VII. Intervene intramarginally, within formal bilateral parity limits, to stabilize the national exchange rate vis-à-vis the DM. Increasingly intervene in DM rather than dollars.

VIII. Keep active exchange reserves in interest-bearing DM open-market instruments such as Euromark deposits, as well as in dollar Treasury bonds.

IX. Adjust short-term national money growth and/or short-term interest rates to support exchange market interventions – whether intramarginal or at the bilateral parity limits.

X. Keep adjusting long-term money growth so that domestic price inflation (in tradable goods) converges to, or remains the same as, price inflation in Germany.

XI. Progressively liberalize capital controls.

Germany

XII. Remain passive in the foreign-exchange markets with other European (EMS) countries: free trade with neither a balance-of-payments nor an intramarginal exchange-rate target.

XIII. Keep German capital markets open to foreign governments or private residents as borrowers or depositors.

XIV. Sterilize (perhaps passively) the effects of German or other EMS countries' official interventions in the European foreign-exchange markets on the German monetary base.

XV. Anchor the DM (EMS) price level for tradable goods by an independently chosen German monetary policy.

---

9 Emminger 1978: 8.
10 Dornbusch 1980: 172, cf. De Grauwe 1994a: 114-5. The subsequent crisis of the mark, when – due to Volcker and Reagan – funds were redirected towards the U.S. on a massive scale, will not be studied here as it had no essential influence on the EMS, except for the fact that the weakness of the mark supported its smooth inception.
11 Reproduced from McKinnon 1993: 37.

Empirically, the above theory on the rise of the key currency status of the mark does not apply before the mid 1980s. The large inflation differentials in the early years of the EMS were compensated by frequent exchange rate realignments, and there were only small balances in Germany's goods and asset market transactions with her European partners (*figure 7.1*).

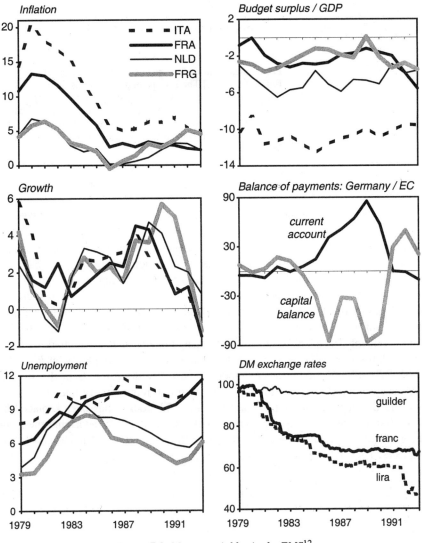

Figure 7.1: Macro variables in the EMS[12]

---

[12] Data from OECD: Economic Outlook, Bundesbank: Monthly Reports, 50 Jahre Deutsche Mark (CD-ROM).

The German surplus began to rise after 1983. After 1987 monetary authorities started to manage the EMS without any further realignments. At that time, the level of European inflation had come down substantially and differentials had narrowed. But the unemployment record showed that the maintenance of monetary stability required a high price.

7.2   The "Advantage" of Fighting Inflation With Tied Hands

> Policy makers in Europe have become mesmerised by the inflation issue. [...] The European policy atmosphere [...] is decidedly unpragmatic, as can be judged from the language of the day: credibility, corsets, targeting, nonaccommodation, restraint, anchors, reputation – a glut of Victoriana. [...] It is difficult to understand the economic benefits of EMS membership.
>
> *Rudiger Dornbusch*[13]

> Better to be a branch of the Bundesbank than an agency of the Tesoro.
>
> *Rudiger Dornbusch*[14]

Contrary to the intentions of its creators the EMS developed into an ordinary, hierarchical key currency system. The actual intervention procedures for analytical purposes can be simplified: central banks in general only keep reserves in "higher ranked" currencies, which as marketable assets can be sold in times of a critical excess supply of the domestic currency. Thus suppose that the Bundesbank neither holds foreign reserves ($f = 0$ in [7.2]) nor intervenes on the market. Its foreign opponent attempts to stabilize the exchange rate as against the mark by varying mark reserves (f^*) and the short-term interest rate; for simplicity let $h^* = 0$ in [7.3]. The solution of the macro model is basically the same as in the Bretton Woods system [6.5-7], but with $\lambda = 0$. Therefore, foreign interest rate policies act only on the distribution of mark assets. The gold stock q has been replaced by some fixed amount of interest bearing mark assets h, which determine the basic level of money supply in both countries. At first, supply and demand shocks are neglected ($w = w^* = g = g^* = 0$).

$$\underline{r} = \underline{r}^* = \frac{1}{\Omega}\left(\mu i - h\right) \qquad\qquad [7.8]$$

$$\underline{f}^* = h + \mu\left(i^* - i\right) \qquad\qquad [7.9]$$

---

[13] Dornbusch 1987: 9-10, 15.
[14] Dornbusch 1989: 358.

$$p = \underline{p}^* = \alpha \underline{y} = \alpha \underline{y}^* = \frac{\alpha \beta}{\Omega}(h - \mu i) \qquad [7.10]$$

The Bundesbank provides the nominal anchor of the system by targeting a constant price level in Germany. The foreign player attaches a weight x^* to his forced target of some optimal quantity of mark assets f_T^*, but mainly prefers to preserve full employment. The loss functions then read:

$$L = p^2 \qquad [7.11]$$

$$L^* = \left(y^*\right)^2 + x^*\left(f_T^* - f^*\right)^2 \qquad [7.12]$$

Inserting the solutions of the macro system (including supply and demand disturbances) and minimizing yields the two reaction functions. The Bundesbank reacts in an unequivocal fashion to shocks as they all endanger price stability. Its absolute supremacy in EMS financial markets, and the lack of any liquidity problem, is expressed by the zero slope of the German reaction function, which says that there is no response to interest rate movements abroad (*figure 7.2*). The foreign central bank however has no autonomy in its interest rate policy with respect to the foreign exchange. It strictly adopts German interest rate moves and responds to various shocks, so that its reserve target is achieved; but according to [7.10] it has no control over output and prices at home.

$$i = \frac{h}{\mu} + \frac{(\delta\beta + \varepsilon + 1/\alpha)\left[\alpha\sigma g + (\beta + \sigma)w\right] + \beta\varepsilon w + \varepsilon\sigma\left(\alpha g^* + w^*\right)}{\mu\beta\Psi} \qquad [7.13]$$

$$i^* = i + \frac{f_T^* - h}{\mu} + \frac{\left[\delta(\beta + \sigma) + 2\varepsilon - 1\right]\left(w^* - w\right) + \left[\delta\alpha\sigma - (1 + \alpha)\right]\left(g^* - g\right)}{\mu\Psi} \qquad [7.14]$$

Since the Bundesbank fixes the level of German interest rates without taking notice of rates abroad, and always can attain a zero loss, the foreign player has the Stackelberg-leader strategy as the best option, which – due to the horizontal form of *RF* – is equivalent to the Nash solution. Without shocks the foreign loss also is zero. Any autonomous supply or demand changes however, at home or abroad, have an effect on output and prices in the foreign country, because the Bundesbank's interest rate responses are designed only to stabilize the German price level[15] and is forced to tolerate only negative repercussions from German wages on

---

[15] A different picture emerges if the Bundesbank should haven taken serious its official money supply target, i.e. $L = (m - m_T)^2$. In that case, the position of its reaction function would remain unaffected by supply and demand shocks. The emerging equilibrium solution at the point of intersection of unchanged *RF* and shifted *RF** would show a lower foreign loss, compared to S*. But actually German interest rate policies served the money supply target only in tranquil times (cf. Bernanke/Mihov 1997).

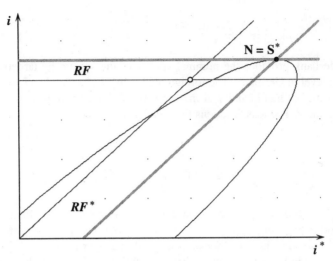

Figure 7.2: Stackelberg solution after a foreign supply shock

home employment (*table 7.1*). The leadership of the Bundesbank, which showed in the timing of its decisions on interest rates and the responses abroad, is to be explained by the lack of foreign player's influence on the relevant macro variables in both countries. Therefore the Bundesbank reacts first to supply and demand shocks, and the central bank abroad adjusts its short-term rate in order to give incentives for capital movements, so that its reserve target can be met.

In particular, a worsening of supply conditions, driven by unfavourable wage or productivity movements, which had been the typical problem of EMS member countries vis-à-vis the German economy, leads to a widening of interest rate differentials; RF^* in general will shift more than RF, and the deterioration of foreign welfare (due to lower output) shows in an expanding loss ellipse (*figure 7.2*). Hence, keeping a fixed nominal exchange rate in times of a disadvantageous inflation differential obviously produces heavy economic costs. But the demonstration of enduring these very costs is said to have formed a "strategy" of fighting inflation which is more *credible* than simply embarking voluntarily on a course of domestic monetary restraint. Because this policy can easily be turned down, inflationary expectations might prove to be sticky. A fixed exchange rate, on the other

Table 7.1: Evaluation of the Stackelberg solution S^*

p	y	y^*	f^*	$r^* - r$
0	$-\dfrac{w}{\alpha}$	$\dfrac{g^* - g - w/\alpha - (\delta\beta + 2\varepsilon)w^*}{\Psi}$	f_T^*	$\dfrac{\delta\left[w^* - w + \alpha\left(g^* - g\right)\right]}{\Psi}$

hand, cannot be varied at will and thus appears as an exogenous constraint for the national economy *and* its policy makers. "For thirteen years the anchoring of the lira [...] served as an intermediate objective on the path to the ultimate goal of disinflation."[16]

This strategy promised to have further crucial advantages:

• Political troubles arising from the side effects of monetary restraint can be limited by using the hard-nosed central bank abroad as a scapegoat. "DM-oriented stabilization policies allowed French politicians to claim the merit of a lowering of inflation, whereas the Bundesbank was made responsible for any negative employment effects of disinflation."[17]

• The exchange rate as the central bank's target can more easily be observed by market agents, compared to some other intermediate monetary policy goals. Thus because the central bank exposes itself to a greater risk of being detected as faulting on its commitments, a policy of disinflation via defending a fixed exchange rate as against a strong currency is said to enhance the credibility of the stabilization goal, to reduce inflationary expectations faster, and therefore to limit the output losses during the period of disinflation.

Both arguments however seem to rely on a sort of policy illusion on the part of the public: it is presumed that market agents cannot trace back a forced monetary restriction to the decision of fixing the exchange rate, and they neglect the possibility of a realignment. That means, the commitment of tying one's hands is not really credible.[18] Actually, weak currencies were devalued until 1987 quite often *(figure 7.1)*. Moreover, inflation came down nearly everywhere during the 1980s; and unemployment was even *higher* in the EMS countries. The trade-off between price stability and unemployment did not improve at all. Maybe the idea that there is a way to disinflate without economic costs by employing institutional reforms and rules is only an illusion.[19]

---

[16] Sarcinelli 1995: 399. The "advantage of tying one's hands" has first been modelled by Giavazzi/Pagano (1988).

[17] Bernholz 1998: 808, cf. Woolley 1984: 14-5.

[18] The story goes that American teenagers in the 1950s often engaged in a "game of chicken". On secluded streets, they would race in their cars one against the other, seemingly heading for a frontal crash. The one lost – and thus proved to be the chicken – who first got scared and tried to get out of the way. According to oral legend some players hit upon a sure-fire recipe to win the game: grasp the steering wheel, pull it out (the cars usually were quite old) and throw it out of the window; make sure that your opponent is able to see what you are doing; as either of you will *have* to make a move, it is him who *must* give in, because you have demonstrated that you *can* not.

[19] "The EMS [...] has in fact worked out to create beachheads for German monetary culture in the member countries' central banks and treasuries. The result may be that tastes have changed. Only in that way can one understand the *growing* enthusiasm for combating inflation even as inflation falls. The explanation is quite obvious from the sociology of clubs. Policy makers fool themselves that joining the club, will by some mystical credibility effects, change the objective trade-offs they face. In fact, it mostly changes

It is obvious that the credibility problem of anti-inflation policies (if there is any) was merely shifted to the foreign exchange market. Expected devaluation takes over the role of inflation expectations in the Phillips-curve model. Note that the foreign output loss is aggravated by expected devaluation which was triggered off by the initial cost push (*table 7.1*). The hypothesis contained in equation [7.1] draws its traditional justification from a trade-balance governed foreign exchange where price differentials cause imbalances, which sooner or later necessitate a change of the relative price of the currencies involved. But if foreign exchange transactions are largely dominated by capital movements, a trade deficit as such will hardly bring about a currency depreciation. Moreover, the implication of the assumption of perfectly interest-elastic portfolio investment is that international markets stand ready to finance *any* trade deficit, as long as offered yields provide a sufficient compensation for any risks.

The exchange rate risk of foreign investors can be derived from the fact that employment consequences of an unfavourable inflation differential add to the loss of the foreign central bank, even without devaluation expectations – but this is exactly the factor which *establishes* the speculation on a realignment. With $\delta > 0$, the speculation becomes self-reinforcing, because employment losses grow, not to speak of the burden of increased interest payments on the public debt. Thus, the general conclusion is: "Monetary stability and credibility are not easily imported, they must be built at home."[20]

7.3   Blowing up the EMS by the Bundesbank's Stabilization Policies

> DM fixation means that France will continue to follow Germany's anti-inflation policy, even though it has no inflation problem. This is the magic spell of gold and the DM or France's lack of confidence in its own policies.
>
> *Rudiger Dornbusch*[21]

> It remains a mystery that the deepest financial markets in the world yielded so remarkably few indications of an imminent crisis.
>
> *Andrew K. Rose / Lars E.O. Svensson*[22]

After 1987 market conditions in the EMS changed in several respects: as already mentioned, realignments were avoided; German interest policies turned on a re-

---

their own cast of mind. [...] EMS membership distorts the mind" (Dornbusch 1989: 16-7, cf. De Grauwe 1994a: 133-40).

[20] Svensson 1994: 465.

[21] Dornbusch 1993: 135.

[22] Rose/Svensson 1995: 111.

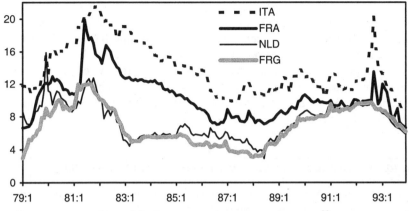

Figure 7.3: Short-term interest rates in the EMS[23]

strictive course, aiming to contain (moderate) inflationary pressures stemming from accelerating growth and, somewhat later, German reunification; and a mounting surplus vis-à-vis her European partners had to be financed by (mainly) short-term capital flows. The macroeconomic consequences of German reunification for the other EMS countries were ambiguous: on the one hand, the German budget deficit grew and the demand-induced redirection of the trade surplus towards the East German Länder, where a large gap between absorption and production opened up, relieved the strain on foreign balances.

The further shrinking of interest rate differentials between 1990-92 can be understood as a proof of the relative strengthening of EMS currencies; credibility gaps apparently were shrinking. But on the other hand, the Bundesbank stubbornly continued to tighten the money market so that the *level* of European interest rates slowly increased – when growth was already faltering throughout Europe (*figures 7.1, 7.3*). Finally the EMS collapsed after two waves of speculative attacks in 1992-93, particularly on the lira, the franc, and the pound, which had entered the system only a short while ago (at an overvalued exchange rate).[24]

The contradictory repercussions of German currency union might have contributed to the fact that the EMS currency crisis had hardly been foreseen in the "for-

---

[23] Call money rates, 6-month rates in Italy until 1989 (data from OECD: Main Economic Indicators).

[24] Technically, the band of permitted exchange rate movements was substantially widened, after the Bundesbank had resorted to the "Emminger letter": before the foundation of the EMS, to dispel the reservations of the Bundesbank, the German government assured that obligatory interventions on the foreign exchange could be suspended if they seriously interfered with the Bundesbank's main task of maintaining price stability. The existence of this escape clause undermined the credibility of the fixed-exchange-rate commitment in the EMS (cf. Eichengreen/Wyplosz 1993, Kenen 1995).

ward looking" financial market. But the asymmetric demand shock originating from the centre country of the EMS required a macroeconomic adjustment: a real appreciation of the mark, as a consequence and containing force of German excess demand. Two of the three possible solutions seemed not to be acceptable on account of national policy preferences: inflation in Germany, or deflation (and more unemployment) in foreign countries. Logically the third route *had* to be taken: the transition to more flexible nominal exchange rates, and some countries temporarily dissolved from the EMS.[25]

Box 16: *The Macroeconomic Consequences of German Currency Union*

The consequences of (fiscal) demand expansion in Germany for the internal and external equilibrium in the EMS countries can be studied by means of goods market equations in Germany and abroad. The foreign market of interest again is affected by inflation-based devaluation expectations. The (fixed) nominal exchange rate of the mark e is specified explicitly.

$$y = g - \beta r + \varepsilon\left(e - p + p^*\right) \tag{7.15}$$

$$p = w + \alpha y \tag{7.16}$$

$$y^* = g^* - \beta\left[r + \delta\left(p^* - p\right)\right] - \varepsilon\left(e - p + p^*\right) \tag{7.17}$$

$$p^* = w^* + \alpha y^* \tag{7.18}$$

From these equations the condition for price stability in Germany, for convenience normalized to $p = 0$, can be derived and visualized as the *PS* line in a *r-e* space (*figure 7.4*). It exhibits a positive slope as a rise in the exchange rate and a rise in the rate of interest have contrary effects on demand; thus both variables have to move in line if some demand-determined level of prices is to be maintained. The curve shifts with autonomous shocks: changes in interest or exchange rates are required to offset their immediate price effect. Points above *PS* represent a deficiency of effective demand causing deflationary tendencies and rising unemployment.

$$r_{PS} = \frac{[\delta\beta + \varepsilon + 1/\alpha](\alpha g + w) + \varepsilon(\alpha g^* + w^*)}{\beta \Psi} + \frac{\varepsilon(\delta\alpha\beta + 1)}{\beta\Psi} e \tag{7.19}$$

Likewise $y^* = 0$, the full employment condition in the foreign country FE^*, can be derived. Its slope is assumed (without affecting the results) to be slightly negative.

$$r_{FE^*} = \frac{(\delta\beta + \varepsilon)(\alpha g + w - w^*) + (1 + \alpha\varepsilon) g^*}{\beta\Psi} + \frac{\varepsilon(\delta\alpha\beta - 1)}{\beta\Psi} e \tag{7.20}$$

A domestic demand shock requires *PS* to shift upwards, more than FE^*. In a flexible-exchange-rate regime the new optimal market equilibrium would move from A to B.

---

[25] Cf. Artis/Lewis 1993, Eichengreen/Wyplosz 1993, De Grauwe 1994a: 121-7, 140-2, Svensson 1994, Rose/Svensson 1995.

But if $\bar{e}$ is kept fixed and the interest rate is raised, point C implies unemployment abroad.

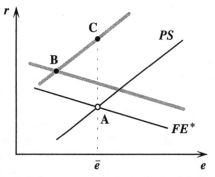

Figure 7.4: An asymmetric demand shock in the EMS

The emerging gap between domestic and foreign prices due to the demand shock

$$dp - dp^* = \frac{2\alpha\varepsilon}{\Psi} de + \frac{\alpha}{\Psi} dg \qquad [7.21]$$

reveals the basic economic policy conflict: if the Bundesbank precludes a rise in German prices ($dp = 0$), the necessary adjustment of the real exchange rate can only be accomplished by deflation (and unemployment) abroad. If however this also cannot be tolerated ($dp^* = 0$), revaluing the mark by $de = -dg / (2\varepsilon)$ remains as the only solution.

In particular, the speculation on the franc may seem puzzling as inflation in France was even lower than in Germany since 1991. But with a high real rate of interest at the same time, unemployment was steadily on the rise (*figure 7.1*). The macroeconomic situation thus could hardly be interpreted as a regime of monetary stability, but rather of "repressed inflation". The strategy of enforcing supply-side reforms and technological progress by means of an overvalued franc throughout the 1980s had not been that successful[26], and political quarters in France pleaded for more expansive macro policies. The relative low rate of French inflation thus could not be taken as a sign of monetary solidity; quite the contrary: it indicated – from the point of view of financial and foreign exchange markets – the risk of a fundamental shift in French policy making.

---

[26] "An overvaluation, created by market forces thus establishing an international reserve currency, backfires, if being imposed by monetary policy. If an overvaluation is no longer the consequence of capital imports, it induces capital export: the more overvalued the currency, the cheaper is the flight from it. [...] At the same time, the rate of interest has to rise in line with the degree of overvaluation in order to prevent a flight from the currency" (Riese 1993: 166, cf. Blanchard/Muet 1993, Fitoussi 1993, Lordon 1998).

France in the early 1990s no longer suffered from an external disequilibrium but from a credibility gap which impaired the sustainability of her strategy of stabilization policy. For political reasons, in times of rising unemployment, the French simply could not *afford* a low rate of inflation, because it undermined the "dogma" of indispensable monetary austerity: if a low rate of inflation is reached, economic policy ought to address the now more urgent problem of high unemployment. But on the other hand, the French government tried to stick to monetary stability, in order not to rekindle inflationary expectations; in that case, the sacrifice in terms of employment losses, made with the aim of reaching a state of low inflation, would have been futile. Immediately before the attack on the franc competent observers demanded concerted devaluation and monetary expansion in EMS countries in order to put the Bundesbank under pressure; a marked revaluation of the mark would have added to the internal economic problems in Germany. "But, in France, this is considered unsound, just as it was in the 1930s to leave gold."[27]

The internal credibility gap nevertheless showed in a speculative in stability on the foreign exchange market. The formulation of the expected exchange rate devaluation should be reassessed. Instead of [7.1] which relied on inflation differentials, the modified interest parity condition should be made dependent on unemployment:

$$r^* = r - \delta y^* \qquad\qquad [7.22]$$

Contrary to the traditional approach [7.22] can be valid only in conjunction with policy preferences, as contained in [7.12]. The failure of economic policy to attain its targets makes the commitment technology vulnerable to speculative attacks. A startling implication is that a fixed-exchange-rate regime may appear to be stable on account of its economic fundamentals for a long time, but when a country is hit by some adverse shock, speculators may guess that it is too expensive for the government to maintain the commitment and that it will renege.[28]

The consequences of the modified foreign-exchange equilibrium condition for the policy game are far reaching. A demand expansion in the home country – as in the above case of rising wages abroad – prompts the Bundesbank to increase interest rates, and the foreign central bank has to adjust, so that with traditional devaluation expectations the equilibrium solution S_1^* emerges (starting from the no-shock constellation S_0^* where the corresponding reaction functions have been omitted; *figure 7.5*). Now substituting [7.22] for [7.1] in the macroeconomic

---

27 Dornbusch 1993: 135, cf. Eichengreen et al. 1995a, Masson 1995.

28 An even more startling implication is that speculators themselves, in principle, have an incentive to attack a currency: the interest rate increases necessary to defend the parity entails output losses which then convince the authorities that a devaluation is the optimal solution. This is the simple outline of the second generation of balance-of-payments crises which in a way are self-fulfilling (cf. Obstfeld 1986).

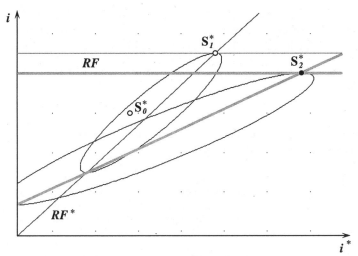

*Figure 7.5: Unemployment-based devaluation expectations
after monetary restriction in the key currency country*

model, changes the position and slope particularly of the foreign reaction function. The new RF^*, leading to the equilibrium solution S_2^*, is flatter, because the lowering of foreign income (due to a monetary restriction on the part of the Bundesbank) further *aggravates* the credibility problem of foreign monetary policy which necessitates a larger reaction coefficient di^*/di, whereas with inflation-based devaluation expectations a rise in interest rates dampens price increases and thus simultaneously the speculative pressure.

The expectation effect [7.22] thus further worsens the market position of the foreign player. The positive feedback between rising interest rates, employment and credibility losses produces a nearly perfect dilemma (even if the monetary restriction of the Bundesbank is somewhat relieved: RF shifts downwards, because the rise in the long rate abroad contributes to the intended dampening of demand dynamics). "An increase in the unemployment rate raises the costs to the government of continuing to pursue policies of price stability. When the public observes unemployment, it revises upward its forecast of the probability that the authorities will deviate in order to reflate the economy; this in turn requires the authorities to raise the discount rate to defend the currency, which only serves to aggravate their unemployment problem."[29]

This last argument has to be qualified however: note that (as in the case of *table 7.1* above) the increase of i^* only contributes to the attainment of the reserve target, whereas the output loss abroad is caused by the joint effect of the policy-induced rise of the long market rate in both countries and the speculation-induced

---

[29] Eichengreen et al. 1995a: 260-1.

additional rise of the market rate in the foreign country. Note also that the collapse of a fixed-exchange-rate regime in general is not due to a lack of foreign reserves, which would make it technically impossible to stick to the external target of monetary policy, but rather due to the economic costs connected with the endurance of devaluation premia on domestic interest rates.[30]

7.4   The Conflict between Internal and External Equilibrium in the Key Currency Country

> The Bundesbank fulfils its European task by accepting its responsibility for providing the nominal anchor; this position is in line with a policy which aims for internal price stability.
> *Otmar Issing*[31]

> A key currency which loses its stability and thus has to be stabilized itself becomes a burden to all.
> *Olaf Sievert*[32]

> The system broke down because other countries were unwilling to go along with the policies of the center country.
> *Michael D. Bordo*[33]

The focus finally is on the key currency country itself. As in the Bretton Woods system, the EMS collapsed because of a basic instability emanating from the centre country. But whereas U.S. monetary policy failed to provide a liquidity constraint for the world economy, the policy of the Bundesbank was too restrictive in the early 1990s, with regard to the EMS, although the chosen path of interest rates might have been appropriate as far as the German problem of excess-demand driven inflation is concerned. It is true, just in order to avoid the Bretton Woods failure, that a key currency country should be characterized by a stable price level, if possible, to provide a nominal anchor for the monetary system as a whole – but it is not paradoxical to add the qualification: the key currency country should never be in a position to need to employ restrictive interest policies in order to *achieve* price stability at home.

The issue can be clarified by comparing three different types of instabilities in key currency systems (*table 7.2*). The problem of a *general* weakness, for whatever reason, of the leading currency on the foreign exchange (case 1) can easily be settled by means of a higher interest rate in the leading country, so that internal

---

[30]   Cf. De Grauwe 1994a: 126-7, Obstfeld/Rogoff 1995.
[31]   Issing 1994: 687, cf. Issing 1992.
[32]   Sievert 1993: 20.
[33]   Bordo 1993: 181.

Table 7.2: Crises in key currency systems

Policy of ... Case	leading country	all member countries	strong member country
(1) Weakness of the key currency with respect to all currencies	restrictive, internal disequilibrium, but external equilibrium by withdrawing the key currency excess supply from the market	no reaction, no substantial consequences for the national economy	---
(2) Weakness of the key currency in relation to a strong member currency	no reaction or restrictive (defending the key currency position)	---	expansive (standard case) or constant/restrictive (currency competition)
(3) Inflation in leading country	internal equilibrium by a rise of key currency interest rates, external disequilibrium	restrictive policy restores external and disturbs internal equilibrium, less employment	---

macroeconomic conditions abroad will be affected only by the dampening of demand in the key currency country. If only one member currency tends to appreciate against the key currency (case 2), policy makers in that foreign country will usually turn to a more expansive course, exploiting the greater latitude granted by the foreign exchange. Only if they refuse to relax the stance of monetary policy, a currency competition (like the sterling-dollar battle in the 1920s) might emerge.

Inflationary pressures in the key currency country, with general external equilibrium at the outset (case 3), produce a rather complicated situation with respect to markets and policies. The prospects for exchange rate realignments are uncertain: the standard response of arising devaluation expectations will hardly apply to a key currency; rather, market agents may bet on a revaluation brought about by the key central bank's monetary tightening. Indeed, it will be difficult for policy makers abroad to explain to the public why they should *deviate* from internal equilibrium at home and deliberately bear employment losses, just for the useless sharing of the burden of anti-inflation policies in the leading country. It is therefore the political logic which urges the uncoupling of the foreign exchange link by which deflationary tendencies are imported. Thus the key currency country becomes the failure of the policy game as it manages to contain its internal inflation problem, but only at the expense of the cohesion of the fixed-exchange-rate system.[34]

---

[34] Cf. Riese 1993, Canzoneri et al. 1997.

In comparison to the gold standard, modern paper standard systems like the EMS are less able to absorb supply or demand disturbances, particularly if they emanate from the leading country. The simple reason is that the Bank of England did not pursue stabilization policies in the modern sense of the term: it did not react to an increase in prices as such, but it only reacted if inflation led to a loss of gold reserves. Therefore the member countries of the international gold standard were not exposed to monetary restrictions to the same degree as has been the case in the EMS. An algebraic inspection of the S^*-solutions reveals that, except for a demand shock in the foreign member country, the gold standard in all countries caused weaker interest rate responses to shocks, if compared to the EMS.

If the Bank of England supported the stability of the gold standard by pursuing the goal of external equilibrium, and if the Bundesbank undermined the stability of the EMS by fighting inflation at home, an obvious question arises: why could the Bundesbank not stabilize the EMS by accepting the character of the mark as an investment currency and give a larger weight to the target of external equilibrium? A simple rule might prescribe that the interest rate, partly, ought to be oriented to the state of the capital balance: decreasing in case of net capital imports, and rising if capital is leaving.[35] But the first case probably comes into conflict with the goal of preserving price stability. Again, this is an implication of the famous $n - 1$ problem: if the key currency central bank in a paper money standard took care of the stability of exchange rates it would lose its influence on income and prices. Thus some other institution (a foreign central bank? the unions?) would have to take over the job of providing the nominal anchor of the system. The second case represents the EMS constellation during the late 1980s where short-term capital exports from Germany financed foreign trade deficits; a *rise* of German interest rates only would have added to the balance-of-payments problems abroad.

The crucial point is that the key currency central bank in a paper money standard according to the solutions given in [7.8] and [7.10] cannot control *relative* macro variables, including trade balances. A loss function of the form

$$L = p^2 + x\left(r^* - r\right)^2 \qquad\qquad [7.23]$$

therefore would not lead to any substantial change of policy making, at least as long as expected devaluation is, following [7.1], assumed to depend on price differentials. The key central bank's monetary policy acts on prices in both countries in the same way. A variation of the key country's interest rate changes the liquidity condition in the whole currency system, and not the state of the home money market relative to conditions abroad.

A somewhat different picture emerges if [7.22] is used to yield

---

[35] Obviously this suggested rule is modelled with regard to the successful Bank of England policy (cf. Riese 1993).

$$L = p^2 + x\left(-\delta y^*\right)^2 \qquad [7.24]$$

This comes down to a course of monetary policy which aims at a compromise between stability (at home) and full employment (abroad). Macro variables in both countries then are affected by shocks; and the definiteness of the home price level as the nominal anchor of the system is lost (*table 7.3*). But the knowledge that the strongest central bank of the international monetary system will take care of each member country's exchange rate will alter the "Rules of the Game": the external constraint is bound to lose its wage-disciplining force; the random-like character particularly of wage shocks[36] would probably vanish, making room for an inflationary bias in wage and price formation.

Table 7.3: Shock effects when monetary policy looks at foreign output

	dy	dp	dy^*	dp^*	dr
dw	−	+	−	−	+
dw^*	+	+	−	+	?
dg	+	+	−	−	+
dg^*	−	−	+	+	+

A final alternative for the Bundesbank would have been to adopt a goal of price stability *in all EMS countries*. In that case, price increases in Germany due to unification excess demand would have had to be assessed as relative, i.e. regional price changes. The adequate degree of monetary restriction applied to contain *average* inflationary pressure in Europe obviously would have had been more moderate. This line of reasoning was also used to support the transition to a monetary union (which can be seen as the final, logical step of a policy of joint price stabilization). However, an average price level of a very large economic area is not very meaningful because market reactions in regions with higher inflation might produce destabilizing feedbacks to be felt in the whole currency area (wage policies, capital flight etc.). This might pose a severe problem for the European Monetary Union if regional disparities should prevail.

---

[36] Bordo's approach (1993) to attribute an endogenous character to demand shocks, and to treat supply shocks as exogenous, appears less convincing.

Summary of Part III

The three famous key currency systems of the 20th century had at least one thing in common: in all cases theories or plans on the design of these systems differed markedly from their factual mode of operation. Theories and plans envisaged competitive systems where none of the member countries had a dominant role to play. The reason for this way of thinking may have been twofold:

• Economic theory tends to apply its deep-seated real-barter approach also to the sphere of international relations and thus postulates that national currencies are merely used as arbitrary transitional vehicles in economic calculations and transactions.

• From a political point of view, the illusion of national currencies equipped with "equal rights" fits to the alleged democratic feature of a private-ownership economy and also corresponds to the aversion of national governments to subordinate themselves to the financial supremacy of some other country.

Actually however, market agents choose a nominal money standard which then is used as a framework of economic behaviour. The need for a point of reference in decentralized decision processes is particularly urgent in the uncertain set-up of an international economic system. The "choice" of a key currency should be seen as the result of an evolutionary process of searching for the most efficient international money of account and medium of payment. The search may take a short cut by historical contingencies, but in general a large and successful trade performance and its implication of building up a creditor position in international relations were a useful initial condition for a national currency to become a key currency. In any case, agents on international markets will permanently assess whether a key currency meets the crucial requirements: offering perfect liquidity (a large asset market) and stability (the lack of any risk of devaluation).

Just because national policy makers in general prefer to be independent from abroad, some explanation is necessary as to how leadership by some country is established and why other countries accept their subordinate position. Even if an international monetary system is not built on a formal agreement, it can only persist if member countries in some way assume that leaving the system (and establishing independently chosen national rules for monetary policy) would not serve their interests. These interests can be "translated" into economic policy goals, targeted on output, employment and prices, on the one hand, and the preservation of the equilibrium of the balance of payments, on the other.

Leadership can be defined in terms of the degree of autonomy in national economic policy making. The issue might be expressed in a slightly paradoxical way: A nation is to be regarded as the leader in international *monetary* relations if it is able to pursue a policy enhancing its *real economic* welfare without facing financial markets constraints resulting from monetary policy decisions of other countries. Contrary to a widespread opinion in the literature, such a state of sovereignty is not necessarily equivalent to a leadership position in terms of game theory. Here, the "Stackelberg leader" finds an advantage in orienting his decisions by an expected policy course of his opponent, who – being the "Stackelberg follower" – adjusts in a passive way by delivering the expected response. But taking up either position has no general implication for the superiority of utility levels.

With regard to currency matters, the key country typically is in the Stackelberg follower position; and foreign countries, for the sake of their own interest, are led to accept the leading country's reaction function as a kind of "budget constraint" in monetary policy making. A further, and potentially misleading, criterion might be the timing of interest rate moves: according to the modern standard wisdom, the key currency central bank always has the "first move"; but actually the sequential order of interest rate changes depends on the kind of shock occurring, and whether the central banks involved in the game can exert a control on the affected macro variables.

In a way, all key currency systems of the 20th century have been "special cases". The Bank of England was an atypical leader of the currency system in the sense that – contrary to the Fed and the Bundesbank in the regimes which followed later – it was also subject to a liquidity problem. Therefore – again contrary to Bretton Woods and the EMS – the leading central bank was not able to control the level of interest rates. But the liquidity problem was perfectly managed so that the pound sterling served as the unchallenged world currency over decades. Nevertheless the belief that the mere use of sterling assets as a "secondary" reserve in the gold standard constituted a stable leader-follower structure was proved analytically unsound. Instead, *economic policy preferences* were the decisive factors. England forced other gold standard countries to choose a ratio of interest rates from her reaction function, because otherwise a battle of rising interest rates, which aimed to attract capital movements, was a severe threat for other countries, which attached some weight to the prospering of the home economy, whereas Britain obviously could afford such a state of markets on account of the overriding importance of the British goal of external equilibrium.

The *neglect* of the target of internal stabilization was another special feature of English leadership in the gold standard, clearly contradicting the definition given above, but compelled by the *lacking* degree of freedom of the $n-1$ problem which usually confers some extra latitude on policy making in the dominating country. And for a long time it seemed that England did not suffer from that renunciation; rather, the discovery of orienting monetary policy by the state of the foreign exchange appeared as a great achievement. In terms of the modern jargon, one might be tempted to argue that British monetary policy was governed by "conservative bankers", endowed with a relatively high interest in monetary stability. But empirically, the problem of unemployment was relatively unimportant from a political point of view; and the trend of the price level in the 19th century was falling, i.e. the problem of inflation simply did not exist.

Thus, a general hypothesis is that the specific market conditions in the classical era of capitalism allowed central banks to dispense with anti-inflation policies, or, to control the level of domestic wages and prices only indirectly through the fixed exchange rate. These peculiarities changed in the interwar period. Democracy and the increasing power of the unions precluded a continuation of a monetary policy strategy in which the only target was to maintain the equilibrium of the foreign exchange, given the old and new parity of the pound. Interest rates could not be increased any further and nominal wages did not come down quickly enough to restore British competitiveness. A major caveat against this line of reasoning is that institutional patterns of wage formation should be treated as endogenous elements of economic development. The credibility of the external constraint of wage setting was undermined by choosing a wrong nominal anchor when re-entering the gold standard.

In any case, after the gold standard national economic policy making was no longer sheltered from unrealistic claims made by various interest groups. Abolishing external constraints was meant to be a precondition for safeguarding the domestic economic system against injurious deflation, but the nationalization of monetary policy later included growth and employment as explicit goals, and many countries failed to preserve monetary stability which then had to be pursued at the policymakers' own accord. The demise of the gold standard marked the historical onset of wage inflation.

The U.S. advanced to the key currency country because they attached a high value to the goal of internal monetary stability (otherwise they would have had to respond to the rise in gold reserves by lowering interest rates which in turn would have alleviated the British predicament in the 1920s). Nevertheless the dollar also kept an official linkage to gold, which sought to maintain the impression of symmetrical constraints of national economic policy and thus support the political acceptance of the Bretton Woods system. In fact, the U.S. was however relieved from balance-of-payments restrictions. Leadership in the Bretton Woods system, again, was executed by the Stackelberg follower. The dominating position of the U.S. in the monetary policy game however was qualified by the lacking influence of foreign interest rate moves on the American macro variables. The U.S. acted as the *n-th* player of the game, determining the macroeconomic conditions for growth and inflation on a world scale.

The obligation for the key country to provide monetary stability for the world economy was neither clearly stated in the rules of the system nor responsibly practised by its leading player. The achievement of the Bretton Woods era: permitting two decades of prosperity, ought to be evaluated against the backdrop of the defect of a system which finally failed to provide a binding monetary budget constraint and compelled its members to finance an inflationary boom. Designed as a half-way house between a metallic and a pure fiat money system, Bretton Woods came down because the gold backing gave rise to unnecessary speculation and paper money in the end was issued without limit.

Whereas the pound and the dollar tended to be overvalued, the mark achieved its key currency status in the EMS by its undervaluation. Inflation differences as against Germany in a fixed-rate system, founded in an explicit democratic and symmetric fashion, left other member countries the awkward choice of either deflating and reforming their economies; of devaluing against the mark; or of financing trade deficits by attracting short-term funds. The ensuing excess demand for mark assets allowed the Bundesbank's interest rate to "rule the roost". Whereas leadership in the gold standard depended on the priority attached to the preservation of external equilibrium at given exchange rates, the emphasis laid on price stability determined that currency which was chosen for intervention and reserve keeping purposes in the EMS as the first pure paper standard.

Disinflation proved to be as painful and costly, in terms of lost output, as in the non-EMS area, because (temporarily) fixing an exchange rate instead of an immediate monetary anti-inflation policy offered little, if any, substantial gains in credibility. Contrary to the gold standard, imposing a liquidity problem on national central banks proved not to be credible, because the external restraint for domestic policy making was *chosen* merely for stabilization purposes, but did not represent a constitutional element of monetary institutions. Nevertheless, it should be stressed that – as it had been the case with respect to the gold standard and Bretton Woods – stabilization problems in member countries generally do not cause a breakdown of key currency systems. They tend to collapse in, or be blown up from, the centre.

The welfare of member countries is always affected by supply and demand shocks emanating from the leading country. But paper standard systems differ substantially from the classical gold standard as they may exhibit a restrictive bias. The reason is that the key central bank in a paper standard fights any disturbances threatening price stability as such, whereas in a metallic standard it reacts only if its external position is endangered. Moreover, the *type* of welfare loss differed significantly:

• Focusing on the external equilibrium, the Bank of England aimed at an optimal *difference* of interest rates, which induced the desired capital flows. This allowed foreign central banks to optimize along the British reaction function and to choose a *level* of interest rates which was consistent with the preservation of internal policy targets.

• The EMS showed the reverse case: the foreign player reached his reserve target but had to bear output losses, if the Bundesbank (in spite of high employment targets abroad) aimed at zero inflation in cases of supply and demand shocks at home. Hence, leadership became a burden for member countries when the key country exported restrictive policies, which in the end could no longer be tolerated.

The dilemma of a paper money standard is that there is no way back for the key central bank to an external anchor which could guide its policy. Whereas a policy which clings to that anchor was a force of circumstance in any resource-based monetary system, adhering to the primacy of external equilibrium merely shams a liquidity problem which no longer exists: the note issue of the leading central bank *is* the reserve – for the member countries. Therefore, the leading central bank *cannot*, as a rule, aim to stabilize exchange rates. The assignment is definitely settled from an economic point of view: member countries practise an external orientation of their monetary policy by importing the nominal anchor which is provided by the leading central bank. The ultimate explanation for the failure of the European key currency system thus is twofold: the nominal anchor itself became unstable and had to be fixed by restrictive monetary policies which caused unjustifiable macro effects in the member countries' economies; at the same time, the willingness to accept a foreign country's leadership in currency matters had waned for political reasons.

PART IV
THE EURO IN THE WORLD ECONOMY

8. A Monetary Union With a Denationalized Currency

8.1 The EMU Project: A Political Reform with Obscure Ends

> The model of a D-mark zone basically is workable and the only true alternative to a monetary union. But it imposes on the single countries [...] a powerlessness, which particularly in times of crises is being felt as shameful.
>
> *Olaf Sievert*[1]

> EMU has gone from being an improbable and bad idea to a bad idea that is about to come true. [...] The costs of getting there are large, the economic benefits minimal, and the prospects for disappointment major. [...] If there ever was a bad idea, EMU is it.
>
> *Rudiger Dornbusch*[2]

> The euro, after all, primarily is no economic project. This is only believed by Waigel, Tietmeyer and other managers of monetary policy. [...] The euro is a strategic project. It is part of the building up of Europe in stages.
>
> *Helmut Schmidt*[3]

The foundation of the European Monetary Union (EMU) followed the lines of political logic. The project was pushed from governmental quarters, and hardly recommended by economic experts. The majority of European nations no longer accepted German leadership; and the Germans themselves, being afraid of political isolation, no longer wanted to bear the sole responsibility in the sphere of European monetary policy.[4] Occasional discussions on the question of an "optimal currency area" actually were misplaced: the choice was not between flexible and fixed exchange rates, but rather between fixed rates and a currency union; and history teaches that the latter, in most cases, was established for non-economic rea-

---

[1] Sievert 1995: 7.
[2] Dornbusch 1996a: 113, 124.
[3] Quoted from Issing 1997.
[4] Cf. Bernholz 1998, Richter 1998, Richter 1999: 135-6, Pierenkämper 1999.

sons.[5] Moreover, politicians promoting the establishment of EMU rightly ignored traditional supply-side preconditions for forming an "optimal currency area", thus unconsciously (?) adopting the Lucas critique according to which market structure and individual patterns of behaviour are endogenous to policy regimes and therefore will change if a new monetary order were to be extended across Europe.

On economic grounds EMU was expected to enhance efficiency and welfare, but mainly should form a community of monetary stability. The "convergence criteria", regulating the admittance of candidates, were centred on the leitmotiv of financial solidity, but without good reason excluded the domestic unemployment rate, although this figure might indicate a future inclination to lax economic policies. Moreover, the approach of forcing each country on the painful road to German stability culture seemed to neglect – rightly or wrongly – the findings of modern macro theory that credibility can be won by institutional reform alone, without previously embarking on a course of domestic disinflation.[6] At the end of the 1990s, an unexpected large number of EMS countries had qualified for EMU entry. Inflation had come down substantially, most probably with the help of a further rise of unemployment. A fiscal tour de force throughout Europe roughly succeeded in reaching the Maastricht criterion for the budget deficit, whereas the continuous adjustment to the Bundesbank's interest rate contributed to reduce the interest burden of the still high stock of public debt (*figure 8.1*).

The political backgrounds and objectives of EMU are manifold; their partly contradictory character did not hamper the process of its institutionalization. Already in 1972 the French were suspected of aiming at an access to the Bundesbank's foreign reserves by propagating a monetary union, which in itself was assessed by some observers as a result of an outdated thinking in terms of superpower conflicts of the cold war era; it was said to have its roots in a "general overestimation of the benefits, economic and political, of the factor of size".[7] Later, in a critical stage before the enactment of EMU, politicians even resorted to the dubious argument that forming a union would prevent an outbreak of war between the participating Western European countries – which surely was not on the agenda.

On a more rational level, the EMU project can be envisaged as a major step in a general *strategy of depoliticization*. To begin with, closing down the foreign exchange markets within Western Europe would remove a trouble spot which had taken up a lot of policy makers' time and energy. None of the participating coun-

---

[5]   Cf. Goodhart 1996a, Kenen 1997.
[6]   "The disappearance of national currencies makes the national inflation rates irrelevant after the monetary reform. It is quite conceivable that a country with an inflation rate of, say, 6 % forms an EMU with countries having an inflation rate of only 2 %, without major problems. When the high inflation country joins EMU, its currency disappears. The fact that this currency used to experience a loss of purchasing power of 6 % a year becomes irrelevant" (De Grauwe 1994b: 170, cf. De Grauwe 1998a, Dornbusch 1996a, Dornbusch 1997).
[7]   Hirsch 1972: 431, cf. Dornbusch 1993.

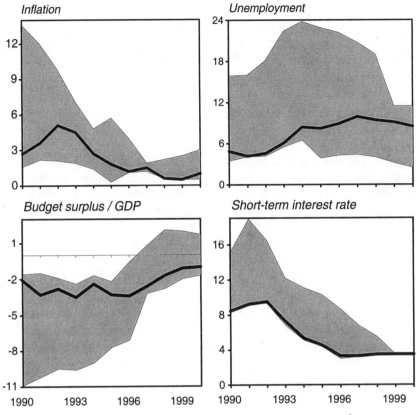

Figure 8.1: Germany and EU11 countries on the road to EMU[8]

tries could be tempted any longer to profit by occasional devaluations of their currencies; and thus governments of neighbour countries, in these cases, would no longer be confronted with demands for compensating subsidies from their home industries.

Or course, simply closing the stage where deficiencies of a national economy are revealed by means of a weak currency, would also not cure these deficiencies.[9] But national governments would no longer dispose of the exchange rate instrument, which in principle could be employed to relieve problems of low competitiveness for a while. Hence, it might be expected that market agents were left to fend for themselves, particularly if stringent rules for competition policies precluded direct payment of subsidies to national industries. It was also argued that

---

[8] Budget figures excluding Luxembourg. Data from OECD: Economic Outlook.

[9] "The most serious criticism of EMU is that by abandoning exchange rate adjustments it transfers to the labor market the task of adjusting for competitiveness and relative prices" (Dornbusch 1996a: 120, cf. Goodhart 1996a, Obstfeld 1997).

the performance of groups of particular (national) market agents would lose some of its former importance, simply because their fate, to some extent, would be submerged in the larger sample of European statistics. "Balance of payment data almost force one to concentrate on the well-being of that sub-entity whose balance is under consideration. Without them, the focus of attention will shift to the larger whole grouping."[10]

Besides the strengthening of competitive forces by obstructing the "easy way out", i.e. devaluation, a second major goal of depoliticization might be the final exclusion of the possibility of financing public deficits by "printing money". Given the high level of public debt in the European welfare states, binding rules for maintaining financial solidity have become an urgent need. Governments should pay their debts in units of a currency which they cannot produce by themselves.[11] The rules of the Maastricht Treaty do not allow governments to run "excessive" budget deficits[12] (thus free-riding on the public good of a still low rate of interest on the European capital markets) and preclude the financing of deficits by resorting to central-bank credits. Moreover, there is a wide-spread consensus that there should be no bail-out, on the part of the European Central Bank (ECB), in the case of a national government's debt crisis.

These precautions however may produce an undesirable side effect: countries suffering from an exceptionally high fiscal burden may feel inclined to demand funds from a central European agency, which in turn may give in for political reasons, for example, in order to prevent menacing national destabilization which may spill over to the European community as a whole. Inconspicuous transfers to national governments thus render bail-outs unnecessary. In general, the limitation of national fiscal policies' room for manoeuvre can be expected to cause political pressure which aims to shift responsibilities from the national to a European level; to create larger or additional central institutions charged with the provision of public goods; and of carrying out structural policies, which are coordinated among national governments.

The centralization of fiscal policies will then require the collecting of additional tax funds; and although there are good reasons to integrate industrial and regional policies into a European master plan, experience shows that inefficiencies (and corruption) rampant, with a growing "distance" between the deciding bodies on, and the final recipients of subsidies. Therefore, in order to preclude moral hazard, i.e. the temptation to shift financial burdens to the community, it might be better

---

[10] Goodhart 1996a: 1087.

[11] This argument was made very forcefully by Sievert (1993: 14): "The history of finance is not a history of evolution towards currencies becoming better an better. Rather, it is a chequered history of the misuse of the right to create money."

[12] Finance ministers found guilty of unsolid housekeeping are to be fined; as an alternative penalty Goodhart (1996b) suggested to oblige them to appear as hosts of the European Song Contest.

to abandon limitations on national fiscal policy, and to keep national governments responsible for financing public spending, preferably by taxation.[13]

Hence, a basic contradiction becomes apparent. Whereas, in the earlier debate on the feasibility of EMU, it was held that a concomitant political union might even be a precondition for a stable common currency, critics now raise objections that EMU might turn out to be a "Trojan horse" for some sort of European government, which is unwelcome on the part of national citizens, but which proves to be indispensable to decide on common policy issues, and to coordinate market regulations in the euro currency area. After all, the modernization of European welfare states might appear not to evolve simply by market forces; political *programmes* seem to be helpful. However, as the European nation states will continue to exist, the result might be an inefficient pattern of policy making: no Olson shock to national coalitions with regard to income distribution, but the rise of a European rent-seeking society.[14]

8.2 Monetary Policy and Price Stability

> The question of the day is whether EMS membership might take Britain all the way to price stability, on an equal footing with Germany. Just as in Germany, the nominal economy [!] would become the exclusive focus of policy makers' attention in an ultimate abdication of responsibility for employment and growth.
>
> *Rudiger Dornbusch*[15]

> In every country and all periods of history, the performance of the central banker is judged to a large extent on the simple yardstick of successful defence of the value of the national currency.
>
> *Mario Sarcinelli*[16]

> In the long run, inflation is always and everywhere an excess nominal GDP phenomenon.
>
> *Robert J. Gordon*[17]

The final, and perhaps most important, objective of a depoliticization strategy arises from the problem of stabilization, which already in the EMS brought national authorities to consent to a subordination to the monetary "corset" provided

---

[13] Cf. Alesina et al. 1995, Eichengreen/Hagen 1996, Goodhart 1996a, Masson 1996.

[14] Cf. Hirsch 1972, Minford 1992, Alesina 1997, Feldstein 1997.

[15] Dornbusch 1987: 10.

[16] Sarcinelli 1991: 515.

[17] Gordon 1997: 17.

by German monetary policy. The Bundesbank was expected to represent a more credible threat to national unions. A generalization of this argument yields a new approach in the "optimal currency area" debate: "A currency area is optimal if it is larger than an area where an effective wage cartel can be established."[18] Thus, the foundation of EMU can be interpreted as a final step in the evolution of European monetary policy towards a more rigid and "impartial" pattern of money supply, in a way comparable to the gold standard. The almost constitutional establishment of price stability as the only legal aim of the ECB emphasizes the fundamental status of the intended regime switch: monetary policy ought to obtain the character of German "Ordnungspolitik", safeguarding the stability and efficiency of a nominal-contract order. After the regime switch from the gold to the wage standard, EMU might be interpreted as a step towards an *institutional* currency standard, where price stability is guaranteed by entrusting monetary authorities with a proper as-signment and wage movements are downgraded to changes of *relative* prices.

Monetary authorities thus expect to gain a strategic advantage vis-à-vis the (groups of) wage earners, since with unchanged structures on the European labour markets, a single union is now degraded to a "marginal" agent in a competitive setting and therefore cannot hope that European monetary policy will "validate" exaggerated wage claims by accelerating the growth of the money supply. It could be argued that this concept is subject to the Lucas critique: the pattern of wage formation might change in response to the more centralized monetary policy mak-ing. But decentralization of wage policies was well under way already on a na-tional level, and thus the rise of a monopolistic union in Europe can hardly be ex-pected. Nevertheless, the rigidity of national, regional and sectoral wages in the process of structural change (driven by forces of diversification and regional spe-cialization) will depend on the generosity of national labour market and social policy regulations.[19]

The institutional design of the ECB itself has been shaped in order to ensure po-litical independence; according to a "classical" definition the bank has "the right to change the discount rate without consultation with or challenge from govern-ment".[20] It has been argued that the position of its Executive Board is relatively weak compared to its Governing Council, so that national economic policy inter-ests, represented by national central banks' governors, might manifest itself in ECB decisions. But the non-regional impact of monetary policy renders attempts

---

[18] Sievert 1993: 18.

[19] Cf. Nardis/Micossi 1991, Obstfeld 1997. On the other hand, De Grauwe (1998b) men-tions that the ECB might choose a higher average rate of inflation, even if equipped with the Bundesbank's policy preferences, in order to take account of the existence of inefficient supply-side conditions in some EMU member countries. This, of course, would be only a short-run solution which shies away from establishing incentives for supply-side reforms.

[20] Capie/Goodhart 1995: 152. In modern terms, this is labelled "instrument independence" (Fischer 1995). For a critical opinion on the general issue see Doyle/Wheale (1994).

to strive for a majority of the Council's votes less attractive. Moreover, the country-specific peculiarities of the monetary transmission process are bound to assimilate by financial market forces.[21]

Since the abandonment of the gold standard it has been felt that some objective or even technical rule might be necessary, or at least convenient, to guide the decision making of a central bank, and to protect it from short-term and short-sighted demands on the part of governmental bodies. The poor performance of the German Reichsbank in the 1920s partly can be explained by the lack of such rules, which made the bank vulnerable to exertion of political influence.[22] The modern game-theoretic literature emphasizes the need to preclude a "surprise inflation", launched by the central bank in order to gain temporary employment effects; anticipating this policy the private sector reacts by establishing prophylactic inflation expectations. This, of course, is a rather naive approach because it ignores the time lags in the transmission process. The rate of inflation cannot be controlled directly. Any monetary expansion has to start by lowering short-term interest rates whereas employment and price effects follow with a lag. If interest rate policies can be observed by market agents, expected and actual inflation would rise long before any additional employment could be gained. Thus even a one-period game makes no sense; there is no temptation to run a surprise inflation. Accordingly, the expectation-driven inflation bias disappears.[23]

It should be stressed however, that market agents in a monetary economy have to be provided with a solid anchor of medium-term expectations of money prices (simply because the allocation of resources is not organized in an auction-like barter where only relative values are of importance, but in a permanent sequence of monetary contracts where money serves as a yard stick and is kept as a buffer stock). For obvious reasons, the ECB tried to draw upon the Bundesbank's success and reputation by taking over a less binding version of the German concept of money supply targeting as one part of its "two-pillar strategy", where the other part is played by some lightened variant of the modern inflation targeting concept. Each component alone, practised with some calmness and flexibility, would have sufficed (and both boil down to a more or less similar way of policy making).[24]

---

[21] Cf. Bean 1998, Dornbusch et al. 1998, Gros 1998.

[22] Cf. James 1998.

[23] Astonishingly it took 15 years before this simple critique was made in the academic debate (cf. Goodhart/Huang 1998, Spahn 1999, Walsh 2000). From the point of view of a practical central banker, Blinder (1998: 50) passed a devastating verdict on the time inconsistency hypothesis. "The academic literature has focused on either the wrong problem or a nonproblem and has proposed a variety of solutions (excluding Rogoff's conservative central bankers) that make little sense in the real world."

[24] "It seems that contrary to some central bankers and economists, market agents have initially believed that IT [inflation targeting] is not a different monetary policy framework, or at least, that in practice nothing has really changed yet with the adoption of IT" (Almeida/Goodhart 1998: 100). A detailed analysis of the inconsistencies arising from running both parts of the strategy is given by Svensson (1999). An important rationale

Price stability nowadays is accepted as an overriding, if not the only, goal of monetary policy. This should not be understood as the outcome of the scientific controversy between Keynesians and Monetarists in the 1970s. Preserving the viability of the society's contract-based way of organizing the production and distribution of resources and income is an absolute need in a market economy. The plea for price stability can be traced back at least to Wicksell who – when designing his vision of a paper money standard at the end of the 19th century – recommended that the central bank should react to the rise or the fall of the general price level, taking these changes as a proxy for the non-observable spread between the "natural" rate of interest and the bank rate. It should be noted however, that even if *changes* in the value of money thus could be avoided, there is no firm anchor for the *level* of prices.[25] Monetarism later propagated the impression that fixing a quantity of money would establish a solid centre of gravity for movements of the price level, but this rests on the assumption of a stable demand for money. And it was, in particular, Keynes who – after the suspension of the gold standard in the First World War – argued vigorously to defend the stability of the internal price level instead of defending the exchange rate.[26]

A cursory inspection might suggest the proposition that it makes no basic difference whether the central bank controls the price of a single good (gold) or the price of a bundle of goods (GDP). Experience of monetary policy after the demise of the gold standard reveals that it makes a substantial difference: defending the stability of the price of a central bank's basic reserve necessarily implies interest rates policies which aim to influence the allocation of stocks of financial wealth, either between bank deposits and cash, or between financial assets denominated in home and foreign currencies (the problem of internal and external drain). In any case, monetary policy acts as *bank policy* aiming to control the liquidity of the economy's basic monetary institution. Varying the rate of interest as the price of financial assets is the appropriate tool for acting on the money and foreign exchange markets; this is supplemented by the use of a stock of reserves which can be sold off or replenished in order to stabilize small-scale disturbances.

On the other hand, whereas the gold price can be stabilized on the asset market, general price level stability can only be achieved by controlling the goods and labour markets; monetary policy instruments have but a vague impact on the process of wage and price formation. The quantity theory of money as the scientific foundation of practical monetarism played down this problem by resorting to the hypothesis of a direct link between money and prices, which later has been refined in a convenient manner by the rational expectation hypothesis. But now there is

---

for sticking at least partly to money supply targeting is that its financial-market technicalities provide a better protective shield against political pressure, compared to a strategy which seems to control directly economic policy targets; this is frankly admitted by Issing (1998).

[25] Cf. Wicksell 1898, Seccareccia 1998, Richter 1999: 4. See also above ch. 2.4.

[26] Cf. Keynes 1923.

overwhelming theoretical and empirical evidence that monetary policy is not neutral, at least in the short and medium run. Finally, of course, there is no possibility of stabilization by varying a stock of reserves – although, in a way, a pool of unemployed labour serves as a substitute for a stock of gold.

This is the tragic irony in – and the basic reason for – the failure of the Keynesian revolution, as far as economic policy is concerned: the recommendation to relieve monetary policy making from the constraints imposed by the "barbaric" relict of an officially fixed gold price, and to let the currency float on the foreign exchange, implied a macroeconomic control of the tightness on the labour market. Keeping money in short supply relative to the central bank's reserve or relative to foreign currencies was replaced by a new pattern of policy making which contained demand, production and employment within the limits given by the endowments of resources. Keynes' subsequent argumentative efforts in favour of full employment (and the practical economic policy designs of his school) could not prevent the spreading "use" of unemployment as a barrier against inflation. Already in the mid 1940s he himself conceded that approaching the state of full employment would inevitably bring about the problem of a rise in inflation; and it was not very helpful for his descendants to learn that Keynes regarded this a more political than economic problem.[27]

But there was hardly an alternative in the evolution of monetary policy strategies. The previous pattern of policy making: monetary control by means of a binding and credible reserve-keeping rule for the central bank, is of no use any longer, particularly in a large currency union which is not bound by a fixed exchange rate. In the history of (central) banking, the commitment to keep a reserve was basically meant to be a reputation-enhancing device. Without the necessity of reserve-keeping, the reputation of any central bank, naturally, is bound to its ability to safeguard the (internal value) of the currency as a precondition for its enduring use on asset, goods and labour markets. Thus, price stability as a norm and performance criterion of interest rate policy represents a final (?) stage in the evolution of monetary institutions, where the former type of bank policy has been superseded.

Surely, price stability represents a specific precondition for maintaining a market economy in a workable order, and therefore is basically different from other macroeconomic policy goals like high rates of growth and employment. But the change of monetary policy institutions forced central banks to widen their field of

---

[27] On the one hand, Keynes (1943b: 33) tried to play down the wage inflation problem: "Some people argue that a capitalist country is doomed to failure because it will be found impossible in conditions of full employment to prevent a progressive increase of wages. [...] Whether this is so remains to be seen. The more conscious we are of this problem, the likelier shall we be able to surmount it." But on the other hand, he admitted to have no economic remedy: "The task of keeping efficiency wages stable (I am sure they will creep up steadily in spite of our best efforts) is a political rather than an economic problem" (Keynes 1943c: 38).

operation from the stabilization of the national money market and the foreign exchange to also include a demand-side control of the dynamics on the goods and labour market. Therefore, much more than in former times, monetary policy comes into conflict with private and political employment interests. After the final EMS failure in the attempt to anchor central bank behaviour in the constraints of an external equilibrium, the EMU (and the effort in many other countries to confer on the goal of price stability an almost constitutional character) marks a turning point in the history of monetary institutions: a stable low rate of inflation, usually envisaged as the (unstable) outcome of the interplay between a discretionary demand management and the unions' wage claims, is to be "institutionalized" in nearly the same way as the sacrosanct bank price of gold in former times.

The gold price however, was defended as a *market* price. If the ECB should likewise be dependent on controlling the rate of inflation by market forces, i.e. by its impact on effective demand, the macroeconomic process will have to be constrained in a narrow corset, which implies poor prospects for long-run growth and employment. Thus, there is a case for public "education" which aims to make market agents *believe* that a low and stable rate of inflation is guaranteed by the central bank, by magic means of reputation and expectations, but without interfering with the dynamics on the goods market. But up to now, we know of hardly any free lunch in macroeconomics.

9. The Multiple International Monetary Standard

9.1 Interest Rate Parity Condition and the Exchange Rate Random Walk

> To determine the short-run outcome for the exchange rate,
> one needs to know its long-run destination.
>
> *Christopher Bliss*[1]

In contrast to the gold standard and the Bretton Woods system, EMS and EMU had been designed as *regional* currency systems. Hence, the monetary relationship between EMU and the rest of the world is an open issue. There have been periods of "multipolar" currency systems (or non-systems) in the interwar years and after the demise of Bretton Woods, but due to the rapid developments on world financial markets it seems less useful to reassess experiences and debates. At the beginning of the new millennium, the time for fixed-exchange-rate regimes seems to have run out. Only very few, or very small, countries manage to peg their exchange rates to a foreign currency, mainly to the dollar.[2]

At first glance, there is no straightforward choice between fixed and flexible exchange rates, because, in the first case, large capital movements force substantial adjustments of home interest rates on the national economy, or, in the second case, lead to considerable distortions of real exchange rates (due to rigid nominal prices). Contrary to the norms of the quantity theory, variations of the nominal exchange rate are not neutral with respect to the "real" economy. A rise of foreign interest rates, or a change of risk premia attached to the currencies involved, for example triggered off by unfavourable trends in public finance, will induce a reallocation of portfolios of international investors and enforce an adjustment of either the domestic interest rate or of the exchange rate.[3] Both policy alternatives can be derived from the basic interest parity theorem

$$r_t = r_t^* + \frac{1}{T}\dot{e}_{t+T}^e + risk = r_t^* + \frac{1}{T}\left(e_{t+T}^e - e_t\right) + risk \qquad [9.1]$$

where T indicates the length of the repayment period of the two financial investments under consideration (which is usually simplified by setting $T = 1$).

---

[1] Bliss 1986: 16.
[2] Cf. Obstfeld/Rogoff 1995, Eichengreen 1999.
[3] "There is a link between indebtedness and the exchange rate; when indebtedness becomes large, people look toward Switzerland; and when they look toward Switzerland, the lira goes" (Dornbusch 1995: 199).

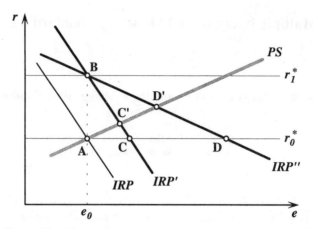

Figure 9.1: A foreign interest shock with varying expected duration

Equations [7.15] and [7.16] give the upward sloping line of the condition for price stability *PS* (with *p = 0*) in an open economy (*figure 9.1*):

$$r = \frac{1}{\beta}\left(\frac{w}{\alpha} + g + \varepsilon\, p^*\right) + \frac{\varepsilon}{\beta}\, e \qquad [9.2]$$

The interest rate parity condition [9.1] yields a downward sloping line in the *r-e* space. This line resembles the Phillips curve: it shows an infinity of *r-e* combinations which represent external equilibrium at *given* exchange rate expectations; and the line *shifts* with changing expectations. A rise of the foreign rate of interest also shifts *IRP* upward. If domestic interest policy aims to defend the exchange rate at e_0, monetary tightening (A → B) implies entering an area of deflation and unemployment (as B is located above *PS*).

If on the other hand the domestic interest rate is kept constant, the currency will depreciate. The degree of devaluation depends on the expected duration of the interest rate differential (*IRP'* or *IRP''*). The longer the foreign lead in interest rates is expected to continue the larger is the initial devaluation (A → D instead of A → C), so that the ensuing revaluation per period compensates for the interest rate spread on foreign assets. In either case, as the temporary devaluation brings about demand-side and (not shown in [9.2]) supply-side driven price increases, domestic interest rates should be raised (depending on the slope of the *PS* condition) in order to maintain price stability (C → C' or D → D', respectively). Note that in the case of flexible exchange rates, interest rate differentials are not to be explained by expected devaluation, but rather by different paths of domestic monetary policy; expected devaluation acts directly on the current spot rate.[4]

---

[4]   Cf. McKinnon 1990.

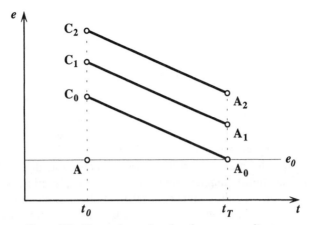

Figure 9.2: Alternative paths of exchange rate adjustment

The preceding analysis builds on the assumption of a given expected future level of the exchange rate. But the required *rate* of appreciation, which is necessary to maintain external equilibrium, is independent of the *level* of its point of destination (A_0, A_1 or A_2 in *figure 9.2*). The expected future level of the exchange rate e^e_{t+T} is the crucial variable in the adjustment process; it serves as its nominal anchor, but is not itself determined in the foreign exchange market. Obviously it cannot simply assumed to be constant. If this questionable assumption is dropped, it becomes apparent that the foreign exchange, being an asset market, determines only the rate of change of the exchange rate, but not its level. "Given the interest rate differential, we have an infinity of paths linking the present spot rate with the expected future one."[5] An equilibrium on international asset markets thus goes along with various equilibria (or disequilibria) on the goods and labour markets, each with different nominal values.

Hence, the critical issue is the direction of causation. If asset holders pick a future exchange rate level at random, this would nevertheless − via the endogenously determined spot rate − have an impact on the "real" economy. According to traditional wisdom this is ruled out by the purchasing power parity theorem, where the equilibrium exchange rate is determined by national price levels of tradable goods. But its empirical validity is restricted to the longer term (20-30 years); and this implies that prices and wages will also adjust to movements of the exchange rate (rather than the other way round).[6] Finally, if capital movements due to their sheer magnitude are found to dominate foreign exchange transactions today, it is awkward to argue that an inflation-based trade imbalance will determine the equilibrium exchange rate tomorrow. The forward solution of the interest rate parity

---

[5] De Grauwe 1996: 106.
[6] Cf. Bliss 1986, Obstfeld 1995, Taylor 1995.

condition [9.1] (where for simplicity risk is ignored, $T = 1$, and E denotes the expectation operator) yields

$$e_t = E \sum_{j=0}^{\infty} \left(r^*_{t+j} - r_{t+j} \right) \qquad [9.3]$$

The equation simply states that "at any point in time the exchange rate embodies the market's best guess about the entire future course of interest rates."[7] This implies that also the expected exchange rate T periods ahead, i.e. the point of reference in [9.1], depends on a guess on the series of interest rate differentials ruling after period T. This further implies that the exchange rate, in principle, can move *independently* of inflation differentials. A relatively high, but controlled, rate of inflation thus may go along with (and is curbed by) currency appreciation; due to a relatively high interest rate which is used to keep inflation in check. Because there is no unequivocal feedback from inflation to the foreign exchange, and goods prices are relatively rigid compared to exchange rates, capital movements mainly determine real exchange rates which may exhibit substantial misalignments over the medium run.

Even if consecutive interest rates *in each country* are serially correlated, following the regularity of booms and recessions, the predicted path of interest rate *differentials* between two countries may nevertheless show a random-like pattern, explaining the random-walk character which has been found to be typical for exchange rate behaviour.[8] On the other hand, if a majority of economic observers in each period extrapolates the probability that one of two countries under consideration will exhibit relatively high interest rates (maybe because of strong growth prospects connected with stability-oriented monetary policy), the spot exchange rate will move continuously in one direction; this has been the driving force of the dollar appreciation in the early 1980s and also (as against the euro) since 1999. Note that such an exchange rate behaviour in no way indicates a foreign exchange crisis, but simple the element of indetermination in a flexible-exchange-rate regime: even if monetary policy in both countries involved manage to control the domestic price level (and thus fix the degree of freedom in the national system of absolute prices), the ratio of these price levels does not exert a strong and unequivocal impact on the exchange rate level.

---

[7] Begg 1989: 29. Information on relative trade performance, prices, and other goods-market-related items may also influence the exchange rate, but mainly through their impact on portfolio investment decisions, based on shifting creditor-debtor relations, increasing risk premia, or doubts on the long-term sustainability of trade imbalances.

[8] Cf. De Grauwe 1996: 131, Rogoff 1996.

9.2 Toward a Bipolar Euro-Dollar System

> International money, any more than domestic, will not manage itself.
>
> *Paul A. Volcker*[9]

> With capital mobility, there may be no comfortable middle ground between full, irrevocable currency union and floating.
>
> *Maurice Obstfeld*[10]

In the light of the instability of flexible-exchange-rate market conditions, "blueprints" for reforming the world's monetary system are obviously very much in demand. McKinnon proposes a price *level* targeting of worldwide tradable goods (thus hoping to profit from the stabilizing virtue of the "Restoration Principle"), pursued by all member central banks, and followed by a fixation of exchange rates on this purchasing power parity basis. Central banks then should ignore the development of the national general price level, and use short-term interest rates to stabilize nominal exchange rates.[11]

What seems odd, is the troublesome distinction between tradables and non-tradables, the recommendation to ignore the *general* price trend in national economies and its link to wage dynamics, and – more fundamentally – the puzzling idea that central banks ought to assign credit volume policies for controlling prices and interest rate policies to defend the exchange rate. This improper "doubling" of monetary policy instruments raises the suspicion that McKinnon dodges a conflict between the internal and external equilibrium: a country with an appreciating currency most probably exhibits high growth rates and rising prices; the prescription to lower interest rates in order to meet the increased international demand for the national currency is incompatible with the task of containing domestic goods market dynamics. In 1999-2000, to prevent the rise of the dollar as against the euro, the ECB would have been forced to curtail its monetary expansion (more than it actually did) in spite of high unemployment and low inflation, whereas the Fed would have had to lower interest rates in spite of a strong boom and rising prices.

Attempts to sterilize foreign exchange interventions would hardly resolve the conflict between external and internal equilibrium. The strong-currency central bank, when buying up excess amounts of a foreign currency which the market threatens

---

[9] Volcker 1978/79: 10.

[10] Obstfeld 1995: 172, cf. Eichengreen 1993.

[11] Cf. McKinnon 1995. Proposals to stabilize *real* exchange rates around "fundamental equilibrium values" (Williamson 1993) are ill-conceived because they ignore the basic problem of *nominal* price level determination. Post Keynesian ideas of banning exports surpluses by taxing creditor nations and also banning unemployment as a "tool" for containing inflation (cf. Davidson 1992/93) simply appear to be a romantic contribution.

to depreciate, may offer deposit facilities to soak up the additional quantity of home currency which has been created during the intervention. It is true that such a facility endowed with a fixed interest rate will prevent an unwanted lowering of market rates. But in an inflationary boom in the home economy, commercial banks acquiring additional reserves through the central bank's intervention might expand their credit business which, in a boom, offers a higher return compared to the central bank's deposit facility. Therefore, the yield of these deposits should be increased drastically in order to curb the domestic volume of credit. This, in turn, would attract further capital imports... The experience of such a destabilizing spiral of events would soon put an end to a joint strategy of exchange-rate fixing and sterilization.

This shows that particularly with respect to the dollar-euro relation a fixed-exchange-rate solution is not available. Even if both central banks agree in general to share the responsibility of foreign exchange intervention, probable imbalances in the current and – even more – capital account, which may not be randomly distributed over the medium term, will put pressure on one of the two players to obtain the necessary foreign reserves. International financial markets will confer a leadership position upon that bank which issues the currency which is in excess demand. But the subordination of the other bank's interest rate policy to the constraints emanating from the exchange rate target would be even less sustainable than it has been the case in the EMS; not only for political reasons, but because – with a low mutual trade share in each country's GDP – it seems economically more reasonable to stabilize the domestic macroeconomic process.

It is true that both policy reactions to a foreign exchange shock, pegging the foreign interest rate or varying the nominal exchange rate, disturb the internal equilibrium. But in the first case monetary policy, the most powerful and flexible macroeconomic tool compared to wage and fiscal policies, is definitely blocked, whereas it still can and has to be used in the second case. In the 1980s and 1990s, economic policy strategies of fixing the exchange rate in order to stabilize the system of nominal prices and to "import" credibility failed in many countries, because real appreciation resulted in non-sustainable current account deficits. A real appreciation through a nominal exchange rate move, brought about by "excess" credibility and strong capital import, is surely to be assessed differently. Some examples in the post-EMS era also show the possibility of successful devaluations, as gains in output were not attained at the expense of accelerating inflation.[12]

In general, flexible exchange rates seem to be more suitable to deter speculative capital movements, because they make foreign investments more expensive via currency appreciation when entering the country, and cause capital losses via depreciation when leaving. But small countries and "young economies" found their

---

[12] England might put up a monument to George Soros whose profitable speculation against the pound forced the country to leave the EMS – and thus enabled the British boom of the 1990s (cf. Dornbusch et al. 1995, Dornbusch 1996b, Obstfeld 1995).

financial markets too weak to carry through a *controlled* devaluation; the sheer volume of capital movements caused large exchange rate changes which could not be dampened by domestic monetary authorities. It was an argument in favour of the gold standard that capital flight brought about an endogenous monetary restriction, whereas in a paper currency standard with flexible exchange rates it might aggravate inflation, thus feeding back on the motives of capital flight. But today even many professionals, instead of calling for a return to fixed rates, would rather allow restrictions to be imposed on capital movements[13] – and Argentina even considered abolishing the exchange rate altogether and, in defiance of traditional justifications for optimal currency areas, forming a monetary union with the U.S.

The strategy of keeping a fixed exchange rate, as an intermediate option between flexible rates and currency union, did not simply run into trouble because of the grown magnitude of capital movements, widespread deregulation and new "technical" conditions on financial markets: "hot money" is not created by modern payment techniques, but by the low credibility of fixed exchange rates. But how can exchange rates in a pure paper money standard ever be credible? Countries which are able to maintain a fixed exchange rate do not need such an external proof of their financial solidity, whereas countries which need an external anchor for credibly stabilizing the path of domestic prices and wages will not be able to defend their nominal exchange rate.

The basic analytical point is: exchange rates are not relative goods prices, but asset prices. Therefore monetary policy should not try to fix them. "Using an asset price as a nominal anchor – whether it be the exchange rate, an interest rate, or the stock market – is very problematic. Asset prices can be extremely sensitive to changing expectations: attempting to fix the exchange rate in the face of volatile expectations can lead to wild gyrations in interest rates and reserves, and, ultimately, to serious ruptures in policy credibility."[14] Thus one might feel inclined to enforce stability by imposing an obligation for reserve keeping for all central banks. But a reintroduction of external restraints as in the gold standard[15] would bring up insurmountable questions as to the character of that reserve, the criteria of its rate of supply, and the world distribution of political influence on its provision. Eventually, again, some country would succeed in gaining particular reputation on financial markets, and the failed history of key currencies would start anew.

The constellation of having two dominating currencies, the dollar and the euro, represents a bipolar monetary standard in the world economy, without a unique means of payment, and where wealth owners will have to bear the risks of capital

---

[13] Cf. Krugman 1999, Hirsch 1978, Eichengreen et al. 1995b.

[14] Obstfeld/Rogoff 1995: 93.

[15] Cf. Mundell 1995.

losses when switching their funds from one "bank" to another.[16] Periods of high volatility and even large swings of the dollar-euro rate are to be expected; but the history of the dollar-mark rate shows that these instabilities can be handled by two strong central banks. In their usual business both remain sovereign because and insofar as (due to the relatively low export and import penetration in GDP) they can afford a behaviour of benign neglect with respect to the foreign exchange. The position of the dollar in that bipolar monetary standard might collapse for many reasons, but hardly because of the U.S. capital-movement-driven trade balance. "The United States does have debts to foreigners, but relative to the size of the U.S. economy they are not large – and anyway (shhh! don't tell anyone) they are in dollars."[17]

---

[16] It is not a *tripolar* standard as Japan seems to be neither able nor willing to play a third role. Even Asian countries preferred to peg their currencies to the dollar, but not to the yen. For a discussion of the new constellation on world currency markets see Bergsten (1997), Fratianni/Hauskrecht (1998), Portes/Rey (1998) and Mundell/Clesse (2000).

[17] Krugman 2000: 14.

Summary of Part IV

Monetary institutions form the core of every market society. Money performs the basic economic function of providing a language of interaction and of assessing the market behaviour of individual agents. Although originating from an evolutionary market process, monetary institutions have always been shaped by political forces. Currency orders have developed in response to growing tensions between different economic policy imperatives; these conflicts arise from the demands to satisfy a widening cluster of policy goals, on the one hand, and to obey to the formal rules and restraints of the financial system, on the other. The impetus to currency reforms typically came from political quarters, not from economic experts, hoping to realize a better compatibility of economic and social aims. The hierarchy of currencies was supported by the structure of weights attached to different economic policy targets, and the transition to a new currency order was driven by the loss of acceptance of balance-of-payments restrictions.

The formation of EMU thus appears as a final, logical step in an era of *nationalization* of economic policy making, which had its incipience already in the 1930s and which in no way contradicts, but rather mirrors, the trend of *globalization*. Since the subordination to the interest rate policy of a dominating country is regarded to be neither economically efficient nor acceptable from a political point of view, the constraints emanating from the obligation of all currency system's member countries to maintain the external equilibrium are being partly internalized and politicized, i.e. are committed into the hands of a European monetary stabilization policy, and they are partly depoliticized, i.e. transformed into adjustment problems to be solved by individual agents on the goods and labour markets. The EMU marks a milestone in monetary history: after the failure of the third key currency system in the 20th century, a group of countries adopted a common currency without giving up their national sovereignty.

EMU thus also stands for the worldwide tendency of relieving monetary policy from the commitment of defending a fixed price of a "reserve", be it a physical good or a unit of a foreign currency. For the sake of preserving confidence in their money issue, central banks for a long time promised to keep it convertible in units of a reserve asset. The history of banking, commercial and public, has shown that this precaution is neither necessary nor sufficient to safeguard the market value of a currency. As the Bundesbank before, and many other central banks at present, the ECB without any "safety net" promises to deliver a stable price level, more precisely: a low rate of inflation. But in a way, the new order resembles the gold standard which has also been regarded as an "impartial" framework for monetary stability: price stability is intended to be likewise obligatory for all EMU member countries as the stable gold price had been in former times; financial market conditions should not be controlled by one country alone (although this proviso contradicts England's dominant position in the gold standard); and the central bank should be protected against political pressure aiming at "easy money" in favour of employment or the state of public finance.

Even if the leitmotif of an "apolitical money" should reflect the politicians' intention, it is by no means obvious that EMU will, in practical terms, turn into a "free market" society without governmental intervention. The abolition of exchange rates may only imply a shift of problems and policies; as national interest rate policies aiming to stabilize the foreign exchange will be substituted by structural, regional and social policies in order to cushion the burden of adjustment on the part of market agents. The problem in EMU is not that there will be no winners, but rather the question of how to deal with those who – at least temporarily – lose jobs and market income. A stability-oriented monetary union might go along with a "transfer union" which in the long run, despite its well-meant intentions, might undermine competitive forces and economic dynamic.

It is true that the traditional preconditions of an *optimal currency area* might endogenously adjust to a regime switch; but Europe with its multiple levels of policy making and its powerful national interest groups has yet to prove that it is an *optimal governmental area* for organizing a European welfare state which exhibits an optimal mix of equity and efficiency. There is more to fear than to hope for from a realization of a political union because a standardization of social and administrative regulations is not efficient, given the variety of European societies; the monetary authorities, in particular, would lose some of their strategic advantage vis-à-vis the still decentralized and competing bodies of policy making.

Compared to the gold standard, the option of "apolitical money" will hardly be attainable because, with price stability instead of exchange rate stability as its explicit target, monetary policy cannot act as a supervisor in the sphere of financial markets, but is forced to control the macrodynamics on goods and labour markets. This is the tragic irony in the legacy of the Keynesian Revolution: Keynes' efforts to come off the gold standard, which he condemned as representing an outdated restraint for maintaining internal equilibrium, i.e. price stability *and* full employment, finally ended up as a concept of stabilization which relied on a stock of unemployment to deter inflation. Thus, although the ECB attempts to present itself as an institution charged with the stability of the monetary "order" of society, it actually executes demand policies and thus cannot avoid coming into conflict with employment interests. The almost constitutional aura of European monetary authorities, cultivated for obvious reasons, might fade by continuing public debates and assessments on the adequacy of interest policies given the state of macroeconomic activity. Therefore the Bundesbank-oriented way of European monetary policy over the years might approach the American way: the Fed explicitly attempts to steer a course which is more willing to compromise with regard to price stability *and* output growth.

The ECB already is in a similar position as the Fed with respect to the problem of external equilibrium. The worldwide tendency toward greater exchange rate flexibility stems from the decline of key currency systems in general and the failure of single strategies of unilateral exchange rate fixing. In a world of paper currencies, which have become emancipated from a metallic backing, the exchange rate peg often served as a substitute for insufficient domestic monetary control and thus was subject to successful speculative attacks. Monetary stability has to be built at home. The exchange rate cannot be fixed by monetary policy for two reasons: first, because there is hardly any alternative policy tool available for controlling inflation, if the central bank is charged with the task of clearing the foreign exchange; second, being an asset price, the exchange rate incorporates preferences, assessments and expectations of current and future trends on all markets of the countries involved and therefore, quite naturally, is subject to substantial volatility. It is true that central banks can win any battle against speculators if they stand ready for an unlimited supply of the currency in excess demand, but that would deprive them of the ability of monetary control on domestic markets.

In a world of unrestricted and interest-elastic capital movements, exchange rates even in the long run cannot be determined by trade balances. At any moment in time, the spot rate depends on all expected future interest rate differentials; in each period, the foreign exchange establishes an equilibrium of actual interest rate differentials and the expected rate of change of the exchange rate. The degree of freedom in the foreign exchange's equilibrium, as to the absolute level of exchange rates, indicates the basic nominal instability of a multipolar international monetary standard, which also spreads out into the national economies. Currency areas with relatively low mutual trade shares in GDP should nevertheless prefer the flexible-exchange-rate regime to preserve their scope for macroeconomic stabilization. Small open economies might opt for a currency boards or a currency union (including its most simple variant of enlarging the operating area of a dominating currency). There are no "blueprints" available which offer an ideal way of organizing a world currency reform.

List of Figures

List of Tables

References

Alesina, A. (1997): Comment. *Brookings Papers on Economic Activity*, 301-4.

Alesina, A. et al. (1995): Together or Separately? Issues on the Costs and Benefits of Political and Fiscal Unions. *European Economic Review*, 39, 751-8.

Almeida, A. / Goodhart, C. A. E. (1998): Does the Adoption of Inflation Targets Affect Central Bank Behaviour? *Banca Nazionale del Lavoro, Quarterly Review*, Special Issue, 19-107.

Andréadès, A. (1909): *History of the Bank of England – 1640 to 1903*. 4th ed., Reprint, Kelley, New York 1966.

Aristoteles (1996): *The Politics and The Constitution of Athens*. Cambridge University Press, Cambridge.

Arrow, K. J. / Hahn. F. H. (1971): *General Competitive Analysis*. Holden, San Francisco.

Artis, M. J. / Lewis, M. K. (1993): Après Le Déluge – Monetary and Exchange-Rate Policy in Britain and Europe. *Oxford Review of Economic Policy*, 9, 3, 36-61.

Auster, P. (1997): *Hand to Mouth*. Faber & Faber, London 1998.

Bagehot, W. (1873): *Lombard Street*. Reprint, Hyperion, Westport 1979.

Balbach, A. B. (1978): The Mechanics of Intervention in Exchange Markets. *Federal Reserve Bank of St. Louis Review*, 60, 2, 2-7.

Balogh, T. (1973): *Fact and Fancy in International Economic Relations*. Pergamon, Oxford et al.

Barro, R. J. (1979): Money and the Price Level Under the Gold Standard. *Economic Journal*, 89, 13-33.

Barsky, R. B. et al. (1988): The Worldwide Change in the Behavior of Interest Rates and Prices in 1914. *European Economic Review*, 32, 1123-54.

Bean, C. R. (1998): Monetary Policy under EMU. *Oxford Review of Economic Policy*, 14, 3, 41-53.

Begg, D. (1989): Floating Exchange Rates in Theory and Practice. *Oxford Review of Economic Policy*, 5, 3, 24-39.

Bergsten, C. F. (1997): The Dollar and the Euro. *Foreign Affairs*, 76, July/August, 83-95.

Bernanke, B. S. (1993): The World on a Cross of Gold. *Journal of Monetary Economics*, 31, 251-67.

Bernanke, B. S. / Mihov, I. (1997): What Does the Bundesbank Target? *European Economic Review*, 41, 1025-53.

Bernholz, P. (1998): Die Bundesbank und die Währungsintegration in Europa. In: Deutsche Bundesbank, ed.: *Fünfzig Jahre Deutsche Mark*. Beck, München, 773-833.

Binswanger, H. C. (1982): Geld und Wirtschaft im Verständnis des Merkantilismus. In: Neumark, F., ed.: *Studien zur Entwicklung der ökonomischen Theorie II*. Schriften des Vereins für Socialpolitik, 115/II, Duncker & Humblot, Berlin, 93-129.

Blanchard, O. J. / Muet, P. A. (1993): Competitiveness through Disinflation – An Assessment of the French Macroeconomic Strategy. *Economic Policy*, 16, 11-44.

Blaug, M. (1995): Why Is the Quantity Theory of Money the Oldest Surviving Theory in Economics. In: Blaug, M. et al.: *The Quantity Theory of Money*. Elgar, Aldershot, 27-49.

Blessing, K. (1962): Das Problem der Geldwertstabilität. In: Erbe, W. et al., eds.: *Währung zwischen Politik und Wirtschaft*. Deutsche Verlags-Anstalt, Stuttgart, 159-77.

Blinder, A. S. (1998): *Central Banking in Theory and Practice*. MIT Press, Cambridge / London.

Bliss, C. (1975): *Capital Theory and the Distribution of Income*. North Holland, Amsterdam et al.

Bliss, C. (1986): The Rise and Fall of the Dollar. *Oxford Review of Economic Policy*, 2, 1, 7-24.

Bloomfield, A. I. (1959): *Monetary Policy Under the International Gold Standard, 1880-1914*. Federal Reserve Bank, New York.

Bloomfield, A. I. (1963): *Short Term Capital Movements under the Pre-1914 Gold Standard*. Princeton University Press, Princeton.

Böhm-Bawerk, E. von (1884): *Capital and Interest*. Reprint, Kelley, New York 1970.

Borchardt, K. / Schötz, H. O., eds. (1991): *Wirtschaftspolitik in der Krise*. Nomos, Baden-Baden.

Bordo, M. D. (1993): The Gold Standard, Bretton Woods and Other Monetary Regimes. *Federal Reserve Bank of St. Louis Review*, 75, March/April, 123-91.

Cairncross, A. (1988): The Bank of England. In: Toniolo, G., ed.: *Central Banks' Independence in Historical Perspective*. De Gruyter, Berlin / New York, 39-72.

Canzoneri, M. B. / Gray, J. A. (1985): Monetary Policy Games and the Consequences of Non-Cooperative Behavior. *International Economic Review*, 26, 547-64.

Canzoneri, M. B. et al. (1997): Mechanisms for Achieving Monetary Stability – Inflation Targeting versus the ERM. *Journal of Money, Credit, and Banking*, 29, 46-60.

Capie, F. / Goodhart, C. A. E. (1995): Central Banks, Macro Policy, and the Financial System. *Financial History Review*, 2, 145-61.

Chick, V. (1983): *Macroeconomics after Keynes*. Allen, Oxford.

Clapham, Sir J. (1944a,b): *The Bank of England – A History*. Vol. 1, 2. Cambridge University Press, London et al.

Clower, R. W. (1967): Foundations of Monetary Theory. in: Clower, R. W., ed.: *Monetary Theory – Selected Readings*. Penguin, Harmondsworth 1973, 202-11.

Coleman, J. S. (1990): *Foundations of Social Theory*. Belknap, Cambridge / London 1994.

Cooper, R. N. (1975): Prolegomena to the Choice of an International Monetary System. *International Organization*, 29, 63-97.

Cooper, R. N. (1982): The Gold Standard – Historical Facts and Future Prospects. *Brookings Papers on Economic Activity*, 1-45.

Cooper, R. N. (1985): Economic Interdependence and Coordination of Economic Policies. In: Jones, R. W. / Kenen, P. B., eds.: *Handbook of International Economics*. Amsterdam. Vol. 2, 1195-234.

Crabbe, L. (1989): The International Gold Standard and U.S. Monetary Policy from World War I to the New Deal. *Federal Reserve Bulletin*, 75, 423-40.

Crafts, N. F. R. (1998): Forging Ahead and Falling Behind – The Rise and Relative Decline of the First Industrial Nation. *Journal of Economic Perspectives*, 12, 2, 193-210.

Davidson, P. (1978): *Money and the Real World*. 2nd ed., Macmillan, London / Basingstoke.

Davidson, P. (1981): Post Keynesian Economics. In: Bell, D. / Kristol, I., eds.: *The Crisis in Economic Theory*. Basic Books, New York, 151-73.

Davidson, P. (1992/93): Reforming the World's Money. *Journal of Post Keynesian Economics*, 15, 153-79.

Davidson, P. (1994): *Post Keynesian Macroeconomic Theory*. Elgar, Aldershot.

Davidson, P. (1999): Global Macro Policies for Reducing Persistent High Unemployment Rates in the OECD Countries. In: Filc, W. / Köhler, C., eds.: *Macroeconomic Causes of Unemployment*. Duncker & Humblot, Berlin, 97-115.

De Grauwe, P. (1994a): *The Economics of Monetary Integration*. 2nd ed., Oxford University Press, Oxford et al.

De Grauwe, P. (1994b): Towards European Monetary Union Without the EMS. *Economic Policy*, 18, 147-85.

De Grauwe, P. (1996): *International Money*. 2nd ed., Oxford University Press, Oxford.

De Grauwe, P. (1998a): Core-Periphery Relations in EMU. In: Duwendag, D., ed.: *Finanzmärkte im Spannungsfeld von Globalisierung, Regulierung und Geldpolitik*. Schriften des Vereins für Socialpolitik, 261, Duncker & Humblot, Berlin, 153-77.

De Grauwe, P. (1998b): The Design of the European Central Bank. *Kredit und Kapital*, Supplement 14: Europäische Währungsunion, 295-315.

De Vroey, M. (1999): The Marshallian Market and the Walrasian Economy – Two Incompatible Bedfellows. *Scottish Journal of Political Economy*, 46, 319-38.

Deutschmann, C. (1995): Geld als soziales Konstrukt – Zur Aktualität von Marx und Simmel. *Leviathan, Zeitschrift für Sozialwissenschaft*, 23, 376-93.

Dillard, D. (1955): The Theory of a Monetary Economy. In: Kurihara, K. K., ed.: *Post-Keynesian Economics*. Allen & Unwin, London, 3-30.

Dillard, D. (1987): Money as an Institution of Capitalism. *Journal of Economic Issues*, 21, 1623-47.

Dornbusch, R. (1980): Exchange Rate Economics – Where Do We Stand? *Brookings Papers on Economic Activity*, 143-85.

Dornbusch, R. (1987): Prosperity or Price Stability. *Oxford Review of Economic Policy*, 3, 3, 9-19.

Dornbusch, R. (1989): Europe 1992 – Macroeconomic Implications. *Brookings Papers on Economic Activity*, 341-62.

Dornbusch, R. (1993): Comment. *Brookings Papers on Economic Activity*, 130-6.

Dornbusch, R. (1995): Comment. *Brookings Papers on Economic Activity*, 197-202.

Dornbusch, R. (1996a): Euro Fantasies. *Foreign Affairs*, 75, September/October, 110-24.

Dornbusch, R. (1996b): The Effectiveness of Exchange-Rate Changes. *Oxford Review of Economic Policy*, 12, 3, 26-38.

Dornbusch, R. (1997): Fiscal Aspects of Monetary Integration. *American Economic Review, Papers and Proceedings*, 87, 221-3.

Dornbusch, R. et al. (1995): Currency Crises and Collapses. *Brookings Papers on Economic Activity*, 219-93.

Dornbusch, R. et al. (1998): Immediate Challenges for the European Central Bank. *Economic Policy*, 26, 17-64.

Dow, S. / Rodriguez-Fuentes, C. (1998): The Political Economy of Monetary Policy. In: Arestis, P. / Sawyer, M., eds.: *The Political Economy of Central Banking*. Elgar, Cheltenham / Northampton, 1-19.

Dowd, K. (2000): The Invisible Hand and the Evolution of the Monetary System. In: Smithin, J., ed.: *What Is Money*? Routledge, London / New York, 139-56.

Doyle, C. / Wheale, M. (1994): Do We Really Want an Independent Central Bank? *Oxford Review of Economic Policy*, 10, 3, 61-77.

Ehrenberg, R. (1896a,b): *Das Zeitalter der Fugger*. Vol. I, II. Reprint, Olms, Hildesheim et al. 1990.

Ehrenberg, R. (1909): Die Banken vom 11. bis zum 17. Jahrhundert. In: *Handwörterbuch der Staatswissenschaften*, Vol. 2, 3rd ed. Jena, 360-6.

Eichengreen, B. (1984): Central Bank Cooperation under the Interwar Gold Standard. *Explorations in Economic History*, 21, 64-87.

Eichengreen, B. (1985): Editor's Introduction. In: Eichengreen, B., ed.: *The Gold Standard in Theory and History*. Methuen, New York / London, 1-35.

Eichengreen, B. (1987): Conducting the International Orchestra – Bank of England Leadership under the Classical Gold Standard. *Journal of International Money and Finance*, 6, 5-29.

Eichengreen, B. (1989): Hegemonic Stability Theories of the International Monetary System. In: Cooper, R. N. et al., eds.: *Can Nations Agree?* Brookings, Washington, 255-98.

Eichengreen, B. (1992): *Golden Fetters – The Gold Standard and the Great Depression, 1919-1939.* Oxford University Press, Oxford.

Eichengreen, B. (1993): European Monetary Unification. *Journal of Economic Literature*, 31, 1321-57.

Eichengreen, B. (1999): Kicking the Habit – Moving From Pegged Rates to Greater Flexibility. *Economic Journal*, 109, C1-C14.

Eichengreen, B. / Hagen, J. von (1996): Federalism, Fiscal Restraints, and European Monetary Union. *American Economic Review, Papers and Proceedings*, 86, 134-8.

Eichengreen, B. / Wyplosz, C. (1993): The Unstable EMS. *Brookings Papers on Economic Activity*, 51-124.

Eichengreen, B. et al. (1995a): Exchange Market Mayhem – The Antecedents and Aftermath of Speculative Attacks. *Economic Policy*, 21, 215-312.

Eichengreen, B. et al. (1995b): Two Cases for Sand in the Wheels of International Finance. *Economic Journal*, 105, 162-72.

Eltis, W. (1995): John Locke, the Quantity Theory of Money and the Establishment of a Sound Currency. In: Blaug, M. u.a.: *The Quantity Theory of Money*. Elgar, Aldershot, 4-26.

Emminger, O. (1934): Die englischen Währungsexperimente der Nachkriegszeit. *Weltwirtschaftliches Archiv*, 40, 270-325.

Emminger, O. (1978): 30 Jahre Deutsche Mark. *Monatsbericht der Deutschen Bundesbank*, June, 5-12.

Feis, H. (1930): *Europe – The World's Banker*. Kelley, Clifton 1974.

Feldstein, M. (1997): The Political Economy of the European Economic and Monetary Union. *Journal of Economic Perspectives*, 11, 4, 23-42.

Fischer, S. (1986): Friedman versus Hayek on Private Money. *Journal of Monetary Economics*, 17, 433-9.

Fischer, S. (1995): Central-Bank Independence Revisited. *American Economic Review, Papers and Proceedings*, 85, 201-6.

Fischer, W. (1981): Internationale Wirtschaftsbeziehungen und Währungsordnung vor dem Ersten Weltkrieg 1870-1914. In: Kellenbenz, H., ed.: *Weltwirtschaftliche und währungspolitische Probleme seit dem Ausgang des Mittelalters*. Fischer, Stuttgart / New York, 163-9.

Fitoussi, J.-P. et al. (1993): *Competitive Disinflation*. Oxford University Press, Oxford.

Foxwell, H. S. (1908): Preface. In: Andréadès (1909), xxiii-xlii.

Frankel, J. A. (1988): International Capital Flows and Domestic Economic Policies. In: Feldstein, M., ed.: *The United States in the World Economy*. Unversity of Chicago Press, Chicago / London, 559-627.

Fratianni, M. / Hauskrecht, A. (1998): From the Gold Standard to a Bipolar Monetary System. *Open Economies Review*, 9, 609-35.

Friedman, M. (1969): *The Optimum Quantity of Money and Other Essays*. Macmillan, London / Basingstoke.

Friedman, M. / Schwartz, A. J. (1963): *A Monetary History of the United States, 1867-1960*. Princeton University Press, Princeton 1990.

Fullarton, J. (1845): Die Regelung der Währung. In: Diehl, K. / Mombert, P., eds.: *Vom Gelde*. Reprint, Ullstein, Frankfurt et al. 1979, 90*-115*.

Galbraith, K. (1975): *Money – Whence It Came, Where It Went*. Penguin, Harmondsworth et al. 1976.

Giavazzi, F. / Pagano, M. (1988): The Advantages of Tying One's Hands – EMS Discipline and Central Bank Credibility. *European Economic Review*, 32, 1055-82.

Giovannini, A. (1989): How Do Fixed-Exchange-Rate Regimes Work? Evidence from the Gold Standard, Bretton Woods and the EMS. In: Miller, M. el al., eds.: *Blueprints for Exchange Rate Management*. Academic Press, London, 13-41.

Giovannini, A. (1993): Bretton Woods and Its Precursors. In: Bordo, M. D. / Eichengreen, B., eds.: *A Retrospective on the Bretton Woods System*. University of Chicago Press, Chicago / London, 109-53.

Goodhart, C. A. E. (1988): *The Evolution of Central Banks*. MIT Press, Cambridge / London.

Goodhart, C. A. E. (1994): Game Theory for Central Bankers. *Journal of Economic Literature*, 32, 101-14.

Goodhart, C. A. E. (1996a): European Monetary Integration. *European Economic Review*, 40, 1083-90.

Goodhart, C. A. E. (1996b): The Transition to EMU. *Scottish Journal of Political Economy*, 43, 241-57.

Goodhart, C. A. E. / Huang, H. (1998): Time Inconsistency in a Model with Lags, Persistence, and Overlapping Wage Contracts. *Oxford Economic Papers*, 50, 378-96.

Gordon, R. J. (1997): The Time-Varying NAIRU and its Implications for Economic Policy. *Journal of Economic Perspectives*, 11, 1, 11-32.

Goschen, G. J. (1861): *The Theory of the Foreign Exchanges*. Wilson, London.

Grantham, G. et al. (1977): On the Microeconomics of the Supply of Money. *Oxford Economic Papers*, 29, 339-56.

Gros, D. (1998): Delivering Price Stability in EMU. *Kredit und Kapital*, Supplement 14: Europäische Währungsunion, 341-63.

Grubel, H. G. (1969): *The International Monetary System*. Penguin, Harmondsworth 1972.

Hahn, F. H. (1977): Keynesian Economics and General Equilibrium Theory. In: Harcourt, G. C., ed.: *The Microeconomic Foundations of Macroeconomics*. Macmillan, London, 25-40.

Hahn, F. H. (1980): General Equilibrium Theory. *Public Interest*, Special Issue, 123-38.

Hahn, F. H. (1982): *Money and Inflation*. Blackwell, Oxford.

Hahn, F. H. / Solow, R. M. (1995): *A Critical Essay on Modern Macroeconomic Theory*. Blackwell, Oxford.

Hamada, K. (1979): Macroeconomic Strategy and Coordination under Alternative Exchange Rates. In: Dornbusch, R. / Frenkel, J. A., eds.: *International Economic Policy – Theory and Evidence*. Johns Hopkins, Baltimore / London, 292-324.

Hamilton, J. D. (1988): Role of the International Gold Standard in Propagating the Great Depression. *Contemporary Policy Issues*, 6, 67-89.

Hankel, W. (1993): Geld – der Entwicklungsmotor. In: Stadermann, H.-J. / Steiger, O., eds.: *Der Stand und die nächste Zukunft der Geldforschung*. Duncker & Humblot, Berlin, 439-48.

Hawtrey, R. G. (1923): *Currency and Credit*. 2nd ed., Longmans & Green, London et al.

Hawtrey, R. G. (1930): Credit. In: *Encyclopedia of the Social Sciences*, Vol. 3. New York, 545-50.

Hayek, F. A. von (1927): Zur Problemstellung der Zinstheorie. *Archiv für Sozialwissenschaft und Sozialpolitik*, 58, 517-32.

Hayek, F. A. von (1928): Intertemporal Price Equilibrium and Movements in the Value of Money. In: Kresge, S., ed.: *The Collected Works of F. A. Hayek*, Vol. V. Routledge, London 1999, 186-227.

Hayek, F. A. von (1931): *Prices and Production*. Routledge & Kegan Paul, London.

Hayek, F. A. von (1968): Competition as a Recovery Procedure. In: Hayek, F. A. von: *New Studies in Philosophy, Politics, Economics and the History of Ideas*. Henley, London 1978, 179-95.

Hayek, F. A. von (1978): *Denationalizing of Money – The Argument Refined*. The Institut of Economic Affairs, London.

Heering, W. (1991): *Geld, Liquiditätsprämie und Kapitalgüternachfrage*. Transfer, Regensburg.

Heering, W. (1999): Privateigentum, Vertrauen und Geld. In: Betz, K. / Roy, T., eds.: *Privateigentum und Geld*. Metropolis, Marburg, 99-143.

Heinsohn, G. / Steiger, O. (1996): *Eigentum, Zins und Geld*. Rowohlt, Reinbek.

Heinsohn, G. / Steiger, O. (2000): The Property Theory of Interest and Money. In: Smithin, J., ed.: *What Is Money?* Routledge, London / New York, 67-100.

Helfferich, K. (1919): *Das Geld*. 4th ed., Hirschfeld, Leipzig.

Hellwig, M. F. (1985): What Do We Know about Currency Competition? *Zeitschrift für Wirtschafts- und Sozialwissenschaften*, 105, 565-88.

Hellwig, M. F. (1993): The Challenge of Monetary Theory. *European Economic Review*, 37, 215-42.

Hellwig, M. F. (1998): Systemische Risiken im Finanzsektor. In: Duwendag, D., ed.: *Finanzmärkte im Spannungsfeld von Globalisierung, Regulierung und Geldpolitik.* Schriften des Vereins für Socialpolitik, 261, Duncker & Humblot, Berlin, 123-51.

Hicks, J. (1946): *Value and Capital.* 2nd ed., Oxford University Press, Oxford.

Hicks, J. (1969): *A Theory of Economic History.* Clarendon, Oxford.

Hicks, J. (1974): Capital Controversies – Ancient and Modern. *American Economic Review, Papers and Proceedings*, 64, 307-16.

Hicks, J. (1982): The Foundations of Monetary Theory. In: Hicks, J.: *Money, Interest and Wages.* Collected Essays on Economic Theory, Vol. 2, Blackwell, Oxford, 236-75.

Hicks, J. (1989): *A Market Theory of Money.* Clarendon, Oxford.

Hirsch, F. (1972): The Political Economics of European Monetary Integration. *The World Today*, 28, Royal Institute of International Affairs, London, 424-33.

Hirsch, F. (1978): The Ideological Underlay of Inflation. In: Hirsch, F. / Goldthorpe, J. H., eds.: *The Political Economy of Inflation.* Robertson, Oxford, 263-84.

Hirschman, A. O. (1977): *The Passions and the Interests – Political Arguments for Capitalism before Its Triumph.* Princeton University Press, Princeton.

Holtfrerich, C.-L. (1988): Relations between Monetary Authorities and Governmental Institutions. In: Toniolo, G., ed.: *Central Banks' Independence in Historical Perspective.* De Gruyter, Berlin / New York, 105-59.

Holtfrerich, C.-L. (1989): Zur Entwicklung der monetären Konjunkturtheorien. In: Schefold, B., ed.: *Studien zur Entwicklung der ökonomischen Theorie VIII.* Schriften des Vereins für Socialpolitik, 115/VIII, Duncker & Humblot, Berlin, 103-40.

Homer, S. (1977): *A History of Interest Rates.* 2nd ed., Rutgers, New Brunswick.

Hume, D. (1739/40): *A Treatise of Human Nature.* Reprint, Clarendon, Oxford 1951.

Ingham, G. (2000): "Babylonian Madness" – On the Historical and Sociological Origins of Money. In: Smithin, J., ed.: *What Is Money?* Routledge, London / New York, 16-41.

Issing, O. (1992): The Impact of German Unification on the Members of the European Community. In: Deutsche Bundesbank, ed.: *Auszüge aus Presseartikeln*, No. 75, Frankfurt, 28.10.92, 3-6.

Issing, O. (1994): Geldmengensteuerung zur Sicherung des Geldwertes – Ein bewährtes Konzept. *WSI-Mitteilungen*, 47, 682-90.

Issing, O. (1997): Der Euro im Weltwährungssystem. In: Deutsche Bundesbank, ed.: *Auszüge aus Presseartikeln*, No. 22, Frankfurt, 16.4.97, 1-7.

Issing, O. (1998): Die Europäische Zentralbank – Das Problem der Glaubwürdigkeit. In: Duwendag, D., ed.: *Finanzmärkte im Spannungsfeld von Globalisierung, Regulierung und Geldpolitik*. Schriften des Vereins für Socialpolitik, 261, Duncker & Humblot, Berlin, 179-92.

Issing, O. (1999a): The ECB and Its Watchers. In: Deutsche Bundesbank, ed.: *Auszüge aus Presseartikeln*, No. 41, Frankfurt, 17.6.99, 10-9.

Issing, O. (1999b): Hayek – Currency Competition and European Monetary Policy. In: Deutsche Bundesbank, ed.: *Auszüge aus Presseartikeln*, No. 36, Frankfurt, 27.5.99, 9-17.

James, H. (1998): Die Reichsbank 1876 bis 1945. In: Deutsche Bundesbank, ed.: *Fünfzig Jahre Deutsche Mark*. Beck, München, 29-90.

Jarchow, H.-J. (1997): Zur Theorie und Realität internationaler Währungssysteme. *Zeitschrift für Wirtschafts- und Sozialwissenschaften*, 117, 443-72.

Jevons, W. S. (1879): *The Theory of Political Economy*. 2nd ed., Reprint, Penguin, Harmondsworth et al. 1970.

Johnson, H. G. (1972): Inflation – A "Monetarist" View. In: Johnson, H. G.: *Further Essays in Monetary Economics*. Allen & Unwin, London, 325-37.

Kaldor, N. (1985): How Monetarism Failed. *Challenge*, May/June, 4-13.

Kenen, P. B. (1960): International Liquidity and the Balance of Payments of a Reserve-Currency Country. *Quarterly Journal of Economics*, 74, 572-86.

Kenen, P. B. (1995): Capital Controls, the EMS and the EMU. *Economic Journal*, 105, 181-92.

Kenen, P. B. (1997): Preferences, Domains, and Sustainability. *American Economic Review, Papers and Proceedings*, 87, 211-3.

Keynes, J. M. (1923): *A Tract on Monetary Reform*. The Collected Writings of John Maynard Keynes, Vol. IV. Macmillan, London / Basingstoke 1971.

Keynes, J. M. (1925): The Economic Consequences of Mr Churchill. In: *The Collected Writings of John Maynard Keynes*, Vol. IX. Macmillan, London / Basingstoke 1972, 207-30.

Keynes, J. M. (1930): *A Treatise on Money, 2: The Applied Theory of Money*. The Collected Writings of John Maynard Keynes, Vol. VI. Macmillan, London / Basingstoke 1971.

Keynes, J. M. (1933): The Distinction between a Co-operative Economy and an Entrepreneur Economy. In: Moggridge, D., ed.: *The Collected Writings of John Maynard Keynes*, Vol. XXIX. Macmillan, London / Basingstoke 1979, 76-87.

Keynes, J. M. (1933/34): Quasi-Rent and the Marginal Efficiency of Capital. In: Moggridge, D., ed.: *The Collected Writings of John Maynard Keynes*, Vol. XXIX. Macmillan, London / Basingstoke 1979, 111-20.

Keynes, J. M. (1934): The Propensity to Invest. In: Moggridge, D., ed.: *The Collected Writings of John Maynard Keynes*, Vol. XIII. Macmillan, London / Basingstoke 1973, 450-6.

Keynes, J. M. (1936): *The General Theory of Employment, Interest, and Money*. The Collected Writings of John Maynard Keynes, Vol. VII. Macmillan, London / Basingstoke 1973.

Keynes, J. M. (1937a): The Theory of the Rate of Interest. In: Moggridge, D., ed.: *The Collected Writings of John Maynard Keynes*, Vol. XIV. Macmillan, London / Basingstoke 1973, 101-8.

Keynes, J. M. (1937b): Alternative Theories of the Rate of Interest. In: Moggridge, D., ed.: *The Collected Writings of John Maynard Keynes*, Vol. XIV. Macmillan, London / Basingstoke 1973, 201-15.

Keynes, J. M. (1937c): The General Theory of Employment. In: Moggridge, D., ed.: *The Collected Writings of John Maynard Keynes*, Vol. XIV. Macmillan, London / Basingstoke 1973, 109-23.

Keynes, J. M. (1938): Letter to Hugh Townshend. In: Moggridge, D., ed.: *The Collected Writings of John Maynard Keynes*, Vol. XXIX. Macmillan, London / Basingstoke 1979, 293-4.

Keynes, J. M. (1942): Proposals for an International Clearing Union. In: Moggridge, D., ed.: *The Collected Writings of John Maynard Keynes*, Vol. XXV. Macmillan, London / Basingstoke 1980, 168-95.

Keynes, J. M. (1943a): Speeches. In: Moggridge, D., ed.: *The Collected Writings of John Maynard Keynes*, Vol. XXV. Macmillan, London / Basingstoke 1980, 206-15, 269-80.

Keynes, J. M. (1943b): The Objective of International Price Stability. In: Moggridge, D., ed.: *The Collected Writings of John Maynard Keynes*, Vol. XXVI. Macmillan, London / Basingstoke 1980, 30-3.

Keynes, J. M. (1943c): Letter. In: Moggridge, D., ed.: *The Collected Writings of John Maynard Keynes*, Vol. XXVI. Macmillan, London / Basingstoke 1980, 38.

Kindleberger, C. P. (1967): The Politics of International Money and World Language. In: Cohen, B. J., ed.: *The International Political Economy of Monetary Relations*. Elgar, Aldershot 1993, 294-304.

Kindleberger, C. P. (1978): *Manias, Panics and Crashes*. Macmillan, London et al. 1981.

Kindleberger, C. P. (1983): Key Currencies and Financial Centres. In: Machlup, F., ed.: *Reflections on a Troubled World Economy*. St. Martin's Press, London, 75-90.

Kindleberger, C. P. (1984): *A Financial History of Western Europe*. Allen & Unwin, London 1987.

Kindleberger, C. P. (1986): *The World in Depression 1929-1939*. 2nd. ed., Penguin, Harmondsworth 1987.

Kindleberger, C. P. (1996): *World Economic Primacy, 1500-1990*. Oxford University Press, New York.

Kiyotaki, N. / Wright, R. (1992): Acceptability, Means of Payment, and Media of Exchange. In: Newman, P. et al., eds.: *The New Palgrave Dictionary of Money and Finance*. London / New York, Vol. 1, 3-5.

Knapp, G. F. (1909): Geldtheorie, staatliche. In: *Handwörterbuch der Staatswissenschaften*, Vol. 4, 3rd ed. Jena, 610-8.

Knight, F. H. (1934): Capital, Time, and the Interest Rate. *Economica*, 1, 257-86.

Kregel, J. A. (1976): Economic Methodology in the Face of Uncertainty – The Modelling Methods of Keynes and the Post Keynesians. *Economic Journal*, 86, 209-25.

Kregel, J. A. (1980): Markets and Institutions as Features of a Capitalistic Production System. *Journal of Post Keynesian Economics*, 3, 32-48.

Kregel, J. A. (1985): Hamlet Without the Prince – Cambridge Macroeconomics Without Money. *American Economic Review, Papers and Proceedings*, 75, 133-9.

Kregel, J. A. (1994/95): The Viability of Economic Policy and the Priorities of Economic Policy. *Journal of Post Keynesian Economics*, 17, 2, 261-77.

Kregel, J. A. (1995): Neoclassical Price Theory, Institutions, and the Evolution of Securities Market Organisation. *Economic Journal*, 105, 459-70.

Kregel, J. A. (1998): Aspects of a Post Keynesian Theory of Finance. *Journal of Post Keynesian Economics*, 21, 111-33.

Krugman, P. R. (1979): A Model of Balance-of-Payment Crises. *Journal of Money, Credit, and Banking*, 11, 311-25.

Krugman, P. R. (1996): Making Sense of the Competitiveness Debate. *Oxford Review of Economic Policy*, 12, 3, 17-25.

Krugman, P. R. (1999): The Return of Depression Economics. *Foreign Affairs*, 78, January /February, 56-74.

Krugman, P. R. (2000): Expect America's Real Economy to Carry On. In: Deutsche Bundesbank, ed.: *Auszüge aus Presseartikeln*, No. 20, Frankfurt, 19.4.00, 13-9.

Kurz, H. D. (1998): Über das "Perpetuum mobile des Volkswirtschaftsmechanismus" und eine "theoretische Verkehrtheit". In: Streißler, E. W., ed.: *Studien zur Entwicklung der ökonomischen Theorie XVIII – Knut Wicksell als Ökonom*. Schriften des Vereins für Socialpolitik, 115/XVIII, Duncker & Humblot, Berlin, 131-86.

Laidler, D. (1988): Taking Money Seriously. *Canadian Journal of Economics*, 21, 687-713.

Laidler, D. (1989): Dow and Saville's "Critique of Monetary Policy" – A Review Article. *Journal of Economic Literature*, 27, 1147-59.

Laidler, D. (1991): *The Golden Age of the Quantity Theory*. Allan, New York et al.

Laidler, D. / Nobay, A. R. (1976): International Aspects of Inflation. In: Claassen, E.-M. / Salin, P., eds.: *Recent Issues in Monetary Economics*. North Holland, Amsterdam, 291-307.

Laidler, D. / Rowe, N. (1980): Georg Simmel's "Philosophy of Money" – A Review Article for Economists. *Journal of Economic Literature*, 18, 97-105.

Laum, B. (1924): *Heiliges Geld*. Mohr, Tübingen.

Law, J. (1720): *Money and Trade Considered*. 2nd ed. Reprint, Kelley, New York 1966.

Leijonhufvud, A. (1977): Costs and Consequences of Inflation. In: Leijonhufvud, A.: *Information and Coordination*. Oxford University Press, New York 1981, 227-69.

Lindert, P. H. (1969): *Key Currencies and Gold, 1900-1913*. Princeton University Press, Princeton.

Locke, J. (1690): *Second Treatise on Government*. Reprint, Blackwell, Oxford 1956.

Lordon, F. (1998): The Logic and Limits of 'Désinflation Compétitive'. *Oxford Review of Economic Policy*, 14, 1, 96-113.

Loyd, S. J. (1844): *Thoughts on the Separation of the Departments of the Bank of England*. Pelham Richardson, London.

Lucas, R. E. (1996): Monetary Neutrality. *Journal of Political Economy*, 104, 661-82.

Luhmann, N. (1988): *Die Wirtschaft der Gesellschaft*. Suhrkamp, Frankfurt 1996.

Lutz, F. A. (1935): Goldwährung und Wirtschaftsordnung. In: Lutz, F. A.: *Geld und Währung*. Mohr, Tübingen 1962, 1-27.

Lutz, F. A. (1936): Das Grundproblem der Geldverfassung. In: Lutz, F. A.: *Geld und Währung*. Mohr, Tübingen 1962, 28-102.

Lutz, F. A. / Niehans, J. (1980): Faktorpreisbildung II – Zinstheorie. In: *Handwörterbuch der Wirtschaftswissenschaften*, Vol. 2, Stuttgart, 530-48.

Macleod, H. D. (1855): *The Theory and Practice of Banking*. Vol. 1, Longman, Brown, Green & Longmans, London.

Macleod, H. D. (1882): *Lectures on Credit and Banking*. Longman, Green, Reader & Dyer, London.

Macleod, H. D. (1889): *The Theory of Credit*. Longmans & Green, London.

Marshall, A. (1920): *Principles of Economics*. 8th ed., Reprint, Macmillan, London / Basingstoke 1982.

Marx, K. (1890): *Capital* (Vol. 1). 4th ed., Reprint, Benton, Chicago, 1952.

Masson, P. R. (1995): Gaining and Loosing ERM Credibility – The Case of the United Kingdom. *Economic Journal*, 105, 571-82.

Masson, P. R. (1996): Fiscal Dimensions of EMU. *Economic Journal*, 106, 996-1004.

McCloskey, D. N. / Zecher, L. R. (1976): How the Gold Standard Worked, 1880-1913. In: Eichengreen, B., ed.: *The Gold Standard in Theory and History*. Methuen, New York / London 1985, 63-80.

McKinnon, R. I. (1969): Private and Official International Money – The Case for the Dollar, 1969. In: McKinnon, R. I.: *The Rules of the Game*. MIT Press, Cambridge / London 1996, 137-59.

McKinnon, R. I. (1988): An International Gold Standard without Gold. In: McKinnon, R. I.: *The Rules of the Game*. MIT Press, Cambridge / London 1996, 111-35.

McKinnon, R. I. (1990): Why Floating Exchange Rates Fail – A Reconsideration of the Liquidity Trap. *Open Economies Review*, 1, 229-50.

McKinnon, R. I. (1993): The Rules of the Game – International Money in Historical Perspective. *Journal of Economic Literature*, 31, 1-44.

McKinnon, R. I. (1995): From Plaza-Louvre to a Common Monetary Standard for the Twenty-First Century. In: McKinnon, R. I.: *The Rules of the Game*. MIT Press, Cambridge / London 1996, 495-526.

McKinnon, R. I. (1996): *The Rules of the Game*. MIT Press, Cambridge / London.

Meltzer, A. H. (1995): Monetary, Credit and (Other) Transmission Processes – A Monetarist Perspective. *Journal of Economic Perspectives*, 9, 4, 49-72.

Menger, C. (1909): Geld. In: *Handwörterbuch der Staatswissenschaften*, Vol. 4, 3rd ed. Jena, 555-610.

Milgate, M. (1982): *Capital and Employment*. Academic Press, London.

Mill, J. S. (1871): *Principles of Political Economy*. 7th ed., Reprint, Kelley, Fairfield 1987.

Minford, P., ed. (1992): *The Cost of Europe*. Manchester University Press, Manchester.

Minsky, H. P. (1979): Financial Interrelations, the Balance of Payments, and the Dollar Crisis. In: Aronson, J. D., ed.: *Debt and the Less Developed Countries*. Westview, Boulder, 103-22.

Minsky, H. P. (1980): Money, Financial Markets, and the Coherence of a Market Economy. *Journal of Post Keynesian Economics*, 3, 21-31.

Minsky, H. P. (1984): Frank Hahn's 'Money and Inflation' – A Review Article. *Journal of Post Keynesian Economics*, 6, 3, 449-57.

Moggridge, D. E. (1972): *British Monetary Policy, 1924-31 – The Norman Conquest of $4.86*. Cambridge University Press, Cambridge.

Moggridge, D. E. (1986): Keynes and the International Monetary System 1909-46. In: Cohen, A. / Harcourt, J., eds.: *International Monetary Problems and Supply Side Economics*. Macmillan, London / Basingstoke, 56-83.

Moore, B. J. (1988): The Endogenous Money Supply. *Journal of Post Keynesian Economics*, 10, 3, 372-85.

Müller, A. H. (1816): *Versuche einer neuen Theorie des Geldes*. Fischer, Jena 1922.

Mundell, R. A. (1995): The International Monetary System – The Missing Factor. *Journal of Policy Modeling*, 17, 479-92.

Mundell, R. A. / Clesse, A., eds. (2000): *The Euro as a Stabilizer in the International Economic System*. Kluwer, Boston et al.

Nardis, S. de / Micossi, S. (1991): Disinflation and Re-inflation and the Implications for Transition to Monetary Union. *Banca Nazionale del Lavoro, Quarterly Review*, 165-96.

Niehans, J. (1978): *The Theory of Money*. Johns Hopkins, Baltimore / London 1980.

North, M. (1994): *Das Geld und seine Geschichte*. Beck, München.

Obstfeld, M. (1986): Rational and Self-Fulfilling Balance of Payments Crises. *American Economic Review*, 76, 72-81.

Obstfeld, M. (1995): International Currency Experience. *Brookings Papers on Economic Activity*, 119-220.

Obstfeld, M. (1997): Europe's Gamble. *Brookings Papers on Economic Activity*, 241-317.

Obstfeld, M. / Rogoff, K. (1995): The Mirage of Fixed Exchange Rates. *Journal of Economic Perspectives*, 9, 4, 73-96.

Patinkin, D. / Steiger, O. (1989): In Search of the "Veil of Money" and the "Neutrality of Money". *Scandinavian Journal of Economics*, 91, 131-46.

Pierenkämper, T. (1999): Der Weg zur Europäischen Zentralbank. In: Simmert, D. B. / Welteke, E., eds.: *Die Europäische Zentralbank*. Deutscher Sparkassen Verlag, Stuttgart, 21-47.

Pigou, A. C. (1933): *The Theory of Unemployment*. Macmillan, London.

Polanyi, K. (1957): Die Semantik der Verwendung von Geld. In: Polanyi, K.: *Ökonomie und Gesellschaft*. Suhrkamp, Frankfurt 1979, 317-45.

Portes, R. / Rey, H. (1998): The Emergence of the Euro as an International Currency. *Economic Policy*, 307-43.

Priddat, B. P. (1993): *Zufall, Schicksal, Irrtum*. Metropolis, Marburg.

Ricardo, D. (1810): The High Price of Bullion. In: Sraffa, P., ed.: *The Works and Correspondence of David Ricardo*. Vol III. Cambridge University Press, Cambridge et al., 47-127.

Ricardo, D. (1824): Plan for the Establishment of a National Bank. In: Sraffa, P., ed.: *The Works and Correspondence of David Ricardo*. Vol IV. Cambridge University Press, Cambridge et al., 271-300.

Richter, R. (1989): *Money*. Springer, Berlin / Heidelberg.

Richter, R. (1998): Europäische Währungsunion – institutionenökonomisch gesehen. *Kredit und Kapital*, 32, 159-91.

Richter, R. (1999): *Deutsche Geldpolitik 1948-1998*. Mohr, Tübingen.

Riese, H. (1986): *Theorie der Inflation*. Mohr, Tübingen.

Riese, H. (1987): Keynes als Kapitaltheoretiker. *Kredit und Kapital*, 20, 153-78.

Riese, H. (1988): Keynesianische Kapitaltheorie. In: Hagemann, H. / Steiger, O., Hg.: *Keynes' General Theory nach fünfzig Jahren*. Duncker & Humblot, Berlin, 377-401.

Riese, H. (1990): *Geld im Sozialismus*. Transfer, Regensburg.

Riese, H. (1993): Schwäche des Pfundes und Versagen der Deutschen Mark. In: Bofinger, P. et al., eds.: *Währungsunion oder Währungschaos?* Gabler, Wiesbaden, 161-88.

Riese, H. (1995): Geld – Das letzte Rätsel der Nationalökonomie. In: Schelkle, W. / Nitsch, M., eds.: *Rätsel Geld*. Metropolis, Marburg, 45-62.

Rieter, H. (1971): *Die gegenwärtige Inflationstheorie und ihre Ansätze im Werk von Thomas Tooke*. De Gruyter, Berlin / New York.

Rieter, H. (1996): *Walter Bagehot – Politischer Ökonom und Publizist im viktorianischen Zeitalter*. Wirtschaft und Finanzen, Düsseldorf.

Ritter, J. A. (1995): The Transition from Barter to Fiat Money. *American Economic Review*, 85, 134-49.

Robinson, J. (1933): The Theory of Money and the Analysis of Output. *Review of Economic Studies*, 1, 22-6.

Robinson, J. (1938): The Economics of Hyper-Inflation. In: Robinson, J.: *Collected Economic Papers*, Vol. 1, Oxford 1951, 69-77.

Robinson, J. (1971): *Economic Heresies*. Basic Books, New York.

Robinson, J. (1980): Time in Economic Theory. *Kyklos*, 33, 219-29.

Rogers, T. (1887): *The First Nine Years of the Bank of England*. Oxford.

Rogoff, K. (1996): The Purchasing Power Parity Puzzle. *Journal of Economic Literature*, 34, 647-68.

Rose, A. K. / Svensson, L. E. O. (1995): Macroeconomic and Political Determinants of Realignment Expectations. In: Eichengreen, B. et al., eds.: *Monetary and Fiscal Policy in an Integrated Europe*. Springer, Berlin et al., 91-117.

Rueff, J. / Hirsch, F. (1965): *The Role and the Rule of Gold*. Essays in International Finance, 47, Princeton University Press, Princeton.

Sarcinelli, M. (1991): Governor Baffi's Monetary Policy. *Banca Nazionale del Lavoro, Quarterly Review*, 179, 513-35.

Sarcinelli, M. (1995): Italian Monetary Policy in the '80s and '90s. *Banca Nazionale del Lavoro, Quarterly Review*, 195, 397-422.

Sargent, T. J. / Velde, F. R. (1995): Macroeconomic Aspects of the French Revolution. *Journal of Political Economy*, 103, 474-518.

Sayers, R. S. (1936): *Bank of England Operations 1890-1914*. King, London.

Sayers, R. S. (1957): *Central Banking after Bagehot*. Oxford University Press, London.

Schefold, B. (1976): Nachworte. In: Sraffa, P.: *Warenproduktion mittels Waren*. Suhrkamp, Frankfurt, 129-226.

Schumpeter, J. A. (1934): *The Theory of Economic Development*. Harvard University Press, Cambridge 1951.

Schumpeter, J. A. (1954): *History of Economic Analysis*. Reprint, Routledge, London 1994.

Schumpeter, J. A. (1970): *Das Wesen des Geldes*. Vandenhoeck & Ruprecht, Göttingen.

Schwarzer, O. (1993): Goldwährungssysteme und internationaler Zahlungsverkehr zwischen 1870 und 1914. In: Schremmer, E., ed.: *Geld und Währung vom 16. Jahrhundert bis zur Gegenwart*. Steiner, Stuttgart, 191-227.

Seccareccia, M. (1998): Wicksellian Norm, Central Bank Real Interest Rate Targeting and Macroeconomic Performance. In: Arestis, P. / Sawyer, M., eds.: *The Political Economy of Central Banking*. Elgar, Cheltenham / Northampton, 180-98.

Setterfield, M. (1997): Should Economists Dispense With the Notion of Equilibrium? *Journal of Post Keynesian Economics*, 20, 1, 47-76.

Setterfield, M. (1999): Expectations, Path Dependence and Effective Demand. *Journal of Post Keynesian Economics*, 21, 479-501.

Shackle, G. L. S. (1982): Sir John Hicks' "IS-LM: An Explanation". *Journal of Post Keynesian Economics*, 4, 435-8.

Sievert, O. (1993): Geld, das man nicht selbst herstellen kann. In: Bofinger, P. et al., eds.: *Währungsunion oder Währungschaos?* Gabler, Wiesbaden, 13-24.

Sievert, O. (1995): Grundzüge der Bundesbankpolitik. In: Deutsche Bundesbank, ed.: *Auszüge aus Presseartikeln*, No. 24, Frankfurt, 28.3.95, 3-9.

Simmel, G. (1889): Zur Psychologie des Geldes. In: Dahme, H.-J., ed.: *Georg Simmel – Aufsätze 1887 bis 1890*. Suhrkamp, Frankfurt 1995, 49-65.

Simmel, G. (1901): Philosophie des Geldes. Announcement of the first German edition. In: Simmel, G. (1991): Philosophie des Geldes. 2nd ed., Reprint, Suhrkamp, Frankfurt, 719-23.

Simmel, G. (1907): *The Philosophy of Money*. Routledge & Kegan Paul, Boston et al. 1982.

Skaggs, N. T. (1997): Henry Dunning Macleod and the Credit Theory of Money. In: Cohen, A. et al., eds.: *Money, Financial Institutions and Macroeconomics*. Kluwer, Boston u.a., 109-23.

Skidelski, R. (1995): J. M. Keynes and the Quantity Theory of Money. In: Blaug, M. et al.: *The Quantity Theory of Money*. Elgar, Aldershot, 80-96.

Skidelski, R. / Nikolov, K. (2000): The Theoretical and Historical Perspectives on the Emergence of the Euro. In: Mundell, R. A. / Clesse, A., eds.: *The Euro as a Stabilizer in the International Economic System*. Kluwer, Boston et al., 21-33.

Smith, A. (1786): *An Inquiry into the Nature and Causes of the Wealth of Nations*. 4th ed., Reprint, Benton, Chicago et al. 1952.

Spahn, H.-P. (1998): Leadership and Stability in Key Currency Systems. In: Arestis, P. / Sawyer, M., eds.: *The Political Economy of Central Banking*. Elgar, Cheltenham / Northampton, 67-82.

Spahn, H.-P. (1999): Central Bankers, Games and Markets. In: Filc, W. / Köhler, C., eds.: *Macroeconomic Causes of Unemployment*. Duncker & Humblot, Berlin, 379-403.

Spahn, H.-P. (2000): Profit und Zins bei John Stuart Mill. In: Streißler, E. W., ed.: *Studien zur Entwicklung der ökonomischen Theorie XIX*. Schriften des Vereins für Socialpolitik, 115/XIX, Duncker & Humblot, Berlin (forthcoming).

Stadermann, H.-J. (1987): *Ökonomische Vernunft*. Mohr, Tübingen.

Stadermann, H.-J. (1994): *Die Fesselung des Midas*. Mohr, Tübingen.

Steuart, J. (1767a,b,c): *An Inquiry into the Principles of Political Economy*. Reprint, Pickering & Chatto, Vol. 2, 3, 4, London 1998.

Stiglitz, J. E. (1997): Reflections on the Natural Rate Hypothesis. *Journal of Economic Perspectives*, 11, 1, 3-10.

Story, J. (1988): The Launching of the EMS. In: Cohen, B. J., ed.: *The International Political Economy of Monetary Relations*. Elgar, Aldershot 1993, 634-49.

Strange, S. (1971): The Politics of International Currencies. *World Politics*, 23, 215-31.

Streißler, E. W. (1983): Stagnation – Analyse und Therapie. In: Bombach, G. et al., eds.: *Makroökonomik heute – Gemeinsamkeiten und Gegensätze*. Mohr, Tübingen, 457-76.

Svensson, L. E. O. (1994): Fixed Exchange Rates as a Means to Price Stability – What Have We Learned? *European Economic Review*, 38, 447-68.

Svensson, L. E. O. (1999): Monetary Policy Issues for the Eurosystem. *Carnegie-Rochester Conference Series on Public Policy*, 51, Amsterdam et al., 79-136.

Taylor, M. P. (1995): The Economics of Exchange Rates. *Journal of Economic Literature*, 33, 13-47.

Tobin, J. (1969): A General Equilibrium Approach to Monetary Theory. *Journal of Money, Credit, and Banking*, 1, 15-29.

Townshend, H. (1937): Liquidity-Premium and the Theory of Value. *Economic Journal*, 47, 157-69.

Townshend, H. (1938): Letter to Keynes. In: Moggridge, D., ed.: *The Collected Writings of John Maynard Keynes*, Vol. XXIX. Macmillan, London / Basingstoke, 289-93.

Triffin, R. (1960): *Gold and the Dollar Crisis*. Yale University Press, New Haven.

Tullio, G. / Wolters, J. (1996): Was London the Conductor of the International Orchestra or Just the Triangle Player? *Scottish Journal of Political Economy*, 43, 419-43.

Tullio, G. / Wolters, J. (2000): Interest Rate Linkages Between the US and the UK During the Classical Gold Standard. *Scottish Journal of Political Economy*, 47, 61-71.

Vilar, P. (1960): *A History of Gold and Money, 1450 to 1920*. Verso, London / New York 1991.

Volcker, P. A. (1978/79): The Political Economy of the Dollar. *Federal Reserve Bank of New York, Quarterly Review*, Winter, 1-12.

Wallerstein, I. (1974): *The Modern World World-System*. Academic Press, New York et al.

Walsh, C. E. (2000): Market Discipline and Monetary Policy. *Oxford Economic Papers*, 52, 249-71.

Weber, M. (1956): *Economy and Society*. University of California Press, Berkeley et al. 1978.

Wicksell, K. (1898): *Interest and Prices*. Reprint, Kelley, New York 1965.

Wicksell, K. (1901): *Lectures on Political Economy*. Vol. I. Routledge & Kegan Paul, London 1934.

Williamson, J. (1993): Exchange-Rate Management. *Economic Journal*, 103, 188-97.

Woolley, J. T. (1984): *Monetary Politics*. Cambridge University Press, Cambridge.

Ziegler, D. (1990): *Das Korsett der "Alten Dame" – Die Geschäftspolitik der Bank von England 1844-1913*. Knapp, Frankfurt.

Ziegler, D. (1993): Zentralbankpolitische "Steinzeit"? Preußische Bank und Bank von England im Vergleich. *Geschichte und Gesellschaft*, 19, 475-505.

Index

Printing: Weihert-Druck GmbH, Darmstadt
Binding: Buchbinderei Schäffer, Grünstadt